Islands Apart

Chronicles of Family Healing

Tim Flood

Illustrations and Cover Design By
Arnon Moscona

KENDALL/HUNT PUBLISHING COMPANY
4050 Westmark Drive   Dubuque, Iowa 52002

DEDICATION

This book is dedicated to the members of any family
who find themselves in pain today,
and to my own family
whose healing presence
graces my life.

CONTENTS

PREFACE

Before we begin this journey together, there are some important things I wish to share with you.

Probably most people who pick up this book will think it's about a residential facility that our teenage son Jacob attended – in particular a program in Western Samoa called "Paradise Cove." While an important backdrop to the stories inside, Paradise Cove is not the subject of this book. Nor do I focus on residential facilities in general. My purpose is not to carefully explain these programs or to delve into the public controversy surrounding them. I expect that all my readers are capable people who can make sense of these matters themselves and fashion whatever opinion they have based on many factors. I will simply say that *I am totally supportive of private residential programs.* One of them helped my son save his life. And in the process I saved my life too. I guess that all this leaves me somewhat biased in their favor!

My intention is rather to write about the process of family disintegration and healing. To take on that challenge requires an emphasis on internal personal processes not programmatic structures and techniques. Family health depends on the internal emotional, psychological, and spiritual health of its members. When a family breaks down, everyone suffers. And when a family heals everyone participates in healing. The Paradise Cove program provided a family healing process that worked for my family. That healing process is the real central character of this book.

For those of you interested how the Program works, the chapter entitled "Journey" awaits you. It explains the basics. The Program you read about here will change. It changed greatly even as I wrote this book. It will change again. The people who run the Program are constantly seeking new ways of making a difference in the lives of the kids and families involved. I like that.

Paradise Cove belongs to a family of programs called "the World Wide Association of Speciality Programs." Some programs, such as Paradise Cove, are for boys only, some are for girls only, and some are co-educational. I chose to focus this book on a few boys at Paradise Cove and their parents for some simple reasons: First, my son was a student there. Second, I made acquaintance with Paradise Cove parents immediately. Third, I thought it would be better to focus my energies. I could just as easily have written about girls and their processes and families.

I tended to focus more on adults than boys. That is because I am writing to an audience consisting mostly of parents of teens or helping professionals who assist those parents. While we all will be heartened by the stories of teens growing and changing, we can all be equally moved when change and growth come later in life – a time when there seems even more to protect, more to lose, more to remember, more to leave behind, more to forgive.

Every story in this book is authentic and true. I couldn't have made up anything this interesting if I tried! I don't write fiction and I didn't need to make anything up. A commitment to authenticity and truth took care of everything just fine. I altered names, locations, and a few details to protect the identity of my benefactors, students at Paradise Cove and their parents.

Much of this book is about my own personal journey from one way of thinking and seeing to another. Writing *Islands Apart* has been a marvelous, maddening, exhilarating, scary, out-of-my-depth experience. Taking courage resulted in discovery of greater depth. Toil resulted in exhilaration. And the madness of it all has made me saner than I've ever been. Writing has been part of the journey itself. It has been powerfully healing. Hours spent at my laptop have seemed like an extended meditation. I will never be the same – not only for the experience I write about but simply for writing it all down. Writing is now a tool I use to make sense of my world rather than a skill I thought I could never master. At a certain point I think I said, "to hell with mastery! I'm gonna do it anyway!" While this book tells the stories of members of my family and other families, in an important sense this book is simply my personal journal. I don't defend it. I *love* it.

It is my belief that this book will benefit the adults and older teens in any family that finds itself in pain. Pain is unnecessary. Nor need it be a permanent condition. There is a pathway leading away from pain into healing. We can learn so much from each other! Thanks to the generosity of a few brave souls, I have opened a few private lives to full view that we might all benefit from the teaching built right into their stories. The open-minded who look for, and see, universals inherent in human processes of self-discovery will find this book useful. Whether it's an adolescent pounding the sand in frustration on the beach of Samoa or a parent struggling to let go of attachments and fears, we can all grow from watching others grapple with life issues. They might be us. And in the end we are all members of one great heart, beating and pulsing.

The idea of this, my first, book came to life about the same time I did – in my fifty-first year. By then I had pretty much given up and sentenced myself to a life of *I can't*. For example, I told myself, "I can't write because …" and I filled in the blank with the self-limiting justification of the moment. So it came as somewhat of a surprise to me when, so far along in my travels, I realized that I had created all my darkly imagined dreams of limitation and black fantasies of rejection. They were simply a part of the package I had assembled thus far and thought about when I looked in the mirror.

At last I learned that I could just as well create another package – a life of *I can*. One of the results of this discovery is the book you hold, for some reason perhaps yet unknown to either of us. There are *many* things we don't know. It has been an important element of my journey to really understand that. So … I wonder. What surprises await us yet?

Tim Flood, San Francisco Bay Area, 1998

ACKNOWLEDGMENTS

*T*here have been three great challenges in my life: raising a family, participating in a family healing process, and writing about it. To meet these great challenges I have required much help. It has come from the generosity and love of many people.

As evermore I must begin with thanks to those who have given so much to me. Many walk before me and have generously given of their wisdom, strength, heart, and spirit. Many walk beside me and with equal generosity share the abundance of their lives. I would have nothing to write about and or say were it not for the radiance of a few living lights in my life.

I must first thank the boys who participated in a residential program called "Paradise Cove" and their parents, who gave me permission to grace these pages with their stories. I owe these selfless individuals everything when it comes to this book. You know who you are, my friends! I thank you for your generosity and trust. Each of you is a gift to me personally and anyone who will read this book. While many of you who consented to my strange interviewing technique will not see your personal stories in these pages, I hope you will nevertheless feel that your efforts were worthwhile and that this book is faithful to your experience too. I gained from each of you.

This book would not be possible without the assistance of a few very special people at the World Wide Association of Specialty Programs. They are Bob Lichfield, Brent Facer, Jean Schulter, Glenda Ikuta, Steve Ikuta, and Karr Farnsworth. Brent, I thank you especially for your support of this idea. Glenda and Steve, I thank you from my heart for believing in me long before I did.

To Brian Viafanua, Dwayne Lee, and all the staff of Paradise Cove, I thank you for returning my son to me and for all you gave to him. In your safekeeping he flourished. Rita Maugatai, how blessed we were to have an angel like you at son's side! Thank you too, Sonja Fullwood, wherever you are. To Cameron and the staff at Spring Creek Lodge, thanks for being there for us in the latter stages of this journey.

To the trainers at Resource Realizations – David Gilcrease, Duane Smotherman, Lou Dozier, and Joyce Christie – I thank you for the gift of your presence in my life and, most of all, for the honesty. David, my big Looney Tune friend, I thank you for your ongoing contribution to my life and to the healing affect you continue to have on the people of our generation. To Ouri Engolz of One, Inc., thank you, buddy.

To the guides of my spirit, Emilia Rathbun and Joan Goddard, bless you for sharing this journey with me. Joan, you stopped to minister to one fallen by his roadside. It was your healing grace that first reached out to me. I was helped as much by whom you are as anything you ever said or did. I will love you always. Emilia, you reminded me where my true home is. My path will ever be brightened by the graceful and loving light you have cast upon this earth for over ninety-three years. I am lucky to be so near it. You will never leave me.

To Arnon Moscona whose artwork adds the mood of experience to pages and cover, thank you for your gifts and for simply being who you are, my friend. I love our work and play together.

To Terri Mesple, thank you for all those hours of transcribing tapes and for being in my space!

To a few beautiful friends, readers, and supporters – Pat and Shelley Tedford, David and Jalane Stoker, Joan and Emilia again, Lance Goddard, Barbara Cochran, Joan Grant, Peggy Crane, Adele and Arnie Moscona, Glenda and Steve again, MacLean Flood, Cathy and Clifford Godwin – thanks for the early reading and ever-important feedback. Where would I be without you? I hope I've done your labors justice.

My special thanks to two young men, David Brothers and Randy Cook. Thank you for being there and sharing your hearts with me.

To Chuck and Sharon Brothers a special thank you for being the ones who first introduced us to a process for healing. You are special friends; we grow together. And to our friend, Jan Presley, what a sight to behold watching you spread your light into the world!

To my mother Doris E. Holm and her husband Harold, thank you for supporting us and never telling us what to do. Thank you for listening and caring, Mom, and for believing in us.

Finally, to my wife Sandy and my two sons, MacLean and Jacob. I thank you for the gift of your being. Not a day passes but what I am thankful to you and blessed by you. You are my greatest teachers! I thank you for the permission to write so revealingly about our experiences together and for your patience with me as husband and father. Thank you for teaching me so much more about love than I could possibly have learned without you. Each of you honors me so. Bless you, my beloved family!

Tim Flood, San Francisco Bay Area, 1998

Principal Families

1. Jacob and MacLean, and their parents Sandy and Tim:

   Jacob (Jake): The younger son, a hippie wanna-be ... graduate of Paradise Cove ... loves poetry, acting, and music.

   MacLean (Mac): The older son ... overcame a depressive childhood ... loves computers and old pickup trucks.

   Sandy: The author's wife ... a special education teacher of language-handicapped elementary school-age children.

   Tim: The author.

2. Ryan and his mother, Susan, and step-father Greg:

   Ryan: Former member of SHARPs (Skin Heads Against Racial Prejudice) ... graduate of Paradise Cove.

   Susan: Divorced mother of Ryan ... raised as "Miss Goodie Two Shoes" ... Ryan educated her to the ways of the world.

   Greg: The committed new man in Susan's life ... loved Ryan as his own.

3. Cary and his parents, Jessica and William:

   Cary: Frequent guest of Juvenile Hall ... former Satan worshipper ... graduate of Paradise Cove.

   Jessica: Always concerned about her son's depressive behavior, she never experienced a serene time with her only child Cary.

   William: His alcoholism challenged family integrity and values.

4. Jonathan and his parents, Mary Beth and Robert:

   Jonathan: Wears a big smile ... longs for approval and belonging ... graduate of Paradise Cove.

   Mary Beth: A take-charge woman who battles bureaucracies to get help for her son.

   Robert: A large, sometimes distant, man with a big heart and temper to match.

5. Anthony and his parents, Katherine and Kyle:

   Anthony: A fragile child confused by the conflicting values of split parents ... gets in trouble at school ... graduate of Paradise Cove.

   Katherine: Raised in a perfectionist household ... left abusive husband to raise Anthony by herself ... until she met Kyle.

   Kyle: An orthopedist living in a small town ... also raised in a perfectionist environment ... loving and caring step-father of Anthony.

6. Paul and his mother Melissa:

   Paul: Confused by the presence of substances in the home ... addicted to computers and drugs ... graduate of Paradise Cove.

   Melissa: Musician living in Sausalito ... her stand against drug use in her home precipitated a crisis for husband and her son.

EVENING TO REMEMBER

Judged by the usual criteria no one would say this was anything other than an ordinary suburban Spring evening. Summer never comes easily to the San Francisco Bay Area and the cool wind nipping at my ears on this Wednesday evening in March, 1997, reminded me that a cold spring had only begun and would stay that way for longer than I liked, impatient as I am for the warmth of summer.

I did not realize at the time that this was no ordinary evening and that I will remember it for the rest of my life. It began simply, my wife and I visiting our favorite haunt, Tokie's Teriyaki Grill, with Jacob, the younger of our two sons.

We took our seats at one of those square Japanese dining tables where patrons sit in community with others, usually strangers. Immediately, we fell into the relaxed and convivial atmosphere of our local dining favorite. We slipped easily into the comfort of each other's company, smiling and laughing. Jacob was trying out some food he'd never experienced before in his eighteen years and fumbling with his chopsticks. He joked and smiled, as charming as ever. Occasionally, he would lean over to me and look at me with a familiar impish look on his face and a wink. The wink was a new addition, I noticed. I liked it. And there was so much more about my son that was new to me.

Sandy obviously enjoyed this experience with her new son. She wore that special girlish smile she has that guys have always loved. I fell in love with her smile in 1966 and I've loved her ever since. As time passed, the girl became woman, developed a career, and answered to a cry for "mommy." Her face changed with time, grew more beautiful, and the smile – her radiant smile! – showed more brightly now than ever, I thought.

So absorbed was I in watching my son and his mom enjoying each other that I paid little attention to others at our table. Like Sandy I was enjoying this precious moment, thankful this was happening to me, thankful that I have a family, *this* family, and most especially my two sons and this woman for my wife. I let myself adore them. I missed my older son and wished he was present, but he had moved to another town, beginning a new life. Tonight was no night for regret, however. I had a feeling that it was going to be one of those picture moments in my life which the camera of my visual memory would record faithfully and which I would remember forever.

The only thing that broke my concentration was a young woman sitting across from us at our table with a young son of her own, a junior high-aged boy. I watched him closely for a time. "He's young enough to be in that state of innocence prior to breaking away from a mother's containment," I thought. But my attention soon returned to my own family, and I paid little attention to our table companions other than occasionally to notice her close observation of us. "A fellow people-watcher," I surmised. When we weren't absorbed in our own little family occasion, we slipped casually into conversation with this woman, who revealed that she was not only a single mother but an executive with a local small bank. "*Two* big jobs!" I thought.

After a while, I sensed there was something important about this woman. Over the years I've learned to become more attuned to the events that life brings and to the people who walk on and off the stage of my life. I've learned that my life, probably very much like yours, is an unfolding drama and that the character who suddenly enters stage left has not appeared there simply by accident.

As it came time to leave I could tell there was something this mother seemed impatient to get off her mind. Intuitively, I felt a kinship with her and realized that probably we are both seekers, she and I. All seekers on this earth share a common bond. We see some mystery that attracts our attention, are drawn by it, and become obsessed with it for a while. I waited for her to tell us what she was she was thinking.

Suddenly, she let it fly! "Well, I'm sitting here wondering what all of you *did so right!* I mean, how often do I see a family of two parents and a teen – how old are you, eighteen? – who so obviously *like* each other so much and who get along so well! I mean, you actually seem to *enjoy each other* and *have fun together!* I need to know how you got there!"

Ha! *No wonder* I had felt drawn to this woman! Jacob and I, who had been giggling all evening, looked at each other and giggled some more. I noticed Sandy had tears of joy in her eyes. This moment of family happiness had *not* come easily to us. And of course we told our younger listeners our story – the brief version, but nevertheless our story. It is only partly the story of a prodigal son. That story is of course very much a story about the parent as well. But, oh! the pride and love of the father! For this, my son, was dead and is alive again; was lost and now is found!

Ours is a story I wish to tell over and over, a story *worth* telling and retelling. From the high-rise apartment in the city to the house in the suburbs to the cottage in the far reaches of the countryside, ours is a story of relevance to families scattered everywhere about our confused and troubled world. It is a story of a family, once broken and wounded, now healing.

The young executive listened attentively and then told a story of her own, a tragic story about a sister never recovered fully from a heroin addiction, a story where the healing force has not yet been invited into a suffering heart. Just about every family has stories like these today. How important to tell stories of the lost who now are found and the blind who now can see!

The conversation shifted and reached its conclusion as Jacob answered her questions about his plans for his life. As we rose to leave, she handed him her card and offered him a job in her bank ... too bad, he just got one with Safeway! ... "But you never know," she said.

As we left to get in the car, tears came to my eyes too. There are two kinds of tears – tears of sorrow and pain and tears of fullness. These tears of Sandy and mine were tears of fullness. Our cups were full to overflowing and the tears of gratitude ran plentifully that night.

The unthinkable

Two years ago an escort service, hired by Sandy and me, came to our house according to plan in stealth in the middle of the night, to secret then seventeen-year-old Jacob against his will to a residential program for "wayward teens." Each of us – Sandy, Jacob, and I – was hurting, angry, crying, in shame and blame, each of us a wounded member of a broken family, wounded by living unconsciously and by living in a world of pain we chose for ourselves.

Yet one year later, to a casual observer like the young mother at Tokie's, we could not have appeared at all like a "normal" family. Because increasingly in our times "normal" means a family which is at least partially, even noticeably, wounded and hurting. Increasingly in our world, "normal" means kids on drugs. It means parents in divorce and custody battles or settling for a kind of peaceful, but uneasy and loveless, coexistence. It means teens dropping out. It means elders without apparent wisdom or influence on the lives of the young. It means kids failing to live up to their potential and frustrated parents feeling powerless to affect the lives of the children they often love more than life itself.

In choosing to place Jake in a residential program, Sandy and I made a choice out of desperation. Not very long before we took this dramatic course of action, doing it would have been unthinkable! Today, because of the healing that has resulted from that choice, all three of us are able to see

3

a blessing both in our desperation and how we dealt with it. Sometimes the unthinkable place is *exactly* the place we need to go!

This is a book about the journey from the pain we felt then to the healing we feel now. This book isn't a clinical treatise and it's certainly *not* about a bunch of perfection and light! It's about ordinary people like you and me – a few boys and their parents and their real struggles together.

Geographically, the setting for our drama alternates between the continental United States and, approximately 4,800 miles away, the small tropical island of Western Samoa where, as I write, over two hundred boys, in a different time zone and with a different understanding of the world, struggle to become men. They are residents of Paradise Cove, a residential school for adolescent boys with problems adjusting to the world. Back home their hopeful parents have struggles of their own, likely more than they initially understood (or perhaps understand). Like their sons in Western Samoa, they too are in varying stages of a journey they did not consciously choose.

The geographical setting of my story could be just about anywhere, however. The *real* setting is inward within the hearts, minds, and souls of these few central figures who occupy the pages of this book.

What exactly is this inner setting? And why is it important?

My purpose is to show you that landscape through the lives of these few families. I believe that our lives are not so different from yours. The high drama of our time is not on stage or screen, Western Samoa, or anyplace exotic we might normally choose as a dramatic backdrop. The real landscape is here – *right here!* – in your life and mine, in our families, and in the lives of ordinary people. In your imagination, remove the roof from any home and silently observe the scene below. Open the door and walk unobserved into the reality of any home – whether it be yours or mine. Open the pages of any family album and look at the *real* life revealed. If you are attentive and look closely, there you will see the masks we wear all too often in order to present ourselves to the world – even to our loved ones. As T. S. Eliot expressed it in his immortal poem, *The Love Song of J. Alfred Prufrock*, we make the decision "to prepare a face to meet the faces that [we] meet." Opening our eyes to the masks we wear is an entry point to the discovery of what ails us individually and as a culture. But the drama is not even contained in the masks we wear. The drama is whether or not we will *remove* the masks and reveal, even to ourselves, our true identity.

Of course, as we look honestly at our lives, we will also see the good times, the successes, the dreams coming true, the sincerity, the intention, the love. And let us savor that sight and cherish it!

But if you and I are truthful we will regard, where they exist, the uneasy and all-too-temporary alliances and truces we make with one another, deceiving ourselves for a moment that we are safe and out of harm's way. We will observe the quick fixes we apply to familial and marital relationships and the breakdowns that issue all too quickly and that we pretend we do not understand. We will see also the compromises, pain, and broken promises, and we will see our dreams broken upon a mirror we gaze into but reluctantly. Far more frequently than any of us would like to admit, we will see father pitted against mother, sister against brother, parent against child, parent against grandparent. Even in the so-called "normal" family.

Was this how we intended it to turn out? Of course not! Yet in the tragicomic unfolding of our brief lives, we spend so much time in pain or in denial of it. Why? So often we have intense feelings of anger and hurt directed primarily at the very people we profess to love the most – a spouse, child, or parent. Why? This book will attempt to answer some of those penetrating questions.

Take heart! For this is a book of glad tidings! While it tells the stories of lives in crisis, *Islands Apart* is mostly about people *succeeding* – succeeding to mend hearts and relationships torn asunder.

BREAKDOWN

*t*he moment I first held each of my two sons at their birth, I fell in love. For several moments, I felt a kind of rapture, separate and distinct from romantic love, and unknown to me until then. All my fear of becoming a father and whether I could be a good one was dissolved by the tiny warm miracle of my first-born whom I held in my arms. To be warmed by our newborn son's warmth, to feel his strong heartbeat, insistent and promising, to understand his complete vulnerability, to realize the trust placed in me — all these I felt as powerfully, in the first few moments of my sons' lives, as I will feel anything in my life. MacLean came first. Three-and-a-half years later his brother Jacob arrived. Sandy and I loved each son beyond all measure and without limit.

Each of our sons began his life journey with his own unique possibility, his own birthright. Each was born free from and unfettered by the conditions and limitations imposed by a life of struggle and compromise. Each was created completely innocent, united with those who gave him birth, vulnerable, strong, total, trusting, and completely focused. Each was a miracle of breath, tears, flesh, and need. Each was born to the soft raindrops of their parents' tears of joy, relief, and complete commitment.

One morning seventeen years later from our living room window I watched Jacob leave the house angrily and amble down the street. He was always angry these days. He looked appalling — his shoulders slumped forward as he walked, one hand in his pocket, the other hand holding the ever-present cigarette, his long, curly, sandy brown hair flopping over his bent-over head with each step. He looked beaten down, mistreated. He was dressed in rags. I felt responsible for the depraved condition of this lost young man, my flesh and blood. He looked so ... *old*. "Probably stoned out of his gourd," I admitted to myself.

I felt guilty stealing up to the window to spy on him as he walked down the street. If he caught me watching him, I'd hear no end of it. But I was worried about my son, the hippie. Every morning he left the house in his leather moccasins and bell-bottoms but never went to school.

I scanned his dress searching for clues. I observed the direction he was headed. Where's he going? What's he feeling? What might occupy his day? Jacob was completely inaccessible. Today would be another frustrating day when I would know nearly nothing about my son or his world. I created just about everything I thought I knew about him through conjecture. It was wholly unsatisfactory – this not knowing and this fearing what I *didn't* know. When I signed up to be father I never thought I'd end up having to be a *detective*! And I really wasn't very good at this detective work either.

Watching him brought up such dark, fearful emotions – emotions which didn't originate in a mere misunderstanding between generations. This kid was not just an adolescent rebel: Jacob was *in trouble* and there I was past denying it. Where was the little one I once held in my arms? Who was this stranger, this strange boarder in my home? "He's probably a stranger even to himself." I choked back tears. I loved him, or at least what once *was* him. I wanted to know him. I wanted to participate in his life. I wanted to help him, but I felt hopeless and sad. And I was angry that he would do this to me. When he injured himself, he injured *me*.

From newborn to lost soul in only seventeen years! When had this abyss between us taken form? Suddenly, quite suddenly, it was so vast. How had the warmth, love, and trust we felt for each other not very long ago been replaced by this fear, anger, and confusion?

Sandy

The remarkable and wonderful woman I fell in love with and married almost thirty years ago, the woman who gave birth to our two sons, had already gone to work that morning. She will begin telling our story. As she speaks I realize that my love and appreciation of her have grown immeasurably. Not that long ago we were in painful conflict. Today I see her as she is, and always was, the perfect wife for me and the perfect mother for our children, two extraordinarily fortunate boys to have such a mother as this! Ever since she was young she dreamed of having children and raising them with love, enlightenment, and opportunity.

> "Our kids were adorable. They played so happily together. We have this picture of Mac, just about four years old, when he held his newborn sleeping baby brother Jake for the first time. Mac's eyes are so wide open with excitement! He adored his little brother, and Jake learned to adore Mac. They did everything together. In Kindergarten, Mac wrote in a classroom exercise that Jake was his best friend. Being the older, Mac always showed Jake how to build things. Mac has always been building and tinkering, fascinated with how things work. We have a large bay window in the front of our house and a chest built underneath

it so you can sit at the window and look out. We still store inside the chest thousands of Legos and wooden blocks, which preoccupied them for hours and hours. As children, a single project they worked on together with friends sometimes occupied them for days. They constantly built and played together. They also loved to create skits and dramatic productions. Mac was always the producer, director, and cameraman, Jake always the lead actor. Mac would frame the scene and videotape the action. Jake was full of lively energy and was so funny and improvisational.

"I set out to be the perfect mother. As a special education teacher of language-handicapped children at the K-1 level, I've devoted my entire career and adult life to loving and caring for kids. My whole self-concept was wrapped up in how successful I was in dealing with children and in creating healthy situations for them to grow and learn.

"As parents, I think each of us at times thought the other was the perfect parent. I thought Tim was the perfect father! He was loving and adoring. He played with the boys constantly. He read to them every night at bedtime. He gave them lots of attention and was gentle with them. He nurtured them maybe too much for a father, but I didn't care. I thought what he did was great. I sometimes thought that he placed a lot of expectations on the boys to appreciate him – not so much when they were little but when they were old enough to say 'thank you.' He seemed to have this big need to be validated and he seemed to look outside himself for validation. He seemed to be looking to Mac and Jake for approval, I thought. Of course, so was I, but less so than Tim. I seemed to look more to the outside world for approval, whereas Tim seemed to need it from the kids.

"Me? I had this mask as a wonderful mother, wife, and teacher. My life was centered around kids eighteen hours a day. I had a loving husband whom I loved, but my emphasis and focus were on kids. That's how I got all my strokes!

"Jake's story really begins with Mac. When Mac began kindergarten, we began to feel that he was really lagging behind the other children. He seemed way too timid. He had a hard time separating from Tim or me; whenever we were in an unfamiliar group situation, he would cling to one of us tightly, well after the age when that is expected. He was smaller than the other kids, physically fragile, and very quiet. As doting parents, we looked forward to his playing Little League and soccer. On the soccer field, he was always the little runt on the outside of the swarm, sort of half-heartedly following the cluster of kids around the ball as the swarm moved from one end of the field to the other. In baseball he just wasn't strong enough to do much damage with the bat. I'd get so excited if he even *made contact* with the ball! Then of course, he'd get thrown out at first because he didn't run fast.

"We tried to encourage him, but he didn't seem to want to try very hard at things. Sometimes when it seemed he wasn't trying, I'd get upset with him. He didn't fit my picture of how it was all supposed to work. He was caring, nurturing, inventive, and so very creative and sensitive; but he didn't care about sports. I didn't appreciate enough the wonderful things about Mac. The more I pushed him and attempted to steer him into 'appropriate' activities, the more he would hide behind me or Tim.

"When his dad took him to Indian Guides, Mac seemed to feel so inferior to the other boys. After a while, I caught on to how he felt and it would break my heart to watch Tim take him to Indian Guides meetings when clearly he didn't want to go. Mac admits today that he sabotaged himself a lot. Some kids would want to be friends with him, but he'd push them away. The older he got the worse it got. By the time I realized he was depressed, he was in a pattern of being a loner. He was identified in the first grade as a loner; he wouldn't play with the other boys; he didn't want to get out and throw the ball and run around. He wanted to stay in one space, play in the dirt and sand, and create something. I see now how wonderful that was. He was unique. I see also that we squashed that magical child who was so precious and so alive inside of him.

"We did the best we knew how at the time. But instead of working with him, his obvious gifts, and his inclinations for individual creativity, we tended to oppose him and try to change him. So *of course* Mac was always a stubborn and recalcitrant child!

"He was kind of in his own world. He read *constantly*. As he grew older, you would seldom see Mac without a book. And he started wearing a parka year round, even in the hot summertime! At school, waiting outside his classroom for the door to be opened, he wore his parka and read a book. The other kids teased him a lot. I knew he didn't feel very good about himself, but I didn't know what to do about it. He was a very frustrating child for us because we wanted him to do all the mainstream kinds of things and be confident with the other kids, but he didn't seem to care at all.

"I couldn't believe that inside he didn't care. In fact, I thought he was depressed but Tim wouldn't hear of that. We didn't see eye-to-eye about our kids. We didn't 'parent on the same page' with either of our kids. It seemed what one of us would do, the other would undo. We lacked consistency, which comes from agreement. We fought a lot and let our emotions fly, often in front of the kids.

"We became really concerned about Mac in the fifth grade. He seemed so out of touch with the rest of the world. Then one night, the worst nightmare I could imagine happened – at ten years old, our little guy tried to commit suicide! He took an overdose of aspirin. He came into our bedroom late at night and woke me up to tell me he was sick. I went with him to his bedroom to talk to him about what was wrong and he told me he'd taken several pills. 'Because I want to die,' he said! I couldn't believe my ears! I rushed into the bathroom and, sure enough, a lot of pills were gone. Tim and I rushed Mac to the hospital. They pumped his stomach out and stabilized him quickly. He was going to be all right.

"It still shakes me to talk about it. Something like this would shake up any loving parent. 'But he is only ten years old!' I kept telling myself. It didn't make sense! We had to understand *why*! What was going on inside that would cause him to try to take his life at such a young age! What had we done wrong?! The counselor we began to see, along with Mac, determined that indeed he had attempted to take his life, that it was a *serious* attempt, and that he truly did not want to live. We had been highly focused on Mac before his suicide attempt. And now we were *intensely* focused on him! Where was Jake in all this?

"Mac's depression and attempted suicide shook me to my core. My identity was so wrapped up in being the perfect mother, and here *my own child* did not want to live! It was unbearable. I became depressed myself. Many times during that period I thought of taking my own life. But I never let myself do it because that would be the most horrible thing I could do to Jake – he was even younger and he needed and depended on me – and because if I gave up on my own life Mac would totally blame himself. He had enough to deal with without also having to cope with a dead mother. I finally realized I was depressed and had been for some time. The psychiatrist prescribed antidepressant medication for me. I realize now that I needed to be on antidepressants. When I began taking them I was amazed that I could feel better ... I hadn't even known I had been depressed. All of a sudden, I had more energy. I didn't have to *go down* with everything and have the temper outbursts I was so prone to have. Before I would always go into these incredible *rages* with Mac, the recalcitrant, frustrating child often on the receiving end. I'd come home from an intense day with very challenging children in my special education class and here, in my own home, was an equal challenge!

"Well ... Mac survived, and over time we survived him and learned to understand him better. He continued to be a very challenging child to raise in many ways. He was depressed and stubborn. He would do only what he wanted to do. He was a highly unusual, very unique child. One summer when he was twelve, he said he wanted to work. Tim got him a job working in the registrar's office at a local university filing documents. We thought he might last for a week or so. But he worked all summer long. He didn't take coffee breaks. He worked diligently and hard at this simple task. Of course, he wore his parka all day long in the building without air conditioning! When he wasn't filing, you might have found him helping some of the older ladies who worked in the office learn about their computers. He saved up his money all summer long and bought his first computer, a MacIntosh. He picked up computers so quickly. We subscribed to *MacWorld* and he read every issue cover to cover.

"Later that year in junior high school he made friends with the teacher in charge of creating the computer lab in the school. Mac helped her order the equipment, they brought the computer lab online, and Mac networked them all together. He was amazing! This was the beginning of an interest that sustained him through those difficult years and helped him pull out of his depression.

"As parents, we were pretty much emotionally exhausted from raising such a challenging child. Of course, we knew that we had created much of the chal-

11

lenge ourselves. At best we were weak and uncertain parents, and just plain out of confidence.

"There was to be no respite. Now that Mac was turning his life around, guess what?! *Jacob* started having difficulties *of his own*! So here we were, two struggling parents trying to recover from having to deal with one child, when the other one begins to change in unexpected ways."

Jacob's difficulties adjusting to life didn't just spring from nothing. Despite Sandy's and my love and care in the best way we knew how, important seeds were planted many years earlier – seeds which waited to sprout above ground when they were ready. It is with MacLean's attempted suicide and its aftermath that Jacob's seeds of self-destruction really began.

"When Mac tried to take his life, Jake was only six. We did the best we knew how. We tried to protect him from knowledge about Mac's situation. 'How could a six-year-old possibly understand?' we asked. 'Or know?' we hoped privately. So there was all this dramatic energy going on in the house and it was directed towards Mac. Jake of course knew that something was different. We now understand just how sensitive and observing a child he was, even at that early age! He has since told us that as time passed he did not feel a part of the family because there were things going on and his parents wouldn't bring him in on it. Being parents devoted to both of our children, we tried to be inclusive of Jake, yet protective. It is the protective part which he experienced.

"Of course, Jake was the opposite of his older brother. He was out there throwing the ball, socializing, laughing, and sparkling with energy all over the place. He was the spark on every sports team. In a room, he drew all eyes. Good looking and fearless, he oozed charisma. And he was funny! He brought laughter and excitement wherever he went. He was the boy I thought a boy should be. So adorable, cute, out there, social, spunky, funny, energetic, and entertaining. So I went the other way with him. I adored him all the time, let him do whatever he wanted, never fussed over him at all, and … never made him accountable!

"I've often thought about what Dr. Barry Brazelton said. Parents should have three children, he said: the first one you go to one extreme, the second you go to another extreme, and with the third child, you've figured out the middle ground, neither over-rescuing nor over-demanding. But such was not my fate. I was really hard on Mac, extreme. But I let Jake get away *with crap*!

"I kept myself real busy adoring Jake, making excuses for his flakiness and lack of accountability, and telling myself that I couldn't hold him accountable for his homework because, poor child, he had a learning disability! The deal was, I myself grew up with a learning disability that I learned to compensate for and work with. And then I specialized in working with learning-disabled children. But your own children are different. I felt sorry for Jake. Clearly, he needed more structure than either of us gave him. I needed to make sure there was work both from school and at home that he could do and I needed to make sure that he *did* the work. Instead, I just sort of threw up my hands and bought into his helplessness. Jake would manipulate me by giving me a hard time whenever I made a lame attempt to introduce structure into his life. Then I'd give up. He was very much into the approval and external validation from his peers. That's where all his energy went and fighting against it was so difficult. Of course, I was all wrapped up in external approval myself!

"By this time Tim had turned his focus onto Mac and buried himself in his work. I really shut down emotionally. Both of us were shut down a lot. We stopped having a social life. We turned all our focus onto our kids. It was sort of like a recipe, when you keep adding more and more of the ingredients hoping it will taste better, but it ends up tasting awful.

"It may not sound like it, but we were fairly sophisticated parents. We could see things about Jake. We could see his issues emerging. But what we couldn't see was how our decisions and actions were affecting him."

In middle school, Jacob was active in school plays, student council, and sports. In his last year of middle school he played the lead part of Sammy Fong in *Flower Drum Song*. Even as a proud father, I could admit that it was kind of funny watching a blond white kid with dyed-black hair play an adult Chinese American! But somehow he brought it off. The most difficult challenge was singing. It was what he most feared. But he held the tune perfectly! It angered me to hear a few titters in the audience when his adolescent voice was a little nasal. Hey, this is my son! He performed beautifully and was the most talked about performer in the whole play. It was a proud day for mom and pop.

The summer before his last year of junior high, Jacob began to attend acting workshops held by a wonderful talent manager with big-time movie connections in LA. I was really enthusiastic about her and her program – a bit more enthusiastic than Sandy! I liked how his manager related to the kids and pushed them to be their best. Jacob adored her and really put himself out during the workshops. He dreamed of being an actor. "Jake needs something to motivate him and this might be it," I thought.

Meanwhile at school, there was special education. Each day, he would leave his regular classroom to attend a couple of periods a day with his special resource teacher. The stigma of being different did not sit well with a boy who looked so much to peers for approval. Those math facts seemed so unattainable. We never succeeded in getting Jacob to sit down to learn them. Even though Sandy faced the problem of learning disabilities growing up herself, even though she became a special education teacher, and even though we had known since early on that academics would challenge Jacob, we could not convince him that he was nevertheless quite intelligent. His special education teachers were extraordinary, dedicated people. Inside, though, he was assimilating his experience in a way none of us could control or influence. By this time, what began as a fear within him had developed into a *conviction* which we were powerless to overcome. Sandy and I always wanted him to succeed – and on his own terms, not ours. Our graduate degrees had not left us with some kind of elitist academic prejudice with which to saddle our kids. We never believed that Jacob had to be some academic superstar. But to know that he felt *stupid*, to watch him turn against reading, to watch him give up so easily – that was extraordinarily difficult! When life challenged us we always tried. It was not within our frame of reference to understand giving up.

It didn't take long for Jacob to be beaten down by experience. The promise and possibility with which he was born became obscured by life's challenging lessons and his response to them. Our perception of the world takes form at an early age. Ask any child of six years old how they perceive the world and they will tell you clearly. The answer is written already in their eyes. One pair of eyes will tell you that this world is a place to fear; another will say it is a place to dominate. The early promise and possibility which is ours at birth too often is torn as we rub against the sharp teeth of living in a complex and unfriendly world. We hide our possibility from others, from ourselves, even from our parents who, breathlessly, saw us as we once were, as we were created to be – complete, loving, pure, innocent, and holy – the *magical children* we once were and always are. At some point early in his life Jacob, like MacLean before him, lost contact with the knowledge of what is magical, childlike, and beautiful about him.

As he encountered the world, he formed beliefs. Over time he shaped those beliefs into a heavy granite hardness almost impossible to penetrate. All of us form these beliefs early on. They protect us from our vulnerability. We polish them for presentation to the world as *our fixed beliefs*. We become extremely attached to these unconscious opinions – so attached that they become solidly ours, to defend, to defend as the *right* beliefs, to defend against *your* beliefs. Our opposition to the world has taken its first step and made its first declaration. Our ego is born. Its walls are up. The natural, inquisitive nature we were born with is buried beneath the weight of a disabling certainty we have about the world we live in.

We not only erect a belief system about the world; we fabricate one about ourselves as well. At what point in the life of a child does the thought "I am stupid" take first form? When and how does it first happen that a child born radiant as a star in the night sky say to himself, "I am *worth less* than this other one over there?"

The initial unity of an infant with his environment becomes a unity that once was but can never be again. It is supplanted with the certainty that I am separate from you.

At an early age. Sandy understood that Jacob had learning disabilities even before his preschool years. After all, she is a professional trained in these matters and all the signs were there. There was no problem with her diagnosis. But because Sandy herself had suffered from learning disabilities, she felt sorry for this little guy. Little by little, she (and I right along with her) rescued this little darling, extricating him from one challenge after another. We held him too close and protected him too much. Soon Jacob's belief *I can* was replaced by the belief *I can't*. Others followed – beliefs such as, *They will do it for me* and *what I do isn't good enough*.

Over time Jacob's life seemed to get more and more out of control. But everything seemed sort of manageable until the latter part of his junior high school after *Flower Drum Song*. Then came summer and a lot of idle time. Once-a-month acting workshops weren't enough to keep him busy.

He entered that phase where a kid doesn't want to be around mom and dad. As sophisticated, well-read parents we realized that a healthy child separates from his family – a painful but necessary part of individuation, of passage from boyhood into manhood – only to return after the process is complete. However, we realized that the period of separation is a potentially dangerous interval in a young man's life. We live in a dangerous time where a young person can get hurt very easily. Watching a child enter this period of his life is a very nervous time for a parent. This nervousness is heightened because, at arm's length from the child, a parent is very out-of-touch with what is going on in the child's life.

One Sunday summer night the phone rang. The mother of a fellow drama student was on the other end, her voice trembling with concern. Jacob had been staying with them that weekend and she told me she had caught the boys drinking. I felt the heavy weight of a long-dreaded fear bear down upon me. This is a door which I had *so* hoped Jacob would not open. Yet I had understood intuitively for some time how easily it would open to him! I knew something about his vulnerability, but it was like the door to a secret room that I pretended wasn't there.

Was not his weakness also mine? Did I not give it to him? Hadn't I been the college kid passed out in the back of the bar most nights at closing time? Hadn't I been the kid who drank with my girlfriend all summer night in West Yellowstone and then drove 110 MPH in a test to see if I'd live? Hadn't I been the drunken kid who drove my friend's car into a cold Montana river, badly injuring my friends that winter night? Hadn't I been the one who continued to drink and drive for several years afterwards,

15

thoughtlessly mixing pot and alcohol? Hadn't I been the kid who wandered around the streets of the San Francisco Tenderloin district stoned out of my mind at three A.M.? Didn't Sandy say to me that she would not marry me unless I cleaned up my life?

It was in his genes, I reckoned. I understood all too well my legacy to Jacob! Like his father, Jacob was a wild one with an addictive personality and an approval need possibly stronger than his will to live! The truth I didn't want to face is that these tendencies were even less controllable in him. "Jacob isn't me," I reasoned correctly.

It took me a while to recognize critical differences between us. My problems didn't surface until I entered college, yet Jacob was only fourteen and beginning to experiment with substances. I had more tools in my tool chest to help cope with my problems — tools like self-confidence and success in school; Jacob wasn't even in high school yet. I had goals I was accomplishing; Jacob had his acting but other than that what was there? I had peers who were succeeding in life; increasingly, I wasn't sure about Jacob's peers. I feared that his journey would be fraught with much more danger than mine — a fear I wouldn't let go of.

I thought that my task as a responsible parent was to stop the behavior immediately, to get into control, to make his decisions for him, to save him from experience. I thought that my task was to change him fast by finding the right buttons to push, fast. I thought my duty was to rescue my son. Jacob had other ideas.

It is often said that one definition of insanity is trying the same thing over and over but expecting different results. I always redoubled my efforts.

Jacob

As I interviewed my own son and asked him to tell his life story into the tape recorder, I felt a father's pride listening to him review his life with such clarity and insight. I appreciated his willingness to share the intimate details of his life with me. What a contrast to the frustrating and inaccessible kid he had been that morning he left the house only two years before, I thought. Now he sat with me in the living room, in front of the same window where I spied upon him previously, and openly shared his life with me.

"There was something more that I wanted in my life that I wasn't getting. There was an empty space that seemed to consume my body. I became lonely and very depressed. Half way through freshman year, I decided not to try out for any school plays and I was not at all interested in academics. I had no focus, no idea where I wanted to go with my life.

16

"Freshman year I went to a drama class and just screwed off, trying to get the acceptance of my peers because I did not feel accepted by anybody. And there were the good kids, the preppy kids, in the class and the bad kids in the class. I mean *good* as in kids who get good grades, dress nice, do good in school, and do as they're told. They're *good* kids. The screw-offs smoked dope, they didn't do anything in the class, but they were very creative people. At the time I got them as more real.

"For a while, I was right in the middle. I wasn't with the good kids or the bad ones. Because I was the class clown and very *out there*, the bad kids kept on saying, 'We gotta get this kid stoned.' And I didn't even know what pot was at the time. I didn't know what you did with it.

"The first time I ever smoked pot was in high school. I still had my four preppy friends. I was getting bored. What I started before I got to high school was TP'ing houses, egging houses and cars, and stealing hood ornaments. But in high school, this wasn't doing it for me anymore. There was still that empty space. I needed something more.

"One time while I was still in middle school and hanging out with my preppy friends, I drank some Xima, drank a whole bottle of wine, and stole my parents' car. I didn't have a license yet. My parents were out that evening. When they got home, they saw that their car was missing and I drove up just as they were going in the front door. I made up this story about having to take this girl home because her father would beat her if she didn't get home on time. They swallowed it. I remember going into my room and realizing how much I could get away with! Next day I went to my special ed class and bragged about it. That was cool. But my preppy friends knew the truth about what I'd done. So now here I was suddenly this very bad kid in their eyes.

"But it all really goes back to my sixth period high school drama class. They were inviting me to parties and wanting to get me stoned. And I really *wanted* to get stoned, but I was just really afraid at the time. I really wanted their acceptance and really wanted to fit into their crowd. They would have accepted me without smoking dope, but I didn't think so.

"So one day, fourth period PE, I turned to two of my new friends that always had pot and said, 'Let's go get stoned.' So we cut out of fourth period, went to these apartments next to my high school, and smoked dope. If anything I didn't feel any different. But the whole thing was so that I could go to sixth period and say, 'Yeah, I smoked dope.' And I probably faked it and said, 'I'm really baked' and stuff.

"So my first saying to myself was, 'I'm only going to do this once a week.' And I was still hanging out with my preppy friends. I had my preppy friends and my stoner friends and I was in this kind of limbo state, which you don't stay in long, in my opinion. The next day I'm with all my preppy friends and my stoner friends walk by and say, 'Hey, we're going to get baked ... you wanna come?' I looked at my preppy friends and they were just doing what they'd been doing

17

for the last year, which is eating in the halls and talking, and that was just getting real boring for me. Here it was an open campus and my preppy friends and I didn't even use that privilege of going off campus. So I said, 'Well, screw this. Hey guys, I'm outa here.'

"So I got stoned. But that was twice in one week. Already I broke my word and my commitment to myself. So after that I said, 'Screw it,' and started getting baked every day. And the third day was the first day I felt it. That was just *awesome!* I *loved* the feeling, I loved the high, I loved smoking it, I loved the things I felt I could do, the person I felt I could be. I wasn't afraid of anything! It was purely awesome! It was the me I always wanted to bring out but I was afraid of. I thought I was more *me* through using. So I kept on using and got addicted really quickly.

"In about two weeks I didn't hang out with my preppy friends any more. I had my stoner friends now. We did stoner things – smoking dope, going to parties, getting drunk, all that stuff. For a while I was known as 'the rookie.' That's what they'd call someone new to dope in my high school. I'd say, 'What's that?' And then they'd explain, 'Well, it's a bong, man, don't worry,' and tell me what a bong is. A big thing for a stoner is to get another stoner to try new things. A couple of my friends were real excited to show me what a bong is, take bong hits, and explain the whole thing to me like, 'This is a pipe' ... 'this is a stem' ... 'you pack the pipe like this' ... you don't smoke these seed things because they're bad.' It was sort of like a baseball player teaching a little kid how to play baseball. And I've done it to all kinds of kids myself and I really enjoyed it too. It was sort of like teaching Drugs 101.

"So that was freshman year. I started rebelling more. I started growing out my hair. I was getting less and less responsible than before, which wasn't much at all, and it just started going down. I didn't see anything happening to me. All I knew was I was having fun and when I was stoned I didn't feel that empty space inside me. The empty space is something I felt missing in my life, that I never grabbed a-hold of. The space was my *magical child* not being able to come out; it was me not fulfilling what I knew I could do and being who I could be. That empty space was waiting for me to fill it with who I am and who I love. That empty space got filled by smoking pot. If I could do drugs, then I could *be* someone, *be* somebody, be validated in some way, have an identity. The whole preppy thing was boring and wasn't doing it for me anymore, and so I thought if I could do drugs it would do it for me. I'm a very fast, very quick, person. My mind races! It's hard to get focused.

"A big part of this began when my brother played a CD of The Doors for me. I liked it a lot. To this day, I still like The Doors. 'This guy's [Jim Morrison of The Doors] cool,' I thought. I got turned onto the Seventies. They smoked dope and all. I started growing my hair long, dressing like a hippie. I wanted to get even with my parents. They paid a lot of attention to my brother who had tried to kill himself at an early age, and I felt ignored. So I felt like I had to do something to get attention. I felt the whole world just wasn't *getting* me, so I felt I had to be *gotten*. And the biggest person who wasn't getting me was myself.

So I started dressing like a hippie. I felt it was an expression of my inner self. Since no one was paying attention to me, I thought this was a way no one could ignore me. I looked straight from the Seventies. Two decades earlier."

Jacob had been attending acting workshops for a little over a year. I saw that he was *really* turned on by them. I hoped he would reverse his downhill direction if he had something that motivating him to excel. I reasoned that we could use the workshops to exert some control over Jacob. Besides, they seemed to be an emotional outlet for him, a release for the anger, fear, and inner demons driving him. Every time he attended a workshop, he returned home upbeat and enthusiastic. For a couple of days afterward he was even respectful to us. But he'd quickly return to the anger and disrespect which typified his behavior towards us and other authorities the rest of the month.

So I was pleased when his talent manager requested that we allow Jacob to move to LA. The theory was that he would live with her, become even more engaged in the workshop process, and attempt to get paying work acting and in commercials – because of her connections, a realistic and probable likelihood if he worked at it. Working hard towards a goal could only do him good. But had he learned to work towards a goal?

"Now before I got into the big hippie image, I was still into acting and enjoyed it a lot. The workshops allowed me to express myself, to express the *real self* inside me. My parents were trying a whole bunch of things at this time. They tried buying me a car, sending me down to LA to live with my talent manager to attempt to become an actor, etc., but none of it worked out. I ended up coming back up to Northern California and I'm glad I did because I was very lonely in LA. So I came back here extremely worn out. I was writing a lot of poetry; I started playing music. I was still going to the workshops. After a while, I was into the hippie thing in full swing. Didn't take long at all. Soon after I returned, things started going down hill, way down hill."

Sandy

"I was watching Jake really closely. I saw a couple of big turning points. First of all, his friends changed *really fast* and I knew that his new friends used drugs heavily. No one had to say anything to me – I just *knew* that was their scene.

"The next big turning point was when Jake went to LA. His talent manager told him that to obtain his Screen Actors Guild card he couldn't have any D's or F's on his report card. All of a sudden, Jake's world collapsed on him. He didn't believe inside that he could achieve anything higher than D's and F's, so he gave up. He shut down and self-medicated. He lasted in LA less than one semester. One night he called us and said that he just *had* to come home, that he was so homesick. Of course, yes, he was a little homesick but the real thing was that he couldn't face getting the low grades he knew he was going to get. He couldn't face asking for help in math. He didn't have the self-discipline to study. Always to the rescue, we brought him home.

"As soon as he returned, there was a brief honeymoon period but then he got heavily into drugs. Of course, we objected. Immediate conflict ensued. Knowing something about drugs ourselves from our own hippie days in the late Sixties and Seventies, we thought that Jake was trying to find some kind of inner peace and validation through drugs. Of course we knew that it is a false way to find what he was looking for. All we could see is that our son was going down, down, down. It didn't seem there was anything I could *do* about it, though.

"That's when I finally started trying to get Tim's attention. I would talk to him and describe what I saw in Jake's behavior. But Tim would say, 'Oh, it's just a phase all kids go through! We simply have to help him work out of it.' He thought that Jake would have to conquer his own demons himself and that he'd eventually accomplish that on his own. In truth, I'd seen the potential for his going downhill before he went to LA. But it seemed like what Jake wanted, and I knew that Tim thought this would be the incentive he'd need to work on his academics and to discipline his life a little. But when Jake failed in LA and we brought him back, I thought to myself, 'Oh no, it's going to get *really bad* now!' And I began to get through to Tim.

"I always thought, and still think, that we were very good, loving, and giving parents. There was nothing abnormal, obsessive, crazy, or violent about us. Sure, there was the depression I had. But as soon as I saw it, I got medication and the medication helped. When as parents we realized we were having difficulties, we got help. We were responsible parents. We never abused; instead, we nurtured. So – why would one child attempt suicide and another get hooked on drugs?! At the time, it baffled and confused me. And it almost destroyed me. A lot to learn lay ahead of me."

Jacob said how much he wanted to be an actor. His honest and caring manager said he had a lot of talent. But how often did we see him actually risk getting on stage? For someone who professed to love acting, he seemed to avoid getting near a stage. Attend acting classes, yes; but try out for a high school play, *no way*! So when he returned from LA he entered high school as another kid with little motivation or direction, lots of time on his hands, and no willingness to risk living his dream.

One of the worst things for me was Jacob's deteriorating relationship with teachers and school authorities. While never a classroom achiever, Jacob had always charmed his teachers. They pulled for him and reached out to him on different levels. But high school was radically different. There was no time for his shenanigans! His classroom behavior worsened, clearly irritating and frustrating his teachers. This was particularly difficult for me to accept because I am someone who cooperates, wins approval, and resolves conflict, not someone who *creates* it! His behavior towards authorities angered and frustrated me! I was mortified and embarrassed. Jacob was clearly making *me* look bad! I tried to reason with him. In return, he scoffed at me and I became *very* angry. Nothing constructive happened.

Sports had always been important to Jacob – soccer, Little League, PONY League, hockey. Jacob was a good soccer player. He was fast and played with joy and intensity. He was fierce and would hurl his body through the air to make a play. I *loved* to watch him and never missed a game. But he was never a star at an age when performance seems so important. I think sports wore him down. When he tried out for high school soccer with a hoard of other try-outs, the coach did not pick him out of the crowd. Of course, Jacob was trying out with leather moccasins on, so he didn't give himself a chance! When the soccer coach asked him back and gave him another chance, he refused. Self-consciousness or disinterest or ... had taken over. Athletics was suddenly a statement of who he was *not* rather than an expression of the physical and emotional joy I knew he could be. His ever-fragile athletic confidence was lost. It hurt me as a father to watch this – but not because I had some big sports agenda for my kid. I remember saying to Sandy, "Well, there goes just one more way he can express himself and be involved in the world." It seemed like he was shutting down his outlets.

The distance between Jacob and me grew immeasurable. Once I held him close to me, once we were inseparable, once we couldn't get enough of each other. Now we had no common ground, no positive bond of feeling.

Especially during their teen years, challenging kids erode a marriage. Struggling children find a way to turn almost unnoticeable cracks into highly visible fissures. In an age when divorce can be a tempting way out of a challenging marriage, it is no surprise that marriages topple when tested by the extreme challenges some children pose. A greater surprise perhaps is that so many marriages *don't* fail! Having had not one but two pretty challenging kids wore us down quickly. Somehow Sandy and I never split up, but as the challenges increased so did the tension between us.

Sandy normally arrived home from work first. Often by the time I arrived home, a conflict between her and Jacob was in full swing. In complete denial of my own emotional state of being, I noticed how emotional *they* were! As I walked in the door, I was frequently greeted with the bad news of the day. "Not much of a loving welcome!" I'd say to myself. I'd immediately begin to feel sorry for myself. What had I done to deserve this? Jacob would be pressuring Sandy to buy something or to extend a privilege he had not earned. Or he would be verbally abusing her. Something negative always seemed to be going on about the time I arrived home. And I always had to hear about it, whatever it was. I resented Sandy's bringing me into these crises. I assumed she was defaulting every problem to me to solve. Couldn't she handle *anything* herself? Did every problem always require *me* to solve it? Could I not even have *five minutes* to myself when I got home without some crisis to attend to? The truth is, I wanted to avoid this stuff because I had no idea what to do about it! Plus, I knew that my solution would always be something different than what Sandy would want to do. Then we'd argue and nothing satisfactory would come out of it.

I did not trust in the problem-solving capacity of anyone else in the family. *They* always seemed to get into negative emotion! Why was it that *I* had to intervene between Jacob and Sandy? Why couldn't *they* ever work things out? How long was I going to be able to jump in and fix things between them? I became frantic wondering how we were going to hang together.

When there wasn't a storm greeting me, silence was – a silence as deafening as the noise. Neither was acceptable. When I came home on the silent nights, Sandy was already asleep, worn out from dealing with the needs of the special children in her classroom all day long followed by some crisis with Jacob. If I got home and she was still available, she had to deal with me too! And I was *plenty* critical of Sandy and the way she handled things. At the time I didn't want to look closely or honestly at myself. I chose to see the picture easiest to develop in the darkroom of my mind. That was a picture of a lazy, weak, and depressed woman, unwilling to face matters head on, unwilling to resolve any form of conflict, unwilling even to remain conscious. I saw a woman choosing to escape and hide. "Great!" I said to myself. "Jacob is escaping and so is Sandy!"

Increasingly, I simply did not want to come home from work. Work was where generally I experienced limited success, home where I experienced failure. But now nothing was doing it for me anymore. Nothing was working. I didn't feel there was anywhere to go where I felt OK.

Often I paused on the doorstep and took a deep breath before walking in the front door at night. I lingered there, wondering how I would make it once I got inside, wondering what the daily crisis would be, hoping that tonight nothing would be asked or required. It just didn't seem right that it was this difficult to walk into my own home! I sensed the household energy immediately as I stepped through the front door and I rarely liked it!

With a habit of pretending formed over the years, it was easy to put false cheer into a greeting. "Hello! I'm home!" But I wasn't happy to be there. I just pretended. I didn't want to deal with pain or trouble, but I didn't want to appear weak either. Beneath my false veneer of cheer lay a cauldron full of fear and dark emotions easily spilled by the tremor of even the smallest household skirmish. In spite of the pretense, I was *furious* and everyone could see it but me, hiding as I was from myself.

I was terrified and intimidated by any form of conflict. I was unprepared and ill-equipped to cope with it in my home. I wanted only peace, quiet, and harmony. Even though I knew it was a fictional existence and would have laughed at the suggestion, I wanted the family ideal as portrayed on tv where father walks in the door to bright, delightful children and a loving, perky, and devoted wife. Any family "crisis" they portrayed on tv wasn't *nearly* the crisis brewing in *my* home! Why couldn't I have a home like that? Surely there were lots of homes where a father looked forward to returning to his sanctuary after a long day at the office. Why wasn't *I* thus privileged? What had *I* done wrong? Had I not given everything to my family? Was I not the Little League coach, the Indian Guides dad, the involved parent? Didn't I read them plenty of stories when they were little? Was this the outcome I deserved? Each day I deposited another little investment in my private bank of self-pity. My deposit was *growing*.

I couldn't seem to point to an area of my life where I felt I had it together. I had no positive excitement in my life. I lacked energy. I had nothing to look to beyond myself. To make matters worse, it became impossible to discuss my problems with Sandy. Increasingly, she seemed to resent me and spent all available time reading in bed, often with the door to our bedroom shut. I had no creative outlet other than work. I felt like a well drying up. I spent long hours working at my computer. It seemed the only way I could medicate myself against everything else. I didn't want to ask my mother or her new husband for advice because I didn't want to worry them. I had few friends. Most of my friends had been in Little League! "How did I *get* myself into this lonely hole?" I wondered sorrowfully.

I longed to talk to someone. But I didn't *even like* people that much anymore. I saw their faults. People seemed so messy to be around. I wanted a friend to talk to whom I could really respect. There were one or two, but I took little advantage of them. It was difficult to talk to anyone because I always felt so weak. I always ended up blaming Sandy or the kids. I knew that wasn't cool, then I'd do it anyway, and feel terrible about it. Or I turned the sharp knife of criticism against myself and cut myself mercilessly. Someone would say, "Don't be so hard on yourself." I'd say, "Well, I deserve it!" I hated myself really.

Life went on. I put one foot in front of another.

Ryan

I've sometimes wondered how I would have dealt with a kid like Ryan. Jacob was one kind of problem, Ryan quite another. I've come to understand that no one is given a challenge he cannot handle. Sandy, Jacob, and Mac-Lean were the perfect challenges I needed. Ryan was *someone else's* obstacle course!

I first had the privilege of interviewing Ryan a few months after he had returned home from his residential program to live again with his family. He's a young man now with a quick, friendly smile. Since I've known only the "after" version of Ryan, I've only experienced his wonderful side. He's a young man I like being around. He would laugh at this description but it's true: He's kind of like a big 6 ft. 2 in. puppy dog – friendly, eager to help out, lovable, loving, loyal, ever ready with a hug and a smile. And he has a wisdom and experience far beyond his years. But things weren't always that way with him ….

"In my life with my family, the good times were when things were not terribly traumatic. There was never a time when there was a sense of peace and harmony. There was no specific day or incident I can remember when things began to fall apart – it was always apart. My mother and dad got divorced when I was eleven. I chose to go to live with my dad for a while because I wanted to straighten some things out. But my dad was more structured and it wasn't a very good atmosphere. Once I left San Diego and moved in with my dad all I could think about was San Diego because I wanted my freedom back.

"My intention was to return home to my mom and stay, but mom's intention was for me to visit and return to my dad. I tried to be on good behavior – for example, to return home on time – so that mom would let me stay, and she agreed to let me stay.

"I had already been getting in trouble a lot at school, but now was when my big decline began. I was hanging out with some friends after school. I was walking by myself up to this restaurant we hung out at after school. This girl came up to me and asked if I'd like to do some speed. I said no, but she persisted. So finally I did it. From then on I became very hooked on all kinds of powder drugs. I became real mean to everybody. I constantly wanted to rip people off, anything I could do to get my drugs. Eventually, I became a skinhead, a SHARP (Skin Head Against Racial Prejudice).

"I had a lot of anger inside me towards everybody and to myself for where I'd gotten myself. Even I knew that. I had something big planned for my life, but here I was not having anybody in my family I felt close to and hooked on some bad drugs. That definitely had no future in it and I knew that. I started treating everybody really bad and pushing them away. No matter what I did, I couldn't accept people's love or trust them. A lot of those relationship issues come from my early beliefs about relationships which grew out of my parents' marriage and divorce. But the big downfall was when I got into powder drugs because they magnified all my emotions to the point where I was only emotions. Some of my anger was specific, but for the most part I just wanted something to be angry at. If somebody got in my way, even if I knew there was no justification for my

24

being angry with them, I'd find a way to be angry at them, because I wanted to vent. It was a feeling of constantly wanting a target. It was my retaliation at the world. Through a lot of my growing-up, I feel I was neglected by my family. My parents had their own stuff going on and never paid any attention to the kids. My sister was off doing the same as me. I don't even remember really seeing my brother as a kid, except for a couple of times. So it was like I spent a lot of my life in loneliness. My anger was an extreme outcome of the loneliness. I was trying to show everybody that they couldn't just walk all over or ignore me. In a wider sense, I was showing everyone how I hurt. It was like the most extreme cry for help I could give, like I was sending out a twenty-four-hour-a-day 9-1-1 call to the world that said, 'Hey, things aren't going right!'"

Over the years we develop dark, *negative emotional responses* to certain behaviors and events. These locked-in emotional responses frequently assume absolute power over our lives. Ryan was this way. Many of us possess far less freedom than we think we do. Apart from the extremity of his behavior, how vastly different are most of us from how Ryan was then? Our emotional reactions can be as invariable, it seems, as the stimulus-response reactions I read about in college describing behavioral experiments with lab animals. Drop a certain kind of pellet into my birdcage and watch me fly off the handle every time! Push my button and you're sure to evoke my fury! Our emotional reactions have formed even before our mothers are packing our lunches for school. Unless we choose differently, they stick with us. All too often we don't get off the treadmill of life enough to consider whether our involuntary emotional responses serve us well. At such a young age, Ryan was destined for an entire lifetime of running his engine on the negative emotion generated out of his parents' divorce. Like Ryan, most of us don't stop to consider choosing differently.

Ryan was certainly dialing for emergency, though. The person who needed to hear his 9-1-1 call was Susan.

Susan

When I first met Susan I understood instantly that she is a woman with a lavish and open heart. She is exceptionally caring and a determined, take-charge woman who easily leads and organizes. When she commits herself to something, it's all the way. All those attributes endear me to her. I have liked her since the moment I met her. I'll lay money that Susan raised all her kids with love and devotion and gave everything she had in the process. But the youngest of her brood was the greatest challenge.

"Like so many others, I saw a 'downward spiral' of behavior occurring over a period of about three or four years. As a child, Ryan was always so loving and kind to others - especially those he thought were the underdog. He would show kindness to smaller, younger children on the playground, to kids not viewed as the 'popular kids,' even to Billy, a mentally retarded man who loved to come to the Little League games. Billy was an idiot savant. His talent was that he had absolute recall of every Little League player, every time they had been on base, their stats, game scores, etc., from one year to the next. He was amazing! But most people didn't take time to find that out about Billy. Most walked a wide circle around him because he was different. Most kids made fun of him. Except my Ryan. My son would spend his own money on Billy at the snack bar, talk to him respectfully, and even seek him out to talk. When Ryan was about thirteen he got in a fight with some kids because they wouldn't stop teasing Billy. After the fight Ryan shared some pizza with him. It would make him really mad when they teased Billy that way. He was always worried how it affected Billy's feelings.

"Ryan had always been a challenge and a handful, very strong-willed. When he was real young, his biggest problems were with school. He didn't understand about learning disabilities and how they worked so he always felt like a failure. This was the origin of a lot of Ryan's problems.

"Things really came to a head, though, after my husband and I divorced. It was a very ugly divorce – worse than most. My husband promptly remarried, and not just anyone. He married my own sister! I had five children with Ryan the youngest. The divorce and the circumstances around it were very difficult for us. It took a toll on me. At eleven, Ryan was young enough to think that everything had been fine between mom and dad. So when the divorce occured it was quite a shock. Then it became one of those typical things where the kid bounces back-and-forth between houses. I know he felt caught in the middle. There were many things he didn't understand, things he did which only resulted in creating fires between his dad and me.

"I tried doing all the right things. Ryan was in sports and I would be the team mom. I always got involved. I always worked closely with his teachers and the school, where he increasingly acted out in class. But the older he got, the more his behavioral problems grew, such as acting out in class. He and I were in and out of counseling a lot. I read a lot of parenting books and tried to adjust my behavior. Every time things started to get just a little bit better, I'd hold onto whatever it is that I had been doing with almost a death-grip and say to myself, 'Oh good, now I've solved the problem and it'll get better now.' As I look back, I see a lot of things I could have done differently. There were a lot of hills and valleys but each valley seemed lower than the one that preceded it.

"Living around Ryan became increasingly difficult. Of course, there were good times. But I've come to learn since then, that a lot of the times I thought were good, really weren't because I was in such denial, naïve, and unaware. For a long time I felt very guilty about the divorce, the weight of twenty-year marriage, along with an extended family structure crumbling in ruin. I chose not to see fully what was really going on around me, particularly with Ryan. In my beaten-down condition, I focused mostly on the day-to-day mechanics of living.

I gave away, or more likely never really tapped, my own personal power. If I'd had even *a concept* of the power I have within me, if I had, as the song says, 'believed I could fly,' I would have intervened with Ryan a lot earlier.

"For a long time I felt guilty from a partial awareness that somehow I was failing my child. After all, I was *the mom*. Moms are supposed to protect their babies – even if that means protecting them from *themselves*. Somewhere deep inside I knew I had to find a way to dig deeper. I also desperately wanted to feel like I was good enough. To feel good enough ... what would that *look* like? What would that *feel* like? It seemed foreign and unfamiliar, that I could look and feel good enough to myself. I so envied those who seem to radiate self-acceptance and love in their lives. I didn't recognize at the time that my child and I shared this internal demon in common. Ryan didn't feel good enough either! But my lack of self-worth was so huge that it blinded me to his similar feelings, to the progressive self-destruction eating away at him from within.

"By the time Ryan was in high school, the counselors knew him very well. Some very wonderful people believed in him, but nobody seemed able to get through. When he was in seventh grade, I got called in for a parent conference early in the school year. He was acting out and having behavioral problems in every class. One very dedicated teacher told me, 'In all my years of teaching, I've never had a student like Ryan. He has such leadership potential. Just by walking into the classroom he doesn't have to say a word. He commands the attention and direction of the entire class. But right now, it's not working for a positive. If we can just turn it around, get him to believe in himself....'

"I had no clue about the amount of self-hatred inside Ryan. I mean, I understood about a poor self-concept and all, but I had no idea at the time about the depth of his problem inside. I've never forgotten that teacher's words to me because it was the first time somebody outside of his dad or me who recognized Ryan's potential. As time went on, I held onto what this teacher told me, knowing that someone else recognized that about my son. I determined not to give up on him. Sometimes things smoothed out and I thought things were going OK, but it was more that I had no clue of what was really happening with him.

"It's not an uncommon occurrence today that we'll have some dinner conversation and he'll recall an incident when he came home drunk or stoned and talked to me in face-to-face conversation. I had been totally clueless. I thought I was a very informed parent. Ha! I was *so ignorant!* I really didn't want to know about what was going on. As a teen, I had never used alcohol or drugs and was never rebellious. My 'image' was Miss Goodie Two Shoes, the perfect daughter. Oh brother! Gag me with a spoon! No one recognized or guessed for a minute how utterly worthless that girl felt inside. I played the role *so* well, so effectively. But what a touch of irony it is that, being so 'good' meant giving up an awareness of reality – so much so that I became a dunce in recognizing the symptoms of my child's pain. Even after all I've been through, it's still hard for me to accept that I did this sometimes.

"I educated myself a lot about parenting – I read a lot of books, took countless parenting classes, stayed up-to-date with news articles, even watched all the applicable talk shows – I did anything I *could* do to be an 'aware' parent. Or so I thought. I thought I was so knowledgeable; I thought I was being so vigilant. But in the end, it was denial – that condition of not knowing that I was lying to myself – which ruled over me."

Sometimes as I talk with Susan it's hard to believe she is the woman she's talking about! She has obviously changed a lot. The person talking to me is very dynamic. As she talks about this fragile side of her, she touches me with her humanity. How forcefully she was imprisoned by her own past! Her upbringing affected nearly everything she did – from choice of occupation to parenting. The Miss Goodie Two Shoes, the perfect daughter who felt she was worth nothing, and knew nothing, was only too willing to deny the reality of her own perception of Ryan. Perhaps Ryan's challenge to Susan was partly to overcome her own history.

"Eventually, I began to get a clue. I started to hate it when the phone rang because it would be some parent calling. Or Ryan would have beaten up some kid. I was hearing from the school all the time. I was in retail with a varied schedule each day. We never established a regular life. I never knew from one moment to the next where he was or what he was doing. By the time Ryan was fifteen, I was aware of drug use and assuming he was drinking whenever he could. I was pretty sure he smoked pot sometimes. Of course, what I *later* learned he was stoned *most* of that time! His school behavior was atrocious. Anything to do with an authority figure was sure to prove trouble. I hated it when the school contacted me because it always was bad news. This only reinforced the message I was giving myself that I wasn't doing well enough.

"By the time he was fifteen, tensions between Ryan and me grew to such a point that he asked to go to live with his dad. I felt just totally beat up; I was whipped. At that point I said, 'I'm not going to fight you on it.' I just couldn't scrape myself together any more. About four weeks later he was telling me, 'Mom, I want to come home again.' That's because his dad and his step-mom laid down the law – 'These are the rules of the house and you're not going to disobey them.' Of course he started causing problems in their home, too.

"He had really bounced back-and-forth between his dad's home and mine for about three years. It was a *terrible* time! He'd stay about six months at a stretch, until his behavior became so unbearable that he ended up at the other parent's house. But I was sensing a different energy from him at age fifteen, and I was feeling a sense of increasing desperation within him. This time something was beginning to go off in my maternal gut. Some inner voice that spoke to me that time was running out. I was trying everything I could think of. I kept having a lot of false hope – hope that his innate sweetness would take over. Something in me said, 'I'm his mom! I'm *supposed* to be able to get through to him. I just have to do it harder, faster, better.' Emotionally, I was so beat up that physically I couldn't do it any more.

"There were many additional developments in my life at that time – positive and negative. I thought I was going to lose my oldest daughter to cancer. My youngest daughter was getting married. My finances were so bleak that I had to rent part of my home to a roommate. I felt like I was being drawn and quartered, and I was drowning in guilt.

"The one bright spot was a brand new relationship with Greg, the new man in my life. Being with him felt so great. It was such a wonderful reprieve. Of course, I didn't trust our relationship yet. More importantly, I didn't trust *myself* yet. Ryan continued to beg, even plead, to come live with me again. I knew what life with Ryan would be like again. It would be great for a short while, and then we'd get right back to where we'd been, or worse. And I believed that having Ryan around would threaten my relationship with Greg and perhaps result in its demise! Besides, it seemed I had reached a saturation point with Ryan. I felt like I had nothing left to give. I was completely out of gas. Just anticipating the thought of having him back was physically exhausting. At least, there was no way I could do this *on my own* any longer. I knew that from the deepest, most guilt-ridden depths of my soul. I knew that I wasn't the one who could stop his self-destruction. I thought that I *should* love him enough that I could make a difference, but that wasn't enough.

"Greg sensed my desperation towards Ryan. I feared to voice my concerns to Greg, fearing he would think me melodramatic, until one day he voiced the same concerns I had. The reality of the situation took on a frightening possibility then and I shared all my fears with Greg. Even though he did not even know Ryan yet, Greg vowed to me that he would do whatever was necessary, whatever was required, to help us. He said to me repeatedly that he was there for us physically, financially, emotionally – whatever Ryan or I needed! This was *two weeks* into our relationship! Somewhere a voice inside me whispered that I could trust this man. My mental voice countered, 'That's a joke! Men aren't to be trusted!' But instinctively I knew I was beginning the fight for my child's life and I knew that this strong man beside me could be a strong helpmate as well as a loving companion."

Paul

Paul always saw himself as different from the rest. We can trace this view of his relationship to the world to his parents. Mom and dad were children of the late sixties, well enmeshed in the counter culture world view popular then in Sausalito where they lived. Melissa and her husband raised their children to think independently. However, both parents developed a deep distrust of "the system" and passed this distrust along to their two children, Paul and a brother four years his senior.

When Paul reached the fifth grade, he began to differentiate himself from his peers. His best friend always had candy. Paul didn't have that good fortune. To possess candy like his friend became an obsession for him. His attempts to convince his parents that he too should be able to have lots of candy were met with refusal. One day in class he confessed his frustration to all his classmates and began to cry before the entire class. That he had allowed himself to cry in front of his peers embarrassed Paul. By this time, he had learned from his father Monty that you do not share your emotions or feelings with others, particularly in front of a whole group. Deeply angry with himself over having crossed his father's stern line, Paul resolved never to let anyone or anything get to him to such an extent again. He decided always to differentiate himself through his innate intelligence.

About the same time Paul began to rebel at school. School had never been difficult. On the contrary, it was seldom challenging enough for his quick mind and frequently he was bored. As he moved on through sixth and seventh grades, Paul showed his disdain for common academic achievement by spending most of his time reading sci fi in class.

> "One day my dad was at school and the social studies teacher complained because I was reading in his class and not doing the work. My dad was already mad because he had just got a two-hundred dollar ticket from this policeman who lived down the street and hassled him all the time. So my dad said to the teacher, 'Is he bothering anyone else in the class?' And the teacher said, 'No.' So my dad says, 'We'll why don't you just let him read, then?' But my social studies teacher kept hassling dad about it and finally dad just went off at him because he was already mad anyway: 'What do you want me to do, lock him up or something?!'

> "Apparently, dad scared the teacher, so the teacher called the school psychologist. Dad doesn't like psychologists with all their 'psycho babble.' That's when I really started clinging to my father's beliefs. He always hated psychologists. And now I was having to deal with them, too, and I decided I wasn't going to like them either. So whenever I had to deal with a psychologist, I just shined it on for them. I always agreed, just to get them off my back, but never really cooperated.

> "My dad's attitude was that you've just got to get through school; you don't have to do well or anything. However, my mom had this big thing about school. She really wanted me to do well."

To Paul's mother intellectual mastery was one of the important ways you win in the world. She frequently implored her son to do his homework. "You gotta do your homework, you gotta do your homework!" she would repeat. But these urgings had little effect on her young independent thinker. "I'd always forget my homework and stuff," reported Paul later.

Dad approached the problem of homework differently. His approach was, "You've just got to do enough to get by, to get these people off your back."

Since schoolwork was rather boring anyway, it was easy for Paul to adopt his father's approach, an approach founded in strongly anti-authoritarian views. Paul never flunked, but he never gave in to teachers, never showed them he cared, seldom excelled on their terms. He would be his own man.

Paul's computer became a sanctuary, a way to escape. His interest in the computer had developed when father and sons built a rocket together and patented it. Now the computer assumed a new significance in Paul's life.

"Dad was always very emotionally explosive and, more and more, there were arguments between mom and dad. When tension started to occur in the family, mom tried to help me, but I'd just sink into my computer. Dad didn't care much for my thing with the computer either. He'd always threaten me, 'I'm going to take an axe to the computer!' And mom would always threaten me, 'I'm going to take *away* the computer!' – mainly because I wasn't doing my homework. So, I'd just say I'd do my homework only to get my computer back. But I only did the minimum and sometimes I'd trick my mom and not even do that. My computer was kind of like my drug, like, I'll go to rehab enough so that I don't get arrested, but then I'll go right back to drugs as soon as I can.

"I hadn't got into drugs or anything like that yet, but things were starting to go downhill for me. There was a lot of tension between me and dad or between me and mom about these issues.

"All during my growing up, my parents smoked pot openly in the house. Dad got caught once and had to go into rehab counseling. He explained drugs to me this way: 'It's OK to use recreationally when you're older but that you should wait until you're finished with school.' Meanwhile, my older brother and dad smoked pot together. I looked up to my older brother as a role model. He always had balance and perspective and seemed able to deal more easily, I thought, with tensions in the household than I could. I wanted to be like him, able to have the pleasures of life and to cope easily with the tensions."

By this time in Paul's family, the themes in the family drama were well established. Dad was angry at forms of authority – police, teachers – and transferred this hostility to his son. Although sharing her husband's fear and distrust of authority, Melissa was more moderate – and less influential – with Paul than her husband. Mom weakened her position in Paul's eyes by continuously harping on the importance of schoolwork, a theme which dad undermined with his just-get-by attitude. Also there was the issue of drugs in the home. Although everyone else in the family used to one extent or another, Paul was instructed to hold off using until later on in life. The rest of his family seemed able to successfully confine their drug use to pot for the most part and to cope reasonably well, though clearly dad had dark emotional outbursts. These were the seeds of family breakdown and, as Paul's life progressed, they would continue to receive all the nourishment they required to reach their full potential. One day Melissa separated from Monty who angrily left the home and became inaccessible to the family.

Melissa

Melissa is a musician living in Sausalito. She thinks carefully as she speaks, vacillates in her decisions, sees many different angles to a problem, and takes her time to sort it all through. Even then she has a difficult time coming to closure – often revisiting a question long after she's come to a conclusion. She is very serious about looking inwardly. She asks lots questions and has no pretense about being an authority. Melissa is a truth seeker who won't settle for half-baked ideas and platitudes. She is perceptive and keenly intelligent, independent and resistant to group pressure. Over the time I have known her, the vestiges of Melissa's old philosophy of rugged individualism and defiance of authority have grown fainter. No longer standing upo the bedrock of this old belief system, Melissa has expanded her capacity to consult, listen, think, and choose freely for herself what seems true according to an inner barometer.

"After Monty and I separated, I made a firm commitment to myself that, even though Paul was becoming increasingly difficult, I would never send him away. He didn't need another parent abandoning him.

"After Monty left, things really got worse. Paul had always been secretive and uncommunicative, but it got *much* worse. He dropped out of school and spent a lot of time away from home, and I didn't know where. Intuitively, I knew that something was pretty bad. I found big boxes of over-the-counter cold medicine around. He was purchasing this stuff at Walgreens. Even the smallest rules in the home seemed impossible to enforce. He became impossible to control. It simply got to the point where I realized that all the love in the world was not going to fix anything.

"I've had to look long and hard at my marital relationship and its contributions to Paul's troubles. As parents, we were diametrically opposed – always were, from Day One. We had been together for twenty years. I was twelve years younger and he was a Vietnam vet. We couldn't agree on anything. My husband has a pretty serious drug habit. He smokes a lot of marijuana and drinks. He was a very loving husband. He wasn't physically violent. But because of his pot-smoking he let many, many things go without trying to correct them either with me or Paul, without telling either of us that something bothered him or that he felt something was wrong. After a while he'd explode in anger, usually when he didn't have anything to smoke. Smoking will, of course, suppress any kind of anger. He smoked because that's how he coped. Or rather *didn't* cope. There was no doubt, however, that we both loved each other very much. It's just that when the threads wore thin, they broke.

"The event that precipitated his leaving was when Paul came home with a report card with almost all F's. My husband's response was just to shrug it off. I asked him if he didn't feel some responsibility. He got very angry and wanted to beat the shit out of Paul. I think that was the only thing he could think of to deal with the situation. The days that followed were pretty awful. My response was to spend the next several days standing between them to protect Paul.

"Education was actually important to both of us. At first when Monty decided to do something, he would do these really weird things. Like he went with Paul to middle school to see what was going on. After doing that, he concluded that the school was really good. Then he had an encounter with one of Paul's teachers during which he went ballistic. He decided all of a sudden that the school was horrible and that they spent all their time calling roll and didn't know what they were doing. So this was the kind of contradiction Paul grew up with. One minute it was one way; the next it was something completely different. And this was coming from the same person!

"I was very hard-nosed about academics with Paul. I was exceedingly concerned about academics. That comes from my own stuff because I didn't finish high school when I was a teenager. I finished it later and it was very hard on me to do it. I could see Paul heading down a path I wanted him to avoid. And of course he rushed headlong into the very path I was attempting to steer him away from.

"At one point I took Paul aside and told him, 'You know, I harp on you every night about your homework. Even if you get it done, you leave it at home or throw it out before you get to school. Obviously, this doesn't work. So it's sink or swim time and I'm going to let you do what you're going to do.' His report card told me that he chose to sink.

"At that point I talked to Monty who responded violently. I told him I wouldn't tolerate violence, so he left. I think he knew of no other way to discipline. I really think he meant well. I fault him only one way – that he never considered the possibility of their being another way than his way. Because obviously when you see things going downhill and you're stuck, you have to seek another way. But he never did that. That's his part of it.

"My part of the relationship failure with Monty is this. I saw very early on in our relationship how out-of-control the pot smoking was. Even though I smoked it myself, I smoked it much less frequently. I smoked daily but only took a couple of hits. Monty on the other hand smoked two to five joints a day. He did this and even held down a job and, in fact, worked very hard. Not only that, he invented and patented a rocket. Monty is a brilliant guy. He's not your average drug addict. He is naturally an extremely hyperactive person. So the dope calmed him down, actually. He was just medicating himself.

"However, there was little control in the moderation of his temper. The way I dealt with these problems was that, over the course of our marriage, I had three affairs. This absolutely killed Monty! It was a good ten years before the situation with Paul erupted. But by the time things got bad with Paul, Monty continued to allow this to eat at him and he would attempt to reciprocate by hurting me in very inappropriate ways. I always felt like I could rise above it and that our relationship could rise above it, but clearly it could not. When I saw that he wanted to beat the shit out of Paul, I felt that really what he wanted to do was beat *me*. It seemed like a lot of old, pent-up stuff. Because Monty's way was to smoke-and-deny, smoke-and-deny … deny that anything painful exists."

Melissa was only eighteen when she met and married the older Monty who assumed the role of father figure and teacher. She grew up under his tutelage and system of belief, adopting it as her own. "Smoke-and-deny" was the technique he taught her. As years passed by, Melissa began to change and seek to establish her own identity.

"The intial way I took power for myself was to have an affair. When Monty and I got into big issues, he'd say, 'Look. If you're not in jail and you don't have a gun to your head, you're OK.' And I'd say to myself, 'Oh man, he's right! What am I *whining* about?! I'm not in jail and I don't have a gun to my head. I guess I must be OK.' It took me many years to realize that there are many shades of gray between being OK and having a gun to your head!"

As Melissa began to differentiate herself from her mentor, she began to use her considerable analytical power to examine all that she had taken for granted as given. She cast an illuminating light that revealed much about the man she married, herself, and their relationship. Illumination threatened status quo.

"You see, his smoke-and-deny technique was how he was coping with Post Traumatic Stress Disorder from his stint in Vietnam. So in effect, I had been maturing under PTSD and was co-dependent in my relationship to him. In fact, I suffered from PTSD by proxy. I had all the nightmares *for him*! When we were first together, he had repetitive nightmares about Vietnam. Over the years they were less and less frequent. The last few years of our marriage I began to have a horrifying repetitive nightmare. Monty and I dug in the dirt with a terrible foreboding feeling. We hit something solid and when we dug it up it was a bag of bones or some body parts or something gruesome. In therapy, I realized I was having these nightmares *for* him. I interpreted this dream in two ways. One was that we had buried our issues and wouldn't talk about them or unearth them. I was trying to dig them up because we couldn't ignore our wounds and expect them to heal. The other was that Monty had a lot of buried issues. For him they were real dead bodies and real body parts. In Vietnam he learned how to deal with problems in a certain way. He learned to protect himself emotionally and physically by putting on emotional blinders on. That's how he got through that war. It was a very good tactic for a war but not such a good one for a marriage. He never got rid of it. He didn't know *how* to get rid of it. And I didn't know how to help. I was willing to get help, but he wasn't. In fact, getting help was very threatening to him.

"Monty was eighteen when he went into the Army. He was avoiding the draft, but they caught up with him and gave him a choice between being hauled off to

Vietnam or going to jail. So he went into the Army. And he *knew* the government was lying to him! And there he was along with all the other boys of his generation, and they all knew the government was lying to them about the war. And here he was fighting in this *ridiculous* war that he wanted no part of! So why would he trust the government?! Why would he trust *any* authority?! *Of course* he had authority problems! And he passed them right along to his son. This had an enormous impact on Paul.

"I tried going to Monty and saying, 'Look, we have these problems. We've got to work them out.' But I wouldn't get anywhere because it was just too threatening.

"I began to change partly through therapy, through my awareness that I didn't want to smoke weed anymore, partly through the Twelve-Step Program, partly through Al-Anon. I was evolving. When I started doing all this stuff, our relationship really became rocky because everything was built on Monty's way, the way he'd taught me. When I no longer wanted to do it Monty's way, when I wanted to remove the veils, it all fell apart between us.

"I deeply, *deeply* regret some of the things I did. I know how hurtful they were to him. I've learned a lot about myself, about being humble and honorable. I learned a lot of it from my husband but I'm sorry these lessons took such a toll on our family."

Paul

Since there were always drugs around the house, it seemed easy and natural for Paul to get started. But there was something different about his use than his family members. Overall, he seemed to have less control than the rest of his family. Then there was the deteriorating relationship with school authorities. His tenuous commitment to keep up with academics, so important to his mother, diminished even further.

"I was about to enter the ninth grade. Things were going to crap in the family. My friend stole some drugs from my dad and dad was all pissed off at me for it. Mom started going to support groups about then. She tried to convince us to join her but we all said 'no way.' We all hated the psychologists. 'They're part of the system and the system's bad,' we thought. Mom stopped using drugs. She tried talking to my dad and telling him to stop using around us, but he wouldn't do it. He'd been doing it for so long. For my whole life I'd been around weed. My dad said, 'I don't think it's going to be a big deal if we stop now.' That's when the real fissures in my family started to develop.

"I was closest to my brother and looked up to him so much. But he had this job and didn't want to get involved in the family anymore because you could tell that the whole thing was about to split in half. My mom was trying to hold it together. My dad was trying to hold onto drugs, but he had a lot of anger about stuff. He ended up leaving. And the thing I did is, I blamed my mom for it all. I said, 'If you wouldn't have got onto this psychiatrist/support group stuff, if you wouldn't have told us all to get off drugs and stuff, then the family wouldn't have got all jacked up.' And that's honestly what I thought then. It seems really weird to me now but that's what I thought then. But my mom said, 'If we can't handle stopping pot and going to a support group, then something's wrong.' This was my freshman year in high school. I was fifteen.

"My dad had been my main motivation for staying in school – through fear, like, 'If you don't go to school, I'm going to axe your computer.' So now that he was gone I said, 'OK, I don't have to do school any more.' I was in a new school now, a real academic high school, real strict. All the teachers loved me, except one. Engineering and computers were my expertise. I got A's in my engineering class. I'd mess around with old, donated NASA computers and fix them up. But I had a real authority problem with the principal and the dean. A *real* authority problem! I'd actually been working on trying to get out of the school. So I'd been wreaking havoc. One day I wanted to go see a friend and give him some drugs. So I went to see the dean and made up some excuse to convince him to let me leave. But he totally surprised me and said, 'You're not in this school anymore.' And just to be defiant I argued with him and said, 'You can't kick me out because I still owe a book fine.' But he hated me just like I hated him. So he took out ten dollars, paid the fine, and kicked me out anyway.

"I started doing a lot of drugs at this point. Then things really started to get bad. I really hadn't done that much before, but when I started it grew real fast, geometrically. And I have to say that I liked drugs, I liked them a lot. I had a lot of fun with them, but they brought bad consequences for me because I really couldn't handle them. All my beliefs were aligned against getting help. 'I'm not going to go to NA or anything,' I'd say to myself. My dad didn't want me to go either because he was afraid that I'd narc him off. He'd gotten arrested once before and didn't want to get arrested again because then they'd force him to go to NA. So I wouldn't get help. Mom got me a tutor so I could pass the GED test and be legally out of school. Well, turns out my tutor used drugs, so pretty soon he started selling me drugs. He was a good guy and all, but he was kind of weak within himself."

As he grew up, a growing lack of agreement between mother and father contributed to Paul's inability to cope with life challenges. As mom became stronger, repotted herself, and brought forth new shoots of her being into the world, dad dug in his heals, locked in his view of the world, unwilling to join Melissa in digging around in the troubling but rich soil her dream revealed. The result was a conflict not just between parents but in how they saw the world. Caught in this conflict, Paul could turn it into opportunity or become a casualty of his parent's war.

❖

Cary

When I met Cary at Paradise Cove, he was well on his way in the program and making great strides with his life. Open and expressive, he spoke rapidly and with obvious sincerity and enthusiasm. His face lit up like a candle whenever the topic of his mother came up. Even the bright sunshine of Western Samoa could not outshine this boy's love for his mom!

"My life has been crazy so far! I've gone through more than most people have by the time they are forty and I'm only eighteen! I've been in and out of Juvenile Hall since thirteen. I've lived on my own and I'm in a tropical island thousands of miles away from home. I've been here for nine-and-a-half months and I was in Juvey (Juvenile Hall) for four months before I came here. I've come from worshipping the devil to finding the Lord Jesus Christ and allowing Him into my heart. I've gone from stealing and hitting my parents to loving them to death!

"As far back as I can remember, my parents always wanted the best for me. They gave me unconditional love. We went on trips as a family all the time. Since I am an only child, I got all the attention I wanted plus more.

"If I didn't like what my parents did or if what they were doing wasn't in my best interest, they would quit doing it. I can remember a specific time when I was in second or third grade. They were teaching us about drugs in school, how dangerous they were. I remember my teacher telling me, if you smoke one marijuana cigarette, you will lose five years of your life. It scared me to death and I didn't ever want to do drugs! But my dad smoked and grew pot at the time. I looked in the closet in the spare bedroom one day and found three grocery bags full of pot. If one joint will take away five years, *imagine what all this will do*! I was convinced my dad was going to die any day. I was so stressed and scared that my back had muscle spasms which hurt really bad. I remember begging dad to quit. He must have thought about it because one day he took me in his truck and together we threw away all his weed in a dumpster behind a supermarket. Later I realized how hard that must have been. It was probably two or three pounds of weed – probably worth $500 or more.

"When I was so scared about my dad's life, I told my friend who lived across the street about my fear. Him and his brother assured me dad would be OK. They told me their dad had been smoking pot for years and it hadn't hurt him. One day I stole some of my dad's pot and gave it to my friend's brother. He rolled some joints and offered to smoke it with me and his brother if we promised not to tell. After thinking it over for a few minutes, I ended up trying it. I was about ten or twelve years old. After that, I didn't smoke pot again for a long time.

"I remember being real far behind in school and getting bad grades. I was feeling hopeless and wanted to give up. But my parents didn't give up on me. They helped me with my homework. They sent me to tutors and even had a tutor come to my house.

"One day after my friend Ryan was telling me about this thing called 'God,' I asked my mom and dad if they believed in God. The answer I got went a little something like this …. 'Well, not exactly. I believe that there is love and other things. I believe that when we die our souls will be happy if we lived a good life. But I don't think there is a heaven or hell and I don't think there is a God who is so powerful.' So for a long time you could say I was an atheist.

"In fourth grade I started getting in a lot of trouble at school. I was always getting negative comments on my report card, like … 'Cary is loud and disruptive. He needs to work on his manners. He doesn't follow instructions well and he's not focusing hard on his work.' I started to make friends with people who were like me – always in trouble. In seventh grade I was in after-school detention more than anyone. I also started smoking pot then. I was suspended often. My GPA at the halfway mark was 0.48 or something. I had straight F's and one D. I started sneaking out at night and had occasional run-ins with the police for curfew and stuff.

"At this point my parents tried grounding me but it didn't work. I'd just run away and they would come looking for me. They were afraid to punish me because I'd react and go crazy.

"Once I got in an argument with mom over looking up the phone number to the Oakland A's ticket agency rather than dialing 4-1-1 to get the number. She got pissed at my stubbornness because she was doing something for me and I was being difficult. She threw the phone book at me. I went crazy temporarily, put my hand through a glass picture, and ran away. I had no intention of coming home. I stayed at a friend's house and we ended up sneaking out and meeting some girls at night. When we went back in the morning, his mom caught us and kicked us out. We slept on the streets in a park the next night and were real hungry. I remembered my parents were going to a barbecue at the neighborhood pool. I knew they wouldn't be home. We walked down the alley near my house and I climbed a tree so I could see when they left. I sat in a tree for two hours watching them pack my dad's truck. As soon as they left, I broke into my garage and stole the spare key to my mom's convertible which was pretty brand new. We took it and some coins that my parents saved. We had no plans of coming back. We picked up this Mexican guy we knew who was going back to Mexico. We planned on driving him there. We drove around and collected money.

"The next day we were in Santa Cruz and almost got a parking ticket at the Beach Boardwalk. We manipulated the meter maid with a pitty story. Then on the way back, an officer pulled me over for driving too fast. At the time I was sitting on two phone books. The officer asked me if I knew what the speed limit was and I told him I didn't. He then told me I was driving too fast and I needed to slow down. Then he let me go. He didn't even ask for a license! Mom's car had been reported stolen. It's pretty strange that they weren't more suspicious of a thirteen-year-old and I didn't look a day older either.

"After we collected enough money and arranged to head for Mexico, we got arrested. I went to Juvey for my very first time. But I didn't even get fully booked by the time my parents came to get me out. I was still mad at my mom over our stupid argument and told her I'd rather stay in Juvey than go home. Plus I knew they were pissed. I was afraid of what they'd do. The next day a case worker drove me to Mountain View and put me in a group home. I met some nice girls there who became close friends. But within two weeks I got kicked out and returned to Juvey on assault-and-battery and vandalism charges. I was in three days, then out.

"At the start of eighth grade a lot of my close trouble-making friends went to community school. I got kicked out and put in opportunity school, which was like a second-chance school. But I really wanted to be with my friends. So I got myself kicked out and got my wish. The majority of kids there were on probation. I'd say most of them were recently out of Juvey or 'the ranch.' I think I went there for about two weeks. One day the meal truck didn't come. About twenty of us walked off campus to the liquor store and bought some food. When we got back they told us to go home, that we were no longer allowed at that school. Since it wasn't even very late in the day, we decided to go to this girl's house. We knocked for a long time on her door but nobody was home. One of the guys knew that her dad had guns under his bed. We broke in and stole guns, a little money, and some cokes from the frig.

"A friend told me that God was mad at me and wasn't talking to me because of what I was doing to my life.

"My best friend had moved to San Francisco. My parents sent me to visit him to get away from kids at home who were a bad influence. But while I visited him, we took LSD and smoked lots of pot.

"I came back and one day me and a few people were walking around with a .22 we'd stolen. We had it sawed off. We were walking by a field and saw a cat. My friend wanted to see if the gun was still accurate now that we'd sawed it off. He shot the cat in the neck but it didn't die. The cat's owner saw us do it and called the cops. Within minutes we were arrested and I was back in Juvey for cruelty to animals, possession of a sawed-off firearm, and firing a weapon within city limits. I was in Juvey for two months. Then they found out that the gun was linked to the burglary we did and sentenced me to six months. But the time I had already done counted against the sentence, plus I was able to work my time off. Overall, I did four months. It felt like one year, for sure! My parents visited me every time they were allowed to.

"During this time two big things happened. One is that I became a Christian. My parents also began attending church, but they were not really Christian. They went for the support and love they got there.

"The other is that when I got out, we immediately moved to _____, a small town of thirty thousand compared to the million or so people in San Jose. I enrolled in a Christian school. I was devoted to God but didn't have what it takes to be in a Christian school. The classes were real hard. They expected a high GPA. Also I had a problem with swearing. In Juvenile Hall swearing was part of life, but not at a Christian school! They kicked me out within a month. I enrolled in independent studies.

"I felt as if I had been rejected by God. I started missing my friends in San Jose. I didn't like small town life. I was used to fast-moving city life, but here I was in the middle of nowhere. The friends I made at the Christian school were no longer allowed to talk to me. My mom introduced me to David, a kid who lived down the street. This kid was the biggest liar I've ever met. I told him my life story and bragged about San Jose to him – more people, more places to go, more drugs to score. David tried to tell me that he smoked pot a lot and that he knew the biggest dealer in town. Depressed as I was, I just wanted to smoke some pot. I asked him to get me some and he ran me in circles for two weeks. He introduced me to this guy he said was the biggest dealer in town, but not to say I knew because the guy would kill me. Well, this guy didn't look or act like a dealer. He was on the high school football team. I asked him if he could get some weed. He said he could. David gave us ten dollars and me and the 'dealer' left. I told him what David said and he told me David was a compulsive liar. We ended up going around to five or six places trying to get some weed but we couldn't get anything. Just some crack. That changed my life forever!"

Just like Cary's parents and just like Sandy and me, many of us think our responsibility is to fix our kids. Maybe if I change jobs, move to another town, give up my addiction, find him a new friend, then maybe my kid will be saved. But is the child ready? And willing? A child has his own inner tasks to accomplish. The questions are: Will he? And when?

Jessica

The easiest thing to adore about Jessica is her smile. She smiles a lot more now than she used to and her whole face brightens. She is likeable, fun-loving, hard-working, and positive by nature. She's got a lot of heart. As with the other parents in our story, being the mother of a challenging boy hasn't been very easy on her. But she has endured and grown.

"Cary was always a difficult child who pushed the limits. I can't really remember a serene time with him. As the parent of a toddler, I was always trying to avoid a catastrophe, always trying to stay one step ahead of him.

"The first couple of years in school went well. The teachers liked him. But about the third or fourth grade, he started getting in trouble, talking back to the teachers, telling the principal what he thought. He spent a lot of time in and out of detention.

"In the seventh or eighth grade, his behavior started to get seriously bad. I didn't know it then but he was getting into drugs. He got kicked out of school several times. I had him in a halfway house but he got kicked out of that.

"After he got out of Juvenile Hall for stealing my car, we saw some changes because being arrested at least got his attention. But the changes didn't last. We thought the problem was the city and city life, so we moved to a small town. But that wasn't the solution either.

"Cary became deeply depressed. He was always talking about killing himself."

Jonathan

Such a likable kid! He wants to give me a hug right away. When we sit down in the shade of the Samoan fale to chat, he adjusts the prosthesis on his leg so he can talk comfortably. I warm up to him instantly. The staff said I'd enjoy Jonathan, and I do. They also hint that after a while he gets on people's nerves, especially his peers. "He wants attention so badly," they say, "he'll do just about anything to get it." He's a large boy who wears a big smile comfortably on his face, but his low self-esteem is quite visible there too. He doesn't think very much of himself and wants desperately for you to think well of him. Maybe then he'll know he's worth something himself.

"I remember early on I was afraid that, if I'd do something wrong, my dad would hit me. I've never been afraid of talking to my mom about my problems or the things I've done. My dad has a lot of explosive anger, though. Whenever he'd find out about something wrong I did, he got very angry, almost to the point that he'd hit me. I was afraid he was going to hurt me. He's a very short-tempered man. So it became that I never wanted to be around him.

"At one time we did a lot of things together, but as the years went by, I got into a lot of things like alcohol, drugs, and things. He'd get very angry but if I was in a real desperate position he'd be supportive. Whenever I really needed help badly, he was there to talk to me. Other times he didn't really want me around. That really hurt me because I'm his son. He shouldn't support the bad things I'd done. But the good things – I expected support for that."

Robert and Mary Beth

Robert is a big man with an enormous reservoir of stored up feeling and emotion inside him. Like his son Robert he wears it all on his face, a face which says, "I have a lot to give. I want more out of life. But I'm afraid to let go, afraid of who or what I'll discover if I do." This big man has a big heart to match. I find myself very drawn to him just as I am to his son.

When I first met Mary Beth she approached me with strength and engagement. "Hi, I'm Mary Beth," she said, offering a warm hand and bright smile – the same smile Jonathan wears. In contrast to father and son, my immediate impression of Mary Beth is that she doesn't shrink from life. Maybe she arrived at an early conclusion that life would require her to be strong. Physically large, like Robert, her eyes and facial expression reveal that Mary Beth is largest on the inside. She communicates a passion for life and a deep love of her family.

As I interview Mary Beth and Robert, she does most of the talking. Robert begins, but Mary Beth jumps right in, then he gets in a word edgewise or at most completes a thought. As our discussion progresses it becomes clear that my new friends are not yet on the same wave length. Both are very willing to talk but they don't agree on a few things. For readability, I've removed much of the back-and-forth banter characterizing their conversation at that point in their relationship.

> **Robert:** "Before placing Jonathan in the Program, things in our house were a total wreck. Jonathan was full of a totally explosive anger. I have the same explosive anger problem. It's something I'm working on. We're not totally there yet. With everything that led up to Jonathan's predicament, I totally cut him out of my life. I did what I could and then gave up on him. After a while, I did anything but what I *needed to do* to be with him. I just went to work. I distanced myself from him. I couldn't even stand to be in the same room with him. Coming home from work and finding the police here – you wouldn't believe the complete nightmare it was for us. His school was calling all the time. Other students and gang members called us threatening his life. He was very vocal to gang members. They didn't want to have anything to do with him."

> **Mary Beth:** "Jonathan's whole thing is that he has never really had a friend. Never. He would do anything to fit in, even alienate someone in hopes it would make him laugh, or pump himself up in front of another in hopes they would think he was this macho, big bad guy – which he's not. He's one of the kindest, gentlest people you'd ever want to meet if he really allows you to see *him*, not his facade. He is desperate for approval from anyone, particularly his dad. When Jonathan would make a poor choice, rather than listen to what he had to say, discuss the poor choice, or give him options of what he do differently, Robert would allow his explosive temper to take over. Then it would be between the two of them and the temperature would rise from, say, one to twenty *instantly*. Robert had this desperate, preset idea of what he wanted from his son. Jonathan in no way lived up to that. Robert created almost a self-fulfilling prophecy by being so afraid that he was going to turn out bad – the way he actually did. Every time the child looked sideways, Robert was on him, trying to correct him when what it did was ..."

> **Robert:** "... hurt him ..."

> **Mary Beth:** "... was just about *kill* him! Robert has a horribly explosive temper. It's something he knows he's got. Even now it comes out. I don't know how much he tries to keep it under control. It's just *there*.

"Jonathan was different almost from birth. Early on I realized he was ADD and everything else. I also realized I was Jonathan's advocate – often his *only* advocate. I think if I hadn't been, he wouldn't be alive today. But it's taken a toll on me, one that I would gladly do again, but I wish it had been different. Jonathan has been a full-time job. Many times in the past couple of years, when Jonathan was talking suicide, I'd have to keep him with me, or take him for a ride and lock the doors until he fell asleep, to keep him safe from himself, or put him in jail when he didn't deserve to be there. I had to lie to protect him from himself! Starting way back with teachers. He's a big kid, big for his age. Teachers thought he was in fifth or sixth grade when he was only in second. He was always expected to act his age. And he *was* – his *age* not his *size!* I always intervened. I quit my job in order to stay home – always a sore spot with Robert. I started a home day-care business so I could take care of him. No one else wanted to, because he's always been such a challenge.

"My best, clearest, earliest memory of Robert blowing up and going totally overboard with Jonathan was the first time he played with matches – a very valid fear, but Robert really lost it. He thought he'd teach him a lesson, so he burned his finger. But this kid wasn't starting fires; he was *lighting matches*. We took him to counseling, to the fire department, did the whole thing. One day I sat him in front of a bucket of water, gave him a box of matches, and said, 'Light all the matches you want.' Finally, I realized that he was trying to figure out how the fire got on the end of the stick. He wasn't being destructive! He was trying to figure out how the damned thing *worked!* And that has been this kid's life. He's smart and always wants to figure things out. When he was two years old, he fixed his tricycle when we thought it couldn't be fixed.

"Whenever anything happened in the neighborhood, the neighbors blamed Jonathan. He became the neighborhood scapegoat.

"A lot of Jonathan's problems had to do with Scott, the live-in friend of our neighbor. Scott's a real charmer, very smooth. He talked to Jonathan as an adult, treated him as a buddy rather than the child he was. The better he treated Jonathan, the less Jonathan wanted to be home with us. Jonathan had complete confidence in him. Scott was kind of a pied piper.

"He let Jonathan smoke cigarettes and swear around him. Jonathan could be one of the guys. But this guy was about thirty-two or something. He built a computer for us but we were leery of him. He was too good to be true. After we got to know him a little, something didn't seem right. I didn't know what it was yet, but I didn't really trust him. After he built the computer, the feeling was, 'Thank God it's done and he doesn't have to come in our house any more.' Yet we still tried to remain friendly. All this time, Jonathan spent more and more time there, and we tried to discourage it. But Jonathan didn't understand why. All through that summer Jonathan ran away several times. Scott was doing cocaine and marijuana and nobody knew it. He was going to stores, stealing things, then returning them – anything to get money."

Robert: "He also had paraphernalia in the bedroom."

43

Mary Beth: "Yeah, I'll get to that. Finally it came out he was having Jonathan steal for him. ..."

Robert: "... like stereos."

Mary Beth: "Well, I don't know how much Jonathan did for this guy or just for the thrill of it. Jonathan stole bicycles, cars, cell phones, and stereos, and everything showed up at Scott's house. At this point, we didn't know this was going on, but we knew that there was something wrong with a thirty-two-year-old having such interest in a fourteen-year-old. I was real concerned. But things started disappearing from their house as well, and our boys started to get blamed for it. What we found out later was that Scott stole things out of the house he was living in and from his girlfriend's children to support his habit. Our relationship with Jonathan became strained. Robert got so upset over things he did. But Jonathan wouldn't listen to us about our concerns."

Robert: "He would walk out of this house on a whim. ..."

Mary Beth: "... and Jonathan would say, as an excuse to himself, that his dad didn't want him. So a lot of that summer of 1995 Jonathan spent on the street. Scott was eventually arrested. Suddenly, Jonathan's best friend is taken away. He wouldn't believe his friend had done all those things. Jonathan's heart was totally broken when he finally realized that his god had fallen and that mom and dad were right. Then he went through a big depression."

katherine and kyle

Kyle is an intelligent, engaging, and charming man, an orthopedist, and stepfather to Anthony since Anthony was three years old. Katherine is a beautiful, energetic mother with a dazzling smile. They live in a small, rural setting. You can tell from the first time you meet them that they care deeply about their son and take their roles as parents very seriously.

I met these two future friends at a support group meeting where we held a beautiful candlelight ceremony. One by one we lit a candle symbolically to rekindle the relationship with a child far away, to awaken our inner spirit, and to spark hope from despair. It was a beautiful evening, a moment when people felt connected to something deep and profound within them.

I recall the deep expression of gratitude on Kyle and Katherine's faces that evening. They arrived feeling isolated and afraid but now felt connected to a community invoking deep, healing energies to soothe broken hearts. It was like they had come home.

As I came to know them, I began to discover the depth of their interest in understanding their experience and learning from it.

Kyle: "We noticed early on that Anthony had a strong will. He was real different than the other two kids I raised. Real defiant. He pushed you to the point of spanking him to get him to mind. This was in part a reflection of his own personality and also a reflection of a very difficult divorce situation."

Katherine: "Anthony was born during a rough period in my life. It was a difficult pregnancy. Anthony's dad was physically abusive and we split up during Anthony's first year. His father did some really mean things and I knew that we had to get away from him. That first year was rough on Anthony. He had cholic and allergies. I felt that his father contributed to Anthony's illness. I felt Anthony was in danger, so I left. His father was very angry. He threatened that he would take Anthony and that I'd never see him again. He would tell Anthony horrible things about me and use the 'F' word in front of him. Even though Anthony was just a baby, I felt that he was affected by that relationship.

"Kyle and I married when Anthony was four. Anthony was by this time in joint custody of his dad on the one hand and Kyle and me on the other. I feel that Anthony very early on felt abandoned by his father. Even at only four years old he had a self-esteem problem. It was just horrible, and I didn't know what to do about it. I tried so hard to figure out what to do. In first grade we really started having problems. We got Anthony into counseling. He begged to live with us. We went into a court battle to gain full custody of Anthony. We won but I don't think any of us really *won* anything. Anthony was used as a guinea pig. He was very hurt by it. He loved his father. He was battered by going back-and-forth between two households. This came out in self-defeating attitudes at school. He was very angry; he would fight with kids. He was suspended in the third grade. He was a chronic bed-wetter, very scared at night, couldn't sleep, didn't like the dark. He was a very caring kid, though, caring and nurturing to younger kids. But he didn't care for himself very much. One day when he was in the third grade he was sitting in my lap and started sobbing, 'Mom, nobody loves me! Everybody hates me!' I told him that couldn't be true. But he didn't believe me. It seemed that there was nothing I could do about it.

"He was very good academically but very small as a child. Sports were difficult for him. He wanted to be Bo Jackson and then Orel Hersheiser. He wrote to Orel and Orel wrote back to him. He had lots of fantasies about which athlete he wanted to be like. But of course he wasn't that great and, you know how kids are, they were brutal with him and they said, 'You're not coordinated, I won't play with you!' His anger started to come out. 'The kids won't throw me the football; they won't play with me!' He was still doing OK academically. We were in counseling, too, dealing with issues of not getting along at school, getting into fights, and not doing homework. His dad was now remarried with a child from that marriage. After a year his dad divorced again and Anthony went through the heat of that split-up.

"In seventh grade I got a call from school saying that they suspected Anthony was using alcohol and had bottles of alcohol in his backpack. I talked to him but he denied it. We had always talked about drinking very openly. He had found bottles of wine my mother had hidden after we had her in recovery, and said to me, 'Mom, I'm never going to do that.' One of the hardest things for me is that I've tried to *teach* him all these things, yet he did it. It isn't as though we weren't *open* about these things – we absolutely *were!* He knew that his grandparents and dad had addiction problems.

"At school the kids didn't like him. He often isolated himself. He was very impulsive and diagnosed with ADD. For a long time before I knew anything about ADD I'd get very impatient. 'Well Anthony, why can't you sit there and behave like your cousins?' Looking back, I was expecting too much of him. I don't think he had the ability to sit still. Then I think he started playing comparison games with me, Kyle, and with his older brother and sister. They are ten and twelve years older, got really good grades, were successful. And then there's Kyle and me – very accomplished in our ways. I think he thought we were all perfect. And we presented ourselves as though we *were* perfect. He couldn't relate to any of us. I think he wondered where he fit in.

"And then of course he wasn't very successful in his relationship with his biological father. I tried to compensate and be both mother and father. I tried controlling and manipulating in order to help him – 'You don't want to be like this, you don't want to be like that....' But I was creating more of a problem than I was solving. He was very impulsive and didn't think through things. Then he'd get angry and turn his anger on me.

"When eighth grade came he decided he was going to live with his dad who was offering a lot more freedom than I was. So, I said, 'OK, I'm not going to take this kind of abuse from you. I'll let you go live with your father. But if you do, you have to stay there at least six months.' Sure enough he started begging to come home soon. He was getting in all the usual trouble at school, then got suspended from junior high. And things weren't going so well with his father either. But we stuck to our guns and wouldn't let him back for six months. By second semester he was back living with us and did OK. Since he didn't have a lot of positive peer interaction, he spent a lot of time with us.

"All of a sudden, however, he found a peer group that he seemed to fit in with. He didn't want to be around us anymore. I think this was the beginning of the really negative influence on him – the type of peer group it was.

"I sensed some trouble. When he got into the ninth grade, I started getting more strict with him, making him earn his privileges. One night I talked to Kyle, and I said, 'Kyle, I know he's using drugs.' The school was telling me that he wouldn't come back to school after lunch. I could smell alcohol on his breath. I confronted him. I got him into counseling. I talked with his dad and tried to get his dad to communicate. It was pretty obvious to me that both father and son were using substances."

As I listened to stories of families breaking down, I recognized how each of us made destructive decisions. But I also wondered how much our culture contributes to the increasingly commonplace breakdown of the family.

❖

Le Mafa Pass Road, Western Samoa

One Pacific island evening after a hot day's worth of interviewing boys at Paradise Cove, the sun was descending into the blue ocean, I headed my rented Suzuki 5-speed up Le Mafa Pass Road over the island's volcanic center in the direction of Apia, the windows rolled down to let the wind dry the sweat from my body. Le Mafa Pass is a relatively deserted stretch of the road, so I revved up the motor to have some driving fun on the winding mountainous highway. I suddenly came upon a pickup in the middle of the road and braked quickly. Several Samoans were standing around with obvious concern and anger instead of the smiles that rest so naturally on their faces. In the brief time I had as I approached this scene, I could not ascertain the cause of their concern. I had been advised to avoid becoming embroiled in local issues, so I passed carefully by, paying little mind.

A little further up the road, I came upon a muscular Samoan in his early thirties walking hurriedly up the road with his hand extended in the universal hitchhiker's gesture. I never pick up riders here in America. But Western Samoa has a completely different feel to it and it seemed perfectly naturally to take on a rider there. All week long I had picked up hitchhikers, finding them good companions. Having forgotten about the stalled vehicle and therefore not connecting this hitchhiker with that scene, I picked him up.

Most Samoans speak English but speak it haltingly. But this man was unusually difficult to understand. It took us a few labored moments to understand each other's English. At last I understood that he needed to go all the way to Apia (an hour's drive from that point). I expressed surprise that he was attempting to walk that long distance. At that point, I also noticed that he seemed fearful. He asked me if I remembered passing the pickup. I indicated that I did. He proceeded to tell me that he had been hired to drive that vehicle but that something had gone very wrong. Had someone died? It wasn't clear. What I did make out was that the family who owned the vehicle blamed him for what had happened. They were very angry, he told me anxiously. He had escaped them but feared they might kill him. There was even something almost childlike about the fear in this adult man.

My immediate thought was to wonder whether I should try to help him get assistance from the police. (That is a very American way of thinking, it turns out.) Then I remembered being warned that in Western Samoa the police are not a strong force. Instead local villages hold the power through the auspices of village chiefs. These villages take matters into their own hands. Best to drive on by a local disturbance, I had been advised. Best not turn to the law in times of trouble. Not here in Samoa anyway!

"I must get back to Apia, to my family," my now tearful and highly agitated companion explained to me. He told me his mother lived in Apia. She was the only family member remaining on the island. His brother and sister had moved to New Zealand, so he could not turn to them for help at all. He was concerned that his only family now was his mother who would not be able to help him very much. It was very easy to tell how alone and abandoned my fellow traveler felt at this moment. No wonder his fear was so strong! There were things I wanted to say to him when I dropped him off in Apia, but I did not know how.

The first noteworthy aspect of this man's behavior was that it was very natural for him to show the extent of his fear. Most men I know, including me, attempt to hide their fear from everyone around them, including their families and their wives. In Western Samoa it is not a sign of weakness for people to show their fear or for a man to cry. To reveal emotion is natural. The Samoans are simpler than we are, less affected, and more real. These are people whose emotional selves are given the expressive freedom to be.

What is also remarkable to me is that, albeit with extreme fear about its present inadequacy, *he looked to the only natural place for him to turn for support: his family*. This is not something unique to this one Samoan hitchhiker; it is a definitive part of the Samoan culture to rely on family first, then village. The family is the sanctuary, the primary source for emotional support, and the abiding structure within which the individual lives. The measure of my companion's fear was in no small measure due to the abandonment he felt on the part of able-bodied family members no longer available to support him in his moment of need. Still, in a time of crisis, he automatically turned to the only family available, an aging mother, for support.

Family, American style

Increasingly in America, we do not think of the family in these ways. My grandmother, born in 1888 and separated as a teen from her sister in England for sixty years, nevertheless wrote faithfully to her every month until her sister died in the 1960s. Although they never saw each other again, each month a letter from the other arrived in the mail. When her sister died, my grandmother shed profound tears of grief. I could not understand this deep feeling for someone so long ago and far away. I now realize that my grandmother had a more profound sense of the importance of family than I. I have been out of contact with several of my relatives for many years, and until recently it has not been a matter of great concern to me. Our culture, me along with it, has evolved into something new and different. And it is not necessarily a good world we have created.

While it is foolish to recommend a return to a more primitive form of existence and easy to idealize that way of life, overlooking its shadowy side, it is clear that we've given up much in our drive to be modern. We've lost touch with our simplicity and naturalness. We're uncomfortable with our emotion and feeling. Even our children quickly become buried in the complexity and compromise accompanying this modern world we've created. Our sense of family and what it is for has been lost entirely or suffers greatly. Family breakdown shows up in answer to the very simple question:

Where do you turn in time of need?

The first question I asked most of the kids at Paradise Cove was a simple variant to that question: "Describe to me the first moment in your life when you encountered some great challenge, some significant problem, and chose *not* to turn to your family for support." You may think this was begging the question. But on a sincere level every young man had a ready answer.

One young man looked at me for a few seconds as if I was serious, then laughed and said, "Man, I *never* turned to my family in time of need! They were too much into their own shit, their own thing, to help *me*! I was on my own from the beginning!"

Without exception, one teen after another had little difficulty recalling that essential moment, at a formative stage in his life, when, no matter the reason, no matter how we evaluate their decision, no matter how it cost him, he chose *not* to turn to mom or dad. At invariably critical junctures in the boys' lives mom and dad were *dealt out* of the picture. Family was not a haven, a source for protection, guidance, and sustenance. And that was just the beginning. At some critical turning point, family was to be *avoided*, eventually at almost all costs. These boys cut themselves adrift and became lost souls in search of answers. Obviously, the seeds of family breakdown had been planted long before these choices were made.

Despite this sad condition, almost universal among us is a deep longing for happiness and well-being within our families. We never cease wanting to be loved by our moms and dads. We never stop wanting to love them back.

In family breakdown, dense, seemingly impenetrable, walls are erected between us – walls that remain for years, perhaps a lifetime. These barriers to real family relatedness are held together by a mortar of betrayal, games, lies, secrets, distrust, unprocessed rage, and a mixture of stored wrongs and opinions about the way things are supposed to be. Our walls are buttressed by often erroneous conclusions and accumulated evidence drawn from our perception about "how things are" with one person and "what I can always expect" from another.

And while these barriers between us may have existed for several years, the pulse of a deep longing for family renewal and healing can still be felt in even the most injured heart. For most of us, however wounded, there is an always-renewable familial bond waiting to be rediscovered and restored to its true, intended state. We simply have to be willing to reach out to touch it with a healing hand. Not only in families with struggling teens, but in countless families throughout our modern and troubled world.

A simple act of family healing

I once had the privilege to witness a big, muscular, intimidating, and out-wardly uncaring, man in his fifties convulse suddenly into tears confessing that all he wanted at this moment in his life was to ask for the forgiveness of his mother and father and to ask them to come back into his life. Ralph had not spoken to his parents for *thirty years* even though they lived in the same community, even though they visited the same relatives, even though they passed by each other crossing the street! Why? His story was simple. He was still mad at them for not sending him to college. For their failure he had driven them from his life in bitterness those many years ago. For thirty years he clung steadfastly to his rage. Fueled by his anger, he successfully developed his own auto repair business to prove to them that he could make something of himself without their help – thank you very much for nothing! "I'll show *them!*"

But there came a time in his life when Ralph began to change. After years of a successful business, he began to realize that there was something vital missing in his life, that there might be something more important than his anger towards his parents. There was an emptiness in his life, a kind of life-less quality, a kind of *not* living. At this moment of awakening, Ralph under-stood that he no longer drew satisfaction from his anger; that it was a hollow victory he had claimed for himself; and that there was still a power-ful need for a relationship with two people he still called "mom" and "dad". With great personal insight he saw that he had passed along his anger to his own children. It was no accident that they really didn't want to have much to do with *him* either! Under the weight of his own insight, this otherwise sturdy man collapsed in convulsive tears and uncontrollable weeping. He would damn up the need for feeling a connection with family no longer!

Within a few moments of this realization, Ralph was on the phone asking his parents through his tears if they would consent to meet him. They said that they would like that very much and told him that they had thought of him every day for thirty years. Ralph organized a barbecue to occur within the following month. He invited his estranged children as well. He called it "a family reunion." It wasn't an easy awakening for this family and this man. Everyone showed up, but it was difficult and strained. Yet it was a start. And what awakening ever is easy?

A few weeks later, I watched Ralph tearfully and joyously recount the reunion. Accompanying him were his mother and father and his children, now with families of their own. Ralph seemed like a man who had come home and who had discovered with great delight what true, honest family relationship and home really *are*. For the first time.

From generation to generation

But for that one act of healing, how many others of us live our lives in anger and suffering today? And how long must it continue?

Frances is in her late sixties now. She's lived a hard life. Her mother Beth who was abandoned as a child had been a hateful, spiteful, selfish woman, cruel to young Frances. Beth gave free reign to her negative emotions but was completely stingy of any positive feelings – choosing never to show them unless she wanted to manipulate Frances for some reason. Beth did not physically abandon her daughter as she had been abandoned; but she abandoned her child emotionally, never providing genuine love and caring.

Frances determined that *she* would never be like her mother and set out to be a devoted mother and wife. She married unfortunately – to a craftsman who installed beautiful hardwood floors. Freddie abused Frances throughout their thirty-five-year marriage. Always the ladies man, Freddie cheated on Frances and wasn't even clandestine about it. He flaunted his manhood openly for all to see that, indeed, he was a "man's man." He treated the floors he installed better than he treated his wife! In clear hearing of others, Freddie told Frances to "shut your mouth," ordered her about like a slave, and beat her if she didn't have everything perfect for him when he came home from a day's labor. No one came to Frances' defense against this vile man, not even Frances' father! She bore Freddie a beautiful daughter Anna. And she endured him until he died of heart failure a few years ago.

Anna meanwhile bore the brunt of her parents' dysfunctional relationship and her father's reign of terror, which kept Anna herself in line as well as "the wife." Of the two parents Anna resented her mom more. She resented not being given privileges and material things. She resented when her friends received nice clothes from their parents but she didn't. She resented not being given a college education. Almost thirty years old now, Anna remained quite voluble in expressing her resentment. Finally Frances, with a stubborn streak strong enough to endure a husband's abuse for thirty-five years, declared enough to her daughter's whining and cut off the relationship completely. She has not spoken a word to her daughter in several years. Her determination resolute, Frances will not make the first move.

Likewise, Anna is adamant herself and will not be the first one to break the silence. Meanwhile, Anna bore a child of her own, Brett. When Brett was seven, Anna divorced her husband and struck out to live on her own, leaving Brett behind to live with his dad.

Free from the domineering husband, Frances travels a lot – living a kind of nomadic existence now with a man who adores her. At least her present life is enjoyable. But what about all that pain from the past? There's no contact with her daughter or grandson. A family history of abandonment continues, one form replacing another. Time is running out on Frances. Is there too much pain inside to bring it all up? A mother and daughter reunion would do that. But both would have to give up *being right!* Both would have to open up to the other's view of the situation. Both would have to be willing to give a little! Neither mother nor daughter will say, "Enough! Let's talk about our pain! Let's face our family history! Let's face each other! Let's face *ourselves!* Let's find a way to build a future together, as a family!" Is each willing to die rather than give up being right?

Frances' mother died a lonely, angry, bitter woman. Is Frances headed for the same fate? Will her daughter Anna be any different? And how about the grandson, Brett? Will *he* be the one to break a family pattern of abandonment? Or will he blindly accept his inheritance of anger and righteousness and, believing that he too has been bruised past all point of forgiveness, pass it along to children of his own?

The face can wear a thousand masks! But just beneath the surface lays the truth waiting to be revealed. It takes *but one act of courage* to break free! Perhaps Frances will awaken to a realization on her own terms that her relationship with Anna is unsatisfactory. Perhaps not. Perhaps she will accept it as inevitable for the rest of her life. It is not for you and I to judge. But if either chooses to experience the pain and break free from it, she may experience that pain as a crisis in her life with as much intensity as Sandy and I felt the pain when we faced the truth about our family and our marriage.

Choices

In this chapter I have told stories of several families where people are wounded, lonely, and self-destructive. Neither Ralph nor Frances nor her daughter Anna has a drug or significant behavioral problem. They're all "making it in the world" by normal standards. But have they not lived much of their years in pain and blame? One of the greatest tragedies of our time is that so many of us choose to *settle* for life on these terms!

But choice always remains an option. Which choice will I make today? Will today be another day of anger, blame, denial, hurt, and vengeance? Will today be another day when I go to work in an attempt to numb myself from an unacceptable pain? Or will today be the day when I choose the simple act of moving forward – bravely into the hurt with ultimate hope for forgiveness, acceptance, healing, and love?

Whether I accept it or not, my family was given to me for a purpose. Our individual roots spring from the soil we call "family." If we neglect the soil, leaving it unattended and undernourished, what happens to the individual shoots called "you" and "me"? With my choice to become a parent I was given both privilege and responsibility. As a gardener tending to this, my most precious garden, I have been granted the privilege of watching a garden grow to its inborn, beautiful potential. We are each given a responsibility to tend the soil in which all of us grow. What are the implications of this responsibility for my life? Or of turning my back on it? Will I receive the full benefit of the privilege if I neglect the responsibility?

I believe that family breakdown, with the commensurate need for healing, is more common than we care to discuss in polite society! One small acknowledgment of the truth of this statement is that millions seek guidance from marriage and family counselors, psychologists, and the like. But these numbers represent only the peak of a heavy and deep iceberg of human pain and suffering. How many never make it onto the counselor's appointment book? How many give up in despair and settle for a protracted or permanent cold war? How many parents with struggling teens simply turn them over to a life in the streets or capitulate to their becoming wards of the juvenile system? How many kids grow up smarting from fresh wounds handed down to them from wounded parents? When do we say "Stop!"?

The families you are reading about here have pushed perhaps more visibly at the boundaries of family experience than is common today. But along with some of the obvious disadvantages of being out there on the painful edge, has come the advantage of looking back at the picture of the "normal" family from outside the frame. For me, this has yielded a lot of insight into the picture itself! Our journey outside the context of the supposedly "normal" has amounted to a great blessing to me and my family! And as I look at the picture of normal family life from outside the frame, I see an increasingly disturbing picture. I see a society in which family breakdown is far more widespread than evidenced by Juvenile Hall rosters and enrollment lists at residential facilities. I see a society where profound and painful family breakdown is accepted all too easily and is all too commonplace.

❖

CRISIS

ithin the context of my own family, I cannot really tell you when what began as a breakdown became a full-blown crisis. For purposes of writing and presentation, I have created a barrier as if there is a clearly visible threshold we stepped across, leaving one definable part of life for another. In real life it's never that way. Yesterday's unlivable moments are forgotten in the respite of today. Yet as the days followed upon each other I saw an overall, discernible difference — an erosion in the quality of individual and family life. Life was less good than it had been, and the living was not like living should be. But at the time I probably could not have told you when we passed from waiting out an uncomfortably bad storm to surviving a hurricane.

Jacob

"Me and my parents had a lot of stuffed feelings, stuffed anger, and stuffed emotions towards each other. And especially there was my hatred towards them.

"I was clearly addicted to pot. I was smoking pot six to eight times a day at least, if not more. It would depend on what I could afford. I was stealing money from my parents, from their credit cards, checks, wallets. Wherever I could get money, I'd get it. I didn't steal money from my friends or anything like that; I stole from my parents. My pot addiction was getting really bad. Some days I didn't have any money and I could only smoke one bowl and those were the days I went nuts. But the majority of the days, I'd buy a twenty-bag and my friend would smoke a twenty-bag and we'd go off, just me and him. And we'd get real stingy with our drugs and smoke bowl after bowl after bowl after bowl — just to keep completely out of it. And I'd have to smoke more and more just to get the same effect. I started doing LSD, mushrooms.

"This was when I was full-out hippie. I had extremely long hair, flowery shirts, bell bottoms, moccasins, beads. I was all into this hippie crap — peace, love, and all that b.s. — because I was really trying to put out this loving vibe, when actually I had all this crap inside me. I wasn't really aware of it. I knew that when I went to acting classes where I was encouraged to express emotion. I had all this rage inside that I had to deal with. But I really had no *awareness* of what it was. So it got really worse. And I couldn't get off the dope.

"Out of all my friends, I was the easiest for the police to spot because of my dress. At the time I never got into dealing because it was a lot easier to steal from my parents than to get into the whole dealing thing and then worry about the cops.

"This was just before my junior year. My parents had tried numerous things. I'd been in about six programs by this time. Outpatient programs. None of them were working. I was cheating on the pee tests they gave me. My parents were making attempt after attempt to no effect. I needed my acting classes so I could let out my emotions, and then I'd go smoke dope and this would cause me to hold them in, and then I'd go to the workshops and let them out again. But there was a point where my parents stopped sending me to acting classes, because they were tired of my b.s., and I went without acting classes for three months. My emotions just took control of me then and I just couldn't deal with them. I was going nuts! I was doing crazy, stupid things I knew I'd get caught for, like forging checks. I knew I'd get caught, but I needed my pot. I knew I was going downhill but I didn't know what to do. All I knew is I wanted the dope.

"At that point I'd tried speed twice but hadn't felt a thing. I know if I'd tried it a couple more times, which I would've when there was nothing else around, I would've gotten addicted to it and that would've started the whole speed-crack-heroin thing. I know I would've gotten into it."

Sandy

"Jake was gone all the time. I knew where he was – he was with those friends – and I knew he was using, too. It frightened me a lot. I had a lot of fear, a lot of denial. I still couldn't get Tim to see the situation clearly. He was in greater denial than I was.

"One of the big reasons Jake wanted to come home from LA was the car we had bought him before he left. Tim thought that buying the car would give him an incentive to work harder. I didn't think it was such a hot idea, but it felt like I was being ganged up on and I didn't feel that I had any power to make a difference. They would just do whatever they wanted to do anyway!

"Tim wrote various contracts on what Jake had to do in school, around the house, etc., in order to have the privilege of driving the car. No one agreed with these contracts. Tim wrote them and thought he was getting our agreement, but he wasn't, not really. I thought Tim would only hear what he wanted to hear, so I just signed the contract to get him off my back. Jake signed the contracts and ignored them. He considered them impossible to achieve. He had no ownership. And the car simply became an object of manipulation and a bone of contention."

Sandy so clearly states the unconscious condition we were in at the time. We acted – but unconsciously. To act unconsciously is to fail to see underlying mechanisms at play within us. On the surface some of my actions, such as the contracts, could have been interpreted as noble. But the people who knew me best – Sandy and Jacob – knew that my actions were prompted out of thinking that I knew better than them. I had to be right; I had to do it my way; I had to be in charge. These impulses were not something I was consciously choosing; they were running *me* not the other way around! On her part some deep impulse within Sandy had taken over and was causing her to sign a document she did not believe in. Would she have signed a document relating to the children in her classroom which she failed to believe in? No way! But things were more unconscious at home. And Jacob? Well, he was seldom sober. How could he act any way *but* unconsciously? He was simply hoping the whole business would go away so he could get on with business as usual. Sandy tells us more ….

"Jake had been on an allowance in L.A. and we continued it when he returned home. But he was frequently asking for more money. He needed it for the drug money, that's why! There was a brief honeymoon after he returned but he quickly started to have an attitude. He began to be so verbally abusive to us. He was emotionally unstable as well. He went downhill really fast.

"It was obvious he was skipping class, failing everything, not attending school at all. So we removed him from his regular high school and tried an alternative school. The idea was that he could get through school at an accelerated rate if he wished, he could get more teacher attention, and he could work in the afternoons after school. Perhaps a job would occupy him and help him feel better about himself. He would have his own money and wouldn't ask us for money all the time.

"But after a short time, he refused to go to alternative school. We started withholding acting classes from him because of his refusal to go to school and his treatment of us.

"That Christmas I bought him a boom box for a gift. Jake said he didn't want it, so I put it in the garage for safekeeping until I could return it. One day it disappeared. I knew Jake sold it for drug money, but Tim kept saying that he needed proof.

"One day Tim decided to look for something in Jake's car. He found a hash pipe in the back seat. That was a big turning point! Finally, Tim had the proof he seemed to need! He was really angry and took away the car.

"We started Jake in a drug and alcohol program offered by our HMO. They insisted we drug test him twice a week. They gave us very specific instructions about how to drug test him. They said we had to be in the room when he urinated in the cup and that we had to watch. Neither Tim or I followed those instructions, though. It was so humiliating to everyone. But it allowed Jake to cheat. He cheated by putting yellow food coloring into the cup and filling it with warm water. He shook it up and it looked just like pee and it was warm like pee. So, we'd turn in the test. Trouble is, the drug test was not testing for the presence of urine, so the tests turned out negative! We couldn't figure it out. We *knew* Jake was using, but ...! After a while, we started to doubt ourselves. Well, maybe he *wasn't* using after all! But there were things I couldn't explain – like, why was money still disappearing from my purse? We began attending Al-Anon on the recommendation of our HMO.

"We did not want to encourage Jake to veg out at home watching tv and talking to friends. Our stance was that he should be in school or working, not at home getting stoned. In order to make home less attractive than alternative school, we removed cable tv hookups and phones every morning, packed them in the trunk, and took them to work. What a way to live!"

And not only that, nothing was working. Jacob wouldn't go to school, and his friends were still *in* school, so he just found other friends – particularly one friend, a former Juvenile Hall resident, nineteen, a very unsavory Pied Piper/Charles Manson-like character. His favorite game was seducing younger girls, getting them high, and having sex with them. One time he and his girlfriend of the moment were out in the woods with another couple and they were all hungry. So, the other couple ate some mushrooms and died. I couldn't help but believe this kid might have put them up to it. But he didn't get into trouble because nothing could be proven. But this was the kind of person, the lifestyle, my son was now choosing to associate himself with! Now Jacob *really* had my attention! He was advancing to a lifestyle that would move well beyond his high school framework!

If he would talk to me at all, it was to scream abuse at me. Imagine this scene repeated several times: He was upset – let's say this time because we had enrolled him in the alternative school against his consent. "Do you *re-alize* where you've sent me?!" he would scream. I'd yell something back. Because the haranguing and insulting wouldn't stop, I'd eventually march him to the door and tell him not to return until he'd calmed down. Then he'd depart using his favorite designation for me. "You're a f-----g rock-head!" It's pretty hard to take that from someone you love.

The experiences of my own youth seemed of little use with this stranger in my home. "Of what use is my experience if it is not to help him?" I wondered. So I gave advice that was not heard and lectures that were scoffed at. I told him stories of my own youthful struggles only to be told that times have changed, old man, and your stories are irrelevant.

I tried everything I could think of. I bought things for him that were not earned and rationalized my overindulgence as "creating incentives." I tried being friends with my son only to be betrayed. I tried being smooth with him. I tried empathy and understanding. I tried psycho-babble. I tried humor – that had *always* worked for me in the past. But my humor only seemed to disgust him now.

I tried resolving conflict between my wife and son. Now, *that* went over *really* well! As if *I myself* was not a big contributor to a family in conflict! I tried being righteous, then indignant. I tried physical intimidation. A couple of times I threw my son up against the wall and threatened to "beat the holy living shit out of" him! All of course in the name of a *peaceful household!*

Nothing I tried worked. Nothing. How had my home turned into this? How had *I* turned into this?!

The only thing that really changed during this period was Jacob's hair. It just got longer, and longer, and longer. You couldn't see his intense blue eyes anymore! If we saw his eyes we would know how stoned he was. It was obvious to everyone that he was hiding behind his hair – even him. It is said that eyes are windows into the soul. Jacob knew how broken he was inside and he was hiding it from everyone, even himself.

I remember the ambivalence I felt. When he walked in my direction, I didn't really want to be around him; but when he walked away, I wanted to hold him tightly and ask how I could take away his torment. When we were apart, I'd imagine how good it could be to be around him again; but when he was near, I saw only how far he had slipped and smelled the repulsive stench of his cigarette habit. During the frequent periods of silence he imposed between us, I longed for him to talk to me, to tell me his feelings, to share an intimacy, to say but one healing word. When at last he spoke to me, I didn't want to hear the hurtful, hateful words he said, the irrationality, the excuses. I didn't want to believe that my son could sum up the world with such glib generalizations, generated from uneducated ignorance, or say the things he said about his mother and me. It was more and more difficult to know who we were dealing with. At times he would be his old charming self and we'd laugh. Once we went to the park to play catch. He would have some friends over and occasionally there would even be laughter. But the good times became fewer and fewer and it wasn't long until there *weren't any* good times. Soon the door to my son closed shut. Tight.

I will never be able to describe adequately the feeling of watching my child, my son, whom I loved so deeply, disappear slowly into a dark hole of his own making. Days and weeks passed by and with them faded one false hope after another of a parent in complete illusion. It seemed at times that the hole called to him and drew him into it with an inevitable, seductive power. But if he was not being drawn, certainly he was *propelling* himself into its dark embrace. I watched helplessly as he responded eagerly to the siren call of his own darkest nature. His hair was a shadow falling across his face.

I felt helpless. Finally, I tried leaving Jacob alone, a tactic which rapidly became my default response. Just leave him alone! It was not my first choice, of course. But there was nothing to do anyway, I reasoned.

Sandy and I began to attend an Al-Anon meeting for parents of addicted kids. At least we could do something for ourselves maybe. We attended Al-Anon only for a short time but it was really helpful – particularly to me. I went to the meeting and cried. It seemed to be the first place, other than therapy, where I could cry and be accepted. The Al-Anon meeting helped me to understand that I was not alone and that many, many good and loving parents were suffering from the same situation as we were.

Jacob was hardly ever at home when we were around. He wouldn't eat at home. Since home wasn't very much fun without a tv and phone, Jacob spent little time at home during the day. We had no idea where he was until late at night when he'd come home to crash.

When she saw Jacob, Sandy had frequent confrontations with him about transportation. He no longer had a car yet wanted Sandy to take him to his friends' houses. He had nothing but hippie and homeless-looking clothes and couldn't go job-hunting dressed like that. He'd want Sandy to give him money to buy clothes to wear job hunting. Sandy wouldn't trust him with money and would say, "You go pick out clothes, call me, and I'll come pay for them." He allowed Sandy to do that a few times, but always insisted on having the receipt. Then he used the receipt, returned the clothes, and got cash for drug money. After a while, Sandy caught on and stopped buying him clothes.

Our HMO dismissed Jacob from its drug counseling program because of his attitude of non-cooperation. They suggested that we join ToughLove and a drug and alcohol clinic. We knew we had to do *something!* Nothing else was working! With ToughLove we heard that you could make your kid go live with another ToughLove family if things got out of hand, perhaps make him earn his way back into our house. It was worth a shot.

In the drug and alcohol clinic sessions we had to listen to other kids just like Jacob justifying their actions and blaming their parents for everything from not having their favorite cereal on hand to not having the freedom to go anywhere, anytime, with anyone. We were just going to hear the same crap over and over – and it was costing us a lot! This program really wasn't aggressive with the kids. It was obvious that the kids manipulated the staff easily who in turn seemed not to challenge the kids' blame. It seemed like we were playing old tapes over and over, going nowhere. Attending individual and group sessions run by a young, well-intentioned counselor whom Jacob easily manipulated only made us angry. Jacob considered it all a useless, boring bother. Sandy felt it was just another place for him to meet more druggies. (Later, Jacob told us that it was at the clinic where he traded war stories with other kids and learned how better to trick us.) As usual, I was trying to bring peace by keeping my family in a process that only seemed to make matters worse rather than better.

We tried one thing after another. You can imagine the energy, the emotional cost, and the resources it took! And nothing was working!

About that time we went to an all-day ToughLove training about letting go and detachment. That's where we heard a couple talking about a program in Western Samoa where their son was being helped. "Those people must be rich," Sandy said. I tuned it out. It seemed awfully extreme.

On dismissing Jacob from the HMO program, the therapist in charge recommended long-term residential placement for Jacob's substance abuse and related problems. We carefully thought about placing him in a residential treatment so that he could get treatment and go to school. Jacob said "no way" and laughed at this possibility when we talked to him about it. So?! We'd put him in a program *anyway!*

Then we discovered that California programs cannot legally keep a minor longer than seventy-two hours unless he consented to be there. *What?!* I didn't feel like I had much power to begin with. But this was *completely* demoralizing! We learned that California is not a "parent-friendly state;" its laws do not support parents' placing a child in an institution within the state against his/her will. In only seventy-two hours, Jacob would just be coming down from his latest high! Besides, how could his *thinking* possibly change in such a short time?! Our hands seemed tied. Why did the law operate against the love of parents for their children? Why didn't the state trust *us* to know what is best for our child? The feeling of powerlessness was overwhelming. We hadn't learned yet that we could place him in a program outside California.

Without the privilege of attending acting classes, Jacob lost the emotional outlet they seemed to provide. He had frequent temper tantrums – crying and pounding against his bedroom walls. During one of these, Sandy entered his room and saw several knives lying on the floor. Jacob sobbed, "I don't want to live!" So she insisted that our HMO provide us a psychologist on an emergency basis. She told them she thought Jacob might attempt suicide and said she wanted him to be picked up and put into emergency care. They said they couldn't do that legally and told her she had to go home to call the police. By the time the policeman came Jacob was calm and portrayed a sane kid with an hysterical mom. The policeman said Jacob didn't appear to be suicidal, gave him a pep talk, and left.

We were on our own. Except in Al-Anon or ToughLove. Al-Anon helped us grieve and begin to let go. ToughLove helped us become resolute and change our behaviors one at a time.

Just prior to turning seventeen, Jacob stopped attending alternative school saying, "I want an education, but I don't want to go to school." Juvenile Hall scheduled a truancy hearing. We *didn't* want Jacob in the legal system. The only education he would get there would be from experts in breaking the law and gaming the system!

ToughLove was an important catalyst for change for me. Its process helped me confront myself. ToughLove helped me realize what Sandy had been saying to me for quite some time: I was still in denial of my son's problems – problems that would not magically go away. I had to detach from my son in order to free myself to act. I had to precipitate a crisis in my son's life. I did not have to remain a victim. I had to end my ceaseless war with Sandy and join her in partnership. We had to work together!

Shortly after I joined ToughLove, I wrote in a journal: "I believe I am freer as a parent than I have ever been. I feel free to allow Jacob to succeed or fail on his own. I will not rescue him anymore. I will not save him from experience. I will not let my happiness or my relationship with Sandy be ruled by my experiences with him." Those were brave words, but *I was* changing. I was becoming ready to take some kind of action, and at last I was ready to work with my wife.

In January, 1996, Sandy and I reached the conclusion that a residential program was the best alternative we had to watching passively as our son continued his downward spiral. All the counselors we consulted affirmed our decision. One of them said that Jacob needs someone "to peel away the layers of the onion" to get to the *real* kid who lies buried inside – the Jacob we all love and adore. We had heard lots of jargon applied to Jacob, such as "oppositional-defiant behavior" and "attention deficit disorder." These words didn't mean much to me. Al-Anon best helped us understand the situation at the time. Jacob had a "disease" requiring treatment. Drugs were just a symptom of an underlying emotional disease. Indeed it seemed that we were battling a phenomenon as powerful as a life-threatening disease! Certainly the quality of his life was threatened. Once we had constructed the disease model in our minds, it was easier to act.

We decided we needed to move fast. He had just turned seventeen. We felt that we had less than a year to save his life.

However, we decided to try one more thing – a ToughLove house rules negotiation process. This is a structured meeting in which parents and child, with the assistance of ToughLove members, determine simple house rules together. If we could just get Jacob to obey a few basic rules in the house, that would be a basis for a turn-around. However, if he would not obey house rules he participated in creating, we'd send him away to some program. But emotionally it was very difficult for us to accept that possibility!

The day of our ToughLove house rules negotiation session arrived. Jacob seemed less-than-enthusiastic but participated. One rule was that he would attend weekly family therapy with us, another that he would go to the half-day alternative school every day.

The next day he didn't attend school and told a long story about why he missed the first therapy session. Day One had come and gone and two of the most important house rules were broken! We wouldn't buy any more stories! At last we realized that he was completely out of our control. We decided to find a residential program.

Sandy recalled the ToughLove parents who had spoken about the Program in Western Samoa. I contacted them and obtained a video on the Program. On the basis of the video and reference calls to a few parents and a former Program graduate, we enrolled Jacob in the Paradise Cove Program. First, he would go to a hospital in Utah for detox, psychological evaluation, and observation. Then he would fly to Western Samoa. Of course, we withheld this plan from Jacob! There was no way he would attend willingly!

A residential program appealed to us for a variety of reasons. Sandy liked the structured day, the mandatory attendance at school, the point system for rewarding behavior and advancing levels, the emphasis on accountably, the requirement that he earn everything beyond a minimum set of privileges. He just might develop a sense of how good he had everything back home! Sandy liked the video. Clearly, Jacob would be in a beautiful setting! But they wouldn't coddle him. It wouldn't be easy. The persuasive factors for Sandy were the emphasis on accountably, the end to entitlement, and the absence of drugs.

I liked the Program's emphasis on inner development and family. I liked the fact that it was located far away; that Jacob could no longer choose to hang out with friends who wouldn't support him in a constructive way; that he'd get a lot of feedback from peers doing something to turn their lives around. Like Sandy I was attracted to the tropical island setting as a peaceful place to reflect on life. I liked the idea of living in, and learning from, a primitive culture where they don't take everything for granted.

The elapsed time between our decision to enroll Jacob and the arrival of the escort service to take him away was only one week.

Ironically, the night before Jacob was taken away, he made it to a family therapy session. He even seemed like maybe he was willing to make some changes. I found myself second-guessing our decision to enroll him in the Program. Maybe we had underestimated him. Perhaps he was ready to change after all! However, he revealed himself pretty clearly in therapy. In so many words, he admitted how lost he was. He was saying, "Help me! I don't have a direction for my life. I'm not sure I've got the skills. I have some real concerns about my life." He seemed ungrounded and out of reality. He talked about his intention to be a hippie and live off the land. Of course, Sandy pointed out to him that he didn't like vegetables! He admitted that he had no realistic plan for this life. The therapist concluded later to us, "He's *not even ready* for therapy! He does not have enough sense of himself yet to benefit from therapy."

When we left the session, Sandy privately questioned the decision to put Jacob in the program. Yet she realized that he said a lot of things that were immature and unrealistic and she realized that it was obvious that he needed help. Interesting! Up to the end it was always *me* dragging my feet. Now that it came time to act, it was *Sandy's* turn! Nobody said this would be easy! But for once, we arrived at a mutual decision to save our boy's life. We were anxious to get started, afraid yet hopeful.

❖

You have to go with these people!

I will always remember the night of March 14, 1996. I remember little of the day, but the *night* ...! The day was a trial of short-breathed fear, anticipation, and endless waiting. I went to work as usual but I was not very attentive to daily tasks.

We had invited Jacob to a "special dinner together." We hoped he would come since we knew that it would be our only chance to spend a last few moments together. I didn't believe that he would show up but when dinnertime arrived there he was! In fact, he seemed to respond somewhat to the importance of the occasion. He helped barbecue hamburgers, his mood subdued and quiet. He was probably stoned. He was a charming son that evening, making it all the more difficult for us emotionally. It was as if he sensed that a change was about to occur and was saying, "See, I'm really all right – you needn't do this!"

After dinner Jacob left for his usual evening out. Sandy and I finished packing his suitcase. I was paranoid that he might burst in and see what we were doing. But we could usually count on him returning home to sleep around ten. We needed him to keep his routine, since the escort service was to arrive at 11:30! To our relief, he arrived home at the usual hour.

Then came the time to wait for the escort to arrive. It was an agony! An exhausted Sandy tried to read a book. We took turns pacing the floor. The phone rang. It was the escort team captain. Their plane had been delayed. They'd be an hour late! Time passed as slowly as it ever has in my life! I sat in the living room close to the street to hear the car as it drove up. I tried unsuccessfully to read. We paced some more. I rehearsed what I would say to Jacob. I triple-checked the thick stack of forms we'd filled out. I worried that something would be wrong with the forms. We worried what the escort people would be like.

At last, I heard the sound of a vehicle stopping in front of the house. I went out to greet these strangers who for a few moments would become part of the intimacy of our home, take one of us away, and become strangers again. My fears began to subside immediately. I instantly felt comfortable with these people – a woman and her husband about our age and a young man in his mid-twenties. They seemed like kind, ordinary, solid people. Sandy then went to sit down in the living room with a supportive friend. I walked the escort team down the hall to Jacob's room, opened the door, and turned on the lights. He didn't stir. I sat on the end of his bed and touched his leg at first gently, then more firmly to wake him. As I write this, I can still feel his touch. That was the last time I touched my son for a long time.

He woke up and looked at me with my small party of interlopers. "What the f---?! ... Oh, man!" He flopped his head back on the pillow and turned away like it was some bad dream – or another contingent of ToughLove people! Now came the moment I had been rehearsing over and over so as to get it just right and real simple. "Jacob, I love you with all my heart but you have to go with these people."

The rest happened quickly and rather easily. I got out of the way and watched as the team captain, the woman, led the way. She had a firm and gentle manner. She left no question in Jacob's mind that he was going to go with them. Given that two of the three were larger and stronger than Jacob, I don't think that he entertained much notion of trying to escape. He was groggy from sleep and compliant. He asked a few disbelieving questions like, "*Now?* I have to go *now?!*" and "Go *where?!*" Each question was answered calmly and efficiently with little information given.

It went far easier than I had imagined. Soon he was dressed and heading down the hall with a man in front of him and the other two behind. The suitcase had already been stashed in the trunk. When we got to the small rental car outside, Jacob was told to get in the middle of the back seat. One escort would ride on each side of him. Before he got in Jacob said, "Look, I'm not getting into this car until I know exactly where I'm going!" The woman said, "You are going to a residential treatment facility." Upon hearing this Jacob looked at me and said, "Just as I'm about to get my life together, you'd do *this*. *It figures!*" The anger in his eyes said everything; the words were just extra baggage. I managed to murmur something lame, like "Yup."

I knew in my head that this was *not* a moment of giving up! This was a moment of turning our child over to community. It very much *does* take a village! But damn it! This was so difficult! I knew that this was a moment that would change our lives forever. We would never be the same. "This could go a couple of ways," I thought.

Then they drove off with my son. I went back into the house and climbed into bed. Sandy and I held each other and sobbed. I remember saying, "I feel so guilty, so dirty!" It was a long and troubling night.

I remembered advice that our wonderful therapist Joan had given me earlier. She said that I might want to pray for a miracle. "Sometimes miracles do happen," she said to me.

That night, while I prayed for a miracle to enter into our lives, Jacob was driven to the hospital. He would have some tests and the drugs would leave his system. He would begin to adjust to the idea of living far away. The hospital took in other young people in similar circumstances. The staff cleaned up the kids, put them on an immediate regimen with discipline, had them shower, cut their hair short, and dressed them in the conservative clothes which we had been instructed to send with our son. Things were not going to be the same for Jacob. Or us.

Susan's story resumed

"Ryan came back from his dad's home to live with us and for awhile it was truly wonderful. Ryan and the new man in my life, Greg, really hit it off. They had fun and played together. I fell comfortably into an illusion that I'd found my solution, that my love for this child would be enough to turn the tide, that we would live 'happily ever after.' My fantasy lasted about two months.

"Again, the problems escalated – disruptive behavior at school; baggy, torn up clothes; violent music; isolation from us; sneaking out at night; horrid language; bursts of rage; trouble in the neighborhood; an increasingly bad reputation; money missing from my wallet. During this time, Ryan's best friend stole his girlfriend and this disturbed him very deeply. He became suicidal, although we didn't realize it until later. Over the next two months the descent into complete chaos accelerated. There was a growing darkness, a desperation, about him.

"He attended a very large high school with a campus of about three thousand kids. School officials began talking to me about placing him in an alternative school, because he was really too much for them. I became suspicious that he was using crystal-meth, a suspicion later confirmed. It seems to me now that crystal-meth was just Ryan's tool of choice for implementing his personal holocaust. He told me later that he once went two weeks without any sleep. Sleep deprivation causes insanity!

"Ryan joined a white supremacist gang and shaved his head. The crystal meth really made him thin. He developed a huge lesion on his forehead. That came from his mixing the crystal-meth with other products. His face was really gaunt. He wore baggy clothes, of course, so it was difficult to tell just how much weight he had lost. He wore a baseball cap pulled way down over his head to cover the lesion between his eyebrows and to cover his eyes from observation. He put a lock on his door and barricaded himself in his room. He was constantly drawing symbols and hate words on his arms and hands. His room was filled with negative posters. Everything inspired hate and violence. We didn't know until later that he had access to guns or that he was simply never sober. At a certain point he refused to go to school anymore. The school finally expelled him. He was a complete power keg of explosive anger, and he exploded frequently.

"So this was what life had become! We were held hostage by our teen in a gruesome nightmare! This was the darkest time in my life.

"The one place of comfort and sanity I had was Greg. Greg gave voice to my, at first unvoiced, gut instinct that something was desperately wrong. He helped me realize that together we needed to make a change, something that would save Ryan's life. He decided that, by not saying anything to Ryan, the boy would think that we approved of his behavior. So, Greg began to confront Ryan fairly soon after the honeymoon phase of their relationship ended. This worried me, because I knew that Ryan would direct his anger towards this wonderful man in my life.

"One morning, I called a school official who had worked with Ryan for several years by that time. We knew him well and Bert liked Ryan. I begged Bert to come to the house to talk to my son. When he finished talking to Ryan, he drew me aside in the kitchen.

"'Susan, I need to tell you something, but it's imperative that you don't panic, because you've got to remain calm. The last time I saw Ryan was two months ago. I deal with about six hundred kids a year. In all my years, I've never seen a kid physically deteriorate as quickly as I've seen Ryan! I am scared to death for him. He needs help! And he needs it *fast!*'

"I knew Bert was right. My maternal gut instinct told me Ryan was just about out of time. After Bert left, Ryan came downstairs and screamed at me. He slammed a note on the counter, packed his back pack, and left to live with his druggie friends. The note, four pages in length, was directed at Greg and me. It began, 'Dear Mr. & Mrs. Manson.' He told us he was leaving and we were not to come after him. He hated us, his letter went on. If we pursued him, he threatened to damage our personal property, such as our vehicles. He threatened to create problems at my work place and to create problems for our landlord that would result in our getting kicked out of our home. He threatened to physically harm Greg. It was a vicious, hurtful, and altogether frightening letter.

"I hated this letter. It made me sick. That day, we changed the locks on the doors, and barred and locked the windows. Greg took his threats very seriously and was scared. In his late-night talks with Ryan, Greg had learned that Ryan, all of fifteen-and-a-half years old, was the leader of his gang. Ryan made no secret of how they resolved their problems with others. Greg knew that Ryan had the resources to retaliate. Every time Greg would approach our apartment door, he would look around to make sure no one was around to come up behind him. The worst thing to me, though, was how wounded Greg's heart was. He felt betrayed. He had opened himself up to my son and made a deep commitment to him, but Ryan now held him in bitter, drug-induced hatred. Still, Greg continued to keep his original commitment to do whatever was asked to help me help Ryan. But I thought then that his relationship with Ryan had been dealt a death blow.

"I knew I had to do something. A voice inside me said that this child would be dead in four to six months max. Over the next six or seven weeks I was consumed by a desperate search to find help for my son. We made no attempt to bring him home, although we knew where he was staying – with his drug buddies at the opposite end of the county. I came across a notebook that, I realized later, Ryan must have left hoping it would be found. In it was evidence of a planned suicide he never followed through on in the aftermath of his friend's betrayal. Several other references indicated that he still thought of suicide. We were running quickly out of time.

"During my search, I was appalled at the difficulty of finding resources. Neither schools, police, or family counselors had any resource to direct us to. I met with a group of fifty counselors, another group of a couple dozen therapists, and the police. None of them knew of resources I could turn to. I couldn't believe it! It didn't take a brain surgeon to determine our family was not an isolated incident. The experts all agreed that Ryan needed help. That comforted me. It helped me realize that I was not reacting hysterically. But I had no idea where to look. I vowed to myself that, if I found a good resource, I would share it with these people. I didn't want some other family to have to wait too long, because they didn't have the necessary information.

"During those weeks I told everyone I could that I needed help, being careful at the same time that the information did not leak back to Ryan. I knew that if he found out, he would be gone and I'd probably never find him. I checked the Yellow Pages – every place I could think of. An inner, instinctive voice screamed out to me that I had only weeks, maybe days, and if I didn't act quickly my son would be dead.

"My answer came in such an unassuming way, I nearly overlooked it. My answer was brought to me by an angel who came in the form of my dear friend, Wendy. She brought me an ad for the residential program and stood there with me while I called. This time, my inner voice told me, 'You've found what you've been looking for.' I didn't know then what that meant. I only knew what I felt – and that was a strong, reassuring, and calming feeling. This program had all three of the resources I had been searching for: people who would transport him, a lock-down intake facility where he could 'dry out,' and a long-term treatment program. I had no idea how I was going to accomplish this from a financial perspective, but I was not about to let that stop me! I simply decided that there was no way I would be stopped. But it was such a weird experience for me! It was as though point A was where we were 'standing.' Point B was where I envisioned my son could be – healthy, happy, loving, safe. Heaven help anyone who would stand in my way! From the first, I believed that my goal would be realized. My belief never changed. Greg was my rock. His support and commitment were constant, which served to further galvanize my resolve.

"The day Ryan was picked up by the escorts was like something out of a very bad movie. All this time he had been living in his drug buddy's house – doing drugs, running around with weapons, raising all sorts of havoc, and deteriorating more each day. The escort service decided not to pick him up there, due to the unknown safety factor for all involved. So on the appointed day I asked Ryan to meet me for lunch at the local Burger King in my area. He reluctantly agreed. Fearing that a concerned citizen might interfere, I advised the local police of my intentions and requested that they stand by to assist. They agreed to help.

"At the appointed hour, everyone was in place. The plan was to get him in my car, pull out of the Burger King, pull up in front of the escorts and police cars. They would pull him out of the car and whisk him to Utah. Well, after over an hour of waiting, it was clear Ryan was going to be a no-show. But I knew he was in the area – I had seen his buddy's car parked near my house early that morning.

"I went home. The police returned to work. I insisted the escorts go grab lunch before they went to wait at my house.

"Due to the hostile and aggressive feelings Ryan now had for Greg, everyone thought it best not to involve him, so Greg had gone to work. Shortly after I returned home, he called me. He was whispering in the phone, saying he had decided to drive by the high school and had spotted the car belonging to Ryan's friend. He was sure he had seen Ryan inside. I flew out of the house, calling the police and escorts on the cell phone to meet me at the high school.

"As I pulled up to the high school, I spotted Ryan hiding in the bushes across the street from the school. He was dressed in a black t-shirt, black pants, and black stocking cap. He spotted me, too. I pulled up and asked him to get in the car with me. He started screaming obscenities, saying he had seen Greg. He ordered me to tell Greg to keep away from him or he would kill him. With that he turned and bolted up the side of a hill, towards a large apartment complex. The police and escorts hadn't arrived yet. Greg joined me and I asked him to show me where Ryan's friend was. I knew there was only twenty minutes until school was out. Once three thousand kids hit the street, Ryan would blend in with the crowd and we'd never find him. So I felt like I had twenty minutes remaining on the time-clock of my son's life.

"We found his friend. I got out of the car. In my own colorful, adrenaline-pumped, way of speaking, I told his friend parked in front of the school, to keep away from Ryan, that Ryan was 'going down,' that I had given the police this boy's name, car description, and license number. What I didn't know at the time was that in the back of this boy's car was an arsenal of guns.

"Suddenly, the police and escorts arrived. A couple of school officials, on noon duty cruising the streets surrounding the high school looking for truants, had spotted Ryan running up the hillside and concealing what appeared to be a gun in the back of his trousers. Now there was an APB out on my son. I said a silent prayer of thanks. This was the break I knew I needed. Now I had lots of police help and attention.

"A few minutes later Ryan was captured. The manager of an apartment complex heard there was a kid running around with a gun. She spotted him 'hiding' in a doorway and alerted the police.

"It didn't take long to have him in handcuffs. That part of the nightmare was over. The police were great. They could have charged him with a concealed weapon, which turned out to be a switchblade instead of a gun, and taken him to juvenile hall. But they knew he wouldn't get any help there. So they turned him over to the escorts. I told my son I loved him. He called me some horrid names and swore he would hate me forever.

"As they drove off, I stood and cried in Greg's arms. I felt such relief! I felt hope for the future for the first time in a long while. My little voice inside gently told me it would be all right. I knew all along that the anger my son had spoken from, had come from a place of self-loathing within him, from his wounded and empty heart, and I knew that the greatest anger he had was at himself. Yes, I knew there were issues he and I would have to resolve, and I knew it would require a large amount of effort and time. But I always had faith it was possible. I knew my son would eventually come to realize the greatness I could see within him. I knew he would eventually come to love and care about himself, to have dignity and self-worth."

Ryan's story resumed

"I tried to commit suicide four times. One time I hung myself but I blacked out. The last thing I saw was my friend coming out to rescue me. I cut myself. I overdosed. One time I stayed up for several days straight trying to OD on crystal. I didn't sleep one minute the whole time. I didn't eat for several days. The reason I'd stay awake is that I was hoping that something would come by that I could live for. I thought that if I put a gun to my head I would miss something. At times I'd get so desperate I wouldn't care. I figured if I just started wasting away, well, something big would come by to save me before I reached the end of the line. I had this big desire to be saved. That was my only hope. I knew I couldn't do it because, right after I stayed up for such a long period of time, I went insane. I didn't know my name or where I was. I went crazy. I feel asleep for forty-eight hours straight. I remember how I went to sleep and woke up in the exact same position. After I got up I stayed up for another several days. And then I got sent away.

"I was living with two brothers when I was escorted. I was fifteen; they were nineteen and twenty-one."

As I listen to stories, I hear more and more tales like these – tales of kids leaving home at an early age, long before they are ready for the responsibilities of living alone. The phenomenon we don't talk about a lot as a society is that the frequency of kids living in the streets is on the rise. Ryan's story is hardly an isolated one.

It also occurs to me that Ryan is a middle class kid from privilege raised by a loving parent. He did not come from an impoverished inner city neighborhood; his parents were not uneducated; he was not beaten or mistreated. Ryan was not one of the disenfranchised people of this earth. He was a wild, uncontrollable son of privilege living a crazy, unhealthy life among two young men who seemed comfortable having a fifteen-year-old for a companion! But did life with his friends bring Ryan what he wanted?

"We had this arrangement whereby if there was a phone call we'd ask who it was and then say their name out loud so we'd know who was calling us. Then if we didn't want to take the call, we'd signal no, we don't want that call. One day my mom called. Josh answered the phone but just handed it to me. I gave him a sign like, you're supposed to signal me! So, man, here is my mom on the phone! Mom was real sweet – 'Oh, hi!' she said, in a cheery voice. She wanted to meet me for lunch. I didn't suspect she was going to have me picked up or something like that. I just didn't trust the tone of her voice. I thought maybe she was just crazy or drunk or something like that. She kept telling me she wanted to meet me for lunch, but I kept telling her the only thing I wanted was to go get my clothes. She was real stuck on going to lunch, but I refused. I got off the phone. Josh told me, 'You better be careful. I don't trust that. You might be going to get picked up.' I said, 'Oh whatever, man. You don't know what you're talking about.'

"That night we drove around and did drugs. I got another kid hooked on speed that night. We drove around all night, stopping about every twenty minutes to do drugs. We did everything from smoking crystal to smoking pot to drinking. I guess it was about four A.M. I was standing on a hill looking over the city and I absolutely *knew* something big was going to happen. I had fear but also a sense of relief. It felt vaguely like there was some hope there.

"The next morning I showered. We were supposed to pick up a friend of ours and drop him off at high school. Well, I'd been kicked out of that high school, and they'd told me that if I showed up there I'd be arrested. I knew that they would, especially since we had a lot of drugs in the car and I was under the influence. So, I told Jamie it wasn't a good idea, but he said, 'No, no, we'll just park in visitor parking, drop him off, and leave. It'll be really quick.' So, I said OK and we went to pick him up. Precisely at noon, right when I was supposed to meet my mom, we showed up at the school. I'm sitting in the passenger seat in the front. I look in the rear view mirror and see a security guard writing down the license number of our car. I told Dan, 'We gotta split.' We had two completely full backpacks filled with all kinds of paraphernalia and stuff – razor blades, straws, an ounce or two of weed, four cans of spray paint, six pipes, all kinds of stuff! Everything except this three-foot bong which we couldn't get in the backpack. In the back we had two shotguns, a .22, and a Russian handgun. We had a lot of stuff that I didn't want to have strapped to my back, because I knew I was a set-up to get arrested. We took the stuff across the street, though. I made a decision to go back to the car because I figured I had a choice of either getting arrested with all the drugs or I'd get arrested for trespassing, and I chose the lesser of the two. So, I went back to the car and sat there waiting for my friends to come out of school.

"The next time I looked in the rear view mirror I saw Greg and he looked real excited. I also saw that a couple of cop cars had pulled up. I knew he was going to go get the cops. I got out of the car and took off. I started crawling underneath the cars because I didn't want the cops to see me. I got across the street and hid in some bushes. I waited for five-to-ten minutes. When the coast was clear, I came back across the street and gave the keys to my friend who owned the car. Suddenly, mom pulled around the corner and drove up. She asked me, 'Why did you stand me up for lunch?' I started yelling F-words at her and asking her what the hell was going on with Greg showing up, the cops and all. She pulled out a cell phone. I knew she couldn't afford a cell phone and that was a tip-off. Something was going on.

"So, I turned around and broke up the hill towards an apartment complex on a hill. I saw my other friend that had come with us sitting on the side of the hill. I said, 'My mom's chasing me, Greg's chasing me, the cops are chasing me! You've got to get the keys to the car, pull around, and get me out of here!' We were starting to get cornered and I knew it. I had a butterfly knife and I got it out, ready to stab anyone who tried to take me. I stood in someone's doorway on the second floor. I saw these people drive by but paid no attention to them. Turns out, this was the escort service and they spotted me. After a bit, I ran back down the hill. I heard a car, looked around and it was a police car with its lights on. The officer told me not in the nicest way to stay still. So, of course I took off. I guess the high school security guard had put in a call to the police saying I had a gun. But I had left the guns back in the car. So, from every direction I had people pointing at me and I said to myself, 'Oh no, this is not good!' I knew that if I could just get out of this situation, I could get to these underground tunnels that even the cops didn't know about and I'd get away. But in the process, I turned down this outdoor hallway between buildings and four cops came out with their guns drawn – .45s and shotguns – because they all thought I had a gun. They started yelling at me and stuff and I said to myself,

'It's over.' They roughed me up, punched me and kicked me for running. I didn't put up a fight. They just all came at me at once and beat my ass. I had three pairs of handcuffs on. They took both backpacks. The escort service was there. I mouthed off at them, telling them this isn't a show, since I thought they were neighbors. Then my mom came up. I called her a 'f------ dike,' and that was the last time I saw her. I was real mouthy with the cops, too, because I was pissed. But I can honestly say that I was happy because I was getting away from everything else that was happening in my life and I knew it. I didn't know I was going to a program. All I knew was that if there were all these cops around, something was going to happen and there would be opportunity in it. I really understood this at the time. The whole situation was like this still water and you put a drop in the middle of it and it ripples out. That drop in the middle was the whole situation that was happening, but with the feeling of opportunity coming into my life, like this is the beginning of a restart of my life. And all these ripples come out, and these ripples are emotions leaving me, the anger I'd been going through the past months. I could feel that leaving. And that's where the attitude was coming from, that last small gasp of 'f--- y--' to the world. But inside I was starting to feel this small light of hope. It was exciting!"

Susan, who had the best current hope of understanding this son-turned-stranger, could only guess at what was really going on within him. The real question now was whether or not he would choose to be honest enough with himself to look within and face himself.

Paul

Like Ryan, Paul developed an entire set of friends around his drug use. But unlike his father, mother, and brother before him, Paul's use was not confined largely to pot.

"Me and my friends were always working towards doing more and more drugs. That was our job, really. That's what we *did*. We'd go on the streets to get drugs if I couldn't get them off my tutor. We wanted to get into the whole romance of it, do acid and everything we could get our hands on. We'd hang out at the park across from my old school where I was able to get acid. All the druggies from the school hung out there. I'd wake up, get dressed, hang out there, go home, do stuff with my computer, go to sleep, get up the next day, do the same thing.

"But inside of me I knew that my life was like crap. I wasn't doing school, I stopped doing the tutor bit, and I was getting hassled by my mom a lot about going to school. 'You've got to go, you've got to go!' she'd always say to me. She'd started going to ToughLove. At one point she started talking to me about going to Outward Bound. I said, 'No, I'm not going to go to that.' I thought that was 'the system' and I was real adamant about refusing."

What do our children hear when we talk about our beliefs? What is "the system" to an unformed young mind of fifteen or sixteen? Indeed, what do we know about our beliefs ourselves? Where did we get them? And how many of them are as unexamined as the beliefs our children pick up on the streets?

> "One day me and my friends got some information on DXM cough syrup off the Internet – about this one brand that doesn't have the stuff in it that Tylenol has that destroys your liver. So I thought, 'Cool, I'll use some of that.' And I did and it was all right. It was real cool, in fact. But the next day I was *really* depressed, like really low, and I slept in until two P.M. And my mom was concerned because here was another day and I wasn't doing anything. She yelled at me to get up. Eventually, she left. I got up, took a shower, got my clothes on, put my leather jacket on, grabbed my bong and put it inside my pocket. So I'm walking down the street to get some drugs wondering what time it was when I realized I'd left my watch in the bathroom after the shower. So I went back to get my watch. I had this feeling that she was up there, that I wasn't going to get out of the house without a hassle. I went up anyway and there she was. I had to force my way past her into my room. It was a really bad scene. She said, 'Where are you going?' She didn't want me to go out and I said, 'Just get out of my way, I'm leaving!' And she was crying. Eventually, I got out and headed up the hill toward the bus stop. On that same hill I ran into my brother."

Paul had always looked up to his older brother. He seemed to have developed a "real peaceful" approach to living which Paul envied. Paul admired the way he seemed to have learned so much about himself and other people. He was amazed at his brother's powers of observation, how he could read people really well. He wanted to be like him and be accepted by him.

> "It seemed like my brother wanted to talk to me so I sat down with him. He said, 'Look, she's going to call the cops on you because she doesn't know what to do. She loves you, she really cares for you, she's trying to do what's best, but she doesn't know that you really don't understand it and that you don't want to do it.'

> "And I didn't *really want* to do the drugs, not really. And that was the thing about my brother. He understood a lot more. I was doing it because I had this belief that you should do drugs, whereas he saw through me and saw what I was doing to myself. He seemed to be able to use drugs just like it was something ordinary you did, like go to the store or something. It didn't seem to get in the way of his vision like it did with me. And he saw exactly what was going on with me.

> "That afternoon with my brother, that's when I realized a lot about my mom. Before I just had these words in my head: 'She loves me' and 'I love her.' But the words weren't that real to me. Every once in a while that feeling between me and her would be real strong and we'd go have an ice cream or something. But most of the time the feeling wasn't that strong. But on this one day sitting on this hill talking to my brother and him saying, 'Your mother really loves

you,' that's when I first *really* thought about it, at least subconsciously, and it sank in. It wasn't enough for me to stop using or to think that sending me to a program would be an act of love or anything, but still I realized, deeper than before, that my mom really loved and cared for me. My brother was also right that she was trying to help me, but that I didn't want the help. And she didn't know how to get me to want it. I know now that if she had left me alone, it would have been all over for me."

After attending ToughLove, consulting with her therapist, and watching her son's downhill slide, Melissa hired a service to take Paul to a wilderness program for three weeks to see what kind of impact it would have.

"This wilderness program had a psychiatrist, and the whole time I was just fighting him off. My whole goal was just to get back home and be left alone. The stuff that my brother had said to me earlier – about how mom loved me and how maybe I needed to look at my drug use – still wasn't very conscious to me. I still didn't get on a very conscious level that my mom was doing this because she loved me. The psychiatrist told me then that they didn't know much about my situation and hadn't had that much contact with my mom and all. And even though it was against my belief system, I believed him. And the next day it was the end of the wilderness program and they said, 'Paul, you're going to go to Western Samoa.' I had no feelings, no shock, no reaction. They were just words."

Cary's story resumed

"When I smoked crack for the first time I was instantly hooked. I ended up getting deep into crank. Mom and dad didn't know for a long time. The need for drugs got stronger and stronger. I ended up doing anything for money – lying, stealing, selling my own stuff – anything for speed! My parents started to know something was going on when stuff kept disappearing and I started getting skinnier.

"I enrolled in continuation school for tenth grade. I began spending a lot of time away from home. My parents were aware of my drug use. They threatened to kick me out because I was sneaking their cars out late at night. I moved in with a girl I knew, got deeper into drugs. I lived with two girls, actually. We continuously moved from one of our houses to another.

"My drug habit worsened to the point that I was doing crank every day. In order to sleep I'd have to smoke marijuana. I started selling drugs to support my habit.

"One day two truckers came to my house to smoke crank with me. When they were filling the glass pipe with crank, some of it got caught near the mouthpiece. One of the guys asked me for something to push it down with. I looked around and picked up my key chain and handed it to him. He put the keys in his pocket after he was done. I told him to give them back. He told me he didn't have them, that I was tripping. After a few days I told my mom that someone stole my keys and that she should change the locks on the house and cars. She didn't.

"I started hanging out with some crazy people who had a lot of drugs – gangsters and Satanists. I started listening to Satanic rap, believing in the devil, and looking up to him. I was told that crank is the devil's drug. Since I loved crank, I must love the devil.

"A month or so afterwards the guy with the keys stole my dad's truck and robbed my house. I remember mom calling me at school while the cops were at my house. I told them who robbed my house but they didn't do anything. A few days later the police recovered dad's abandoned truck. When the guy finally got arrested, he told the police that I owed him money for crank, so I gave him my keys and told him to call it even. The police knew that I did crank and believed their story, because they had heard similar stories about me selling my parents' stuff. They arrested me for grand theft auto and burglary. I did two weeks in Juvenile Hall and it pissed me off. My hatred towards cops grew and my love for the devil grew as well.

"At this point in my life I had nowhere to go except to stay at drug dealers' houses with the girls. One time we stayed up for more than two weeks without sleep. One day I was at this guy's house and a local narcotics task force, called 'Net Five,' raided the place. The police knew me on a first-name basis and were constantly harassing me.

"During this time, I could always come back home whenever the real world got too tough or I was tired and wanted to sleep. My parents were devastated with what was going on. But through all, they still loved me. I screwed them over time after time and they still let me back in. I hurt my mom and dad so bad that I permanently scarred their hearts."

Of course, these words were spoken by Cary after he had considerably reshaped his life. Most likely he never actually verbalized those thoughts in the moment. Yet his actions spoke his emotional truth: He came home because home was a sanctuary of love when "the real world got too tough."

For long stretches of time, I was certain that Jacob had no love for us at all. The empty space between us was vast! I thought it likely never to be filled, and figured he might feel the same towards us when he is thirty or forty as he did at sixteen. Yet night upon night without fail, no matter how difficult things were between us, Jacob came home to sleep. Didn't this reveal that something of great value to him, beyond a mere place to crash, was here for him at home? I did not think this way then. I wonder how it affects our children when we ourselves lose perspective and, along with it, hope?

"I started getting sick of living my life this way. I was tired of always hurting my parents. But the fact remained that I was hooked on crank and I couldn't quit.

One day the police pulled me over and arrested me for possession of metham-phetamine and paraphernalia. They gave me a court date.

"I wanted to quit doing crank. At my court appearance, I was expecting to get thirty days but the judge just put me on probation with drug testing. I knew I couldn't pass a drug test. The first thing I wanted to do when I got out of court was some crank. I told the judge I wanted to quit, but I felt I needed a period of time to recover. I asked him to put me in Juvey for thirty days.

"When I got out I spent a lot of time with my mom and dad. They enjoyed be-ing around me. I stayed one hundred percent sober for a week. Then I couldn't resist temptation. Some friends were smoking pot and I smoked some. I felt that I screwed up but then I figured as long as I only smoked weed it would be OK. But within a month I ended up doing crank again. This time I hid it from my parents. I didn't want to let them down.

"The last day I had with my mom was Christmas, 1995. My dad was sick so he didn't come to my grandma's with me and mom. It was a great Christmas; I enjoyed it. I got a lot of nice presents. My family thought I was drug-free now and told me how proud they were. It hurt because I knew I couldn't keep it a secret forever.

"That night me and my mom drove home. We had a good talk and I drove most of the way. When I got home I went to spend the night at my friend's house. I met up with another friend and we went out for a midnight walk around town. No one was awake anywhere. We stayed up all night at his house and I didn't wake up until 1:30 the next afternoon. My mom was going to pick me up at ten A.M. to go to some appointment. I called her up quick and told her some story of why I forgot. She was suspicious, but didn't want to hear that I was doing drugs again, so she told herself I wasn't using."

We hear what we want to hear and see what we want to. Sometimes our choices favor *anything* but reality! How often I too chose to put on the blinders like Cary's mom! It's called *denial*. It is a parent's way of escaping the obligation to see our children clearly.

"Later that day I borrowed her car and gave my friend a ride so he could sell some drugs. He always carried a sawed-off shotgun everywhere because he had been shot before. I was stoned and I did a 'California stop' at a stop sign. A cop pulled me over. In the car they found the shotgun and a ten dollar bag of crank on me. They didn't find the eight balls and half ounce of weed on my friend. When we got to the holding cell in Juvey, he showed me what he had and I told him to give it to me because he was going to get busted with it. I ate most of the weed. The rest we scattered around the edge of the room. I keister'ed the crank. They took us to our rooms. I couldn't sleep because I was too stoned. I hid the crank in the pocket in my underwear.

"That morning my probation officer came to see me. I was so stoned from eating all that weed that I was stumbling all over the place and running into the walls. I was standing up while he was talking to me and I fell and caught myself on the wall. My eyes were solid red and I couldn't talk, my mouth was so dry. He told me I looked screwed up. He showed me some form that had my charges on it. Later that day I started passing out some crank to people so I could get rid of it. I did a lot myself. I had it in my possession for about eight days before they moved me to the other side of the facility – the side for people who had been sentenced. To this day I'm not positive why they moved me, but I think it's because they suspected people were wired and they thought I was responsible. Anyway, I knew all the people on the other side because I had just been there two months before. One guy snitched on me for extra behavior points. They searched me and found the crank on me – it was about a sixteenth, or a sixty dollar rock. I knew I was screwed now.

"They put the whole Juvey on lock-down for two days and searched the whole place good. They found out that the weed in the holding cell was mine and my friend's. I got two more felonies – sneaking drugs into a detention center and possession. They drug tested everyone and everyone got caught. As a result, some people went to California Youth Authority (a prison for kids under age twenty-one). I had already been sentenced for six months. They were going to sentence me as an adult now because I was seventeen-and-a-half. I had four felonies and two misdemeanors against me. I was looking at going to state prison or, if lucky, CYA. When I first realized the mess I was in I thought about killing myself or maybe trying to run. I was still into the Satanic stuff. I carved '666' into my wrist. They found this and added it to my court report."

While I will spend no energy blaming "the system," note that there was little or no systemic intervention on behalf of Cary's mental health. Anyone who reads this story will picture a boy facing a critical stage of his life with serious mental health and behavioral issues. He was a desperate young drug addict completely out of control, attempting suicide, worshipping evil, and desperately crying out for someone to help him. To such an extent as there *was* institutionally-provided mental health assistance, *it was not working!* Cary's critical mental health issues went unaddressed, while the state merely housed him between crimes. But after another crime, Cary would be brought back, stored away, and punished further – another recidivism statistic. But is there a statistic, a word, for the repetitive behavior of a society that uses the same method over and over yet expects different results? Commit another crime? Well, add it to his record, give out more punishment, but let's not actually *do anything different as a society* – something that might actually assist our young to find themselves!

"Carving '666' on my wrist may have been one of the best things I've ever done for this reason: When my mom found out, she realized that the devil had my soul. She didn't want the devil in our lives. She called a pastor and told him she didn't want the devil in her life. He told her, 'Well, that's no problem. As a Christian you can tell the devil to get out of your life.' She told him, 'Well, there is a problem – I'm not a Christian.' 'You can become one,' he said. 'All you have to do is pray to the Lord and ask him into your heart and confess that you are a sinner and that Jesus died on the cross for you.' That day my mom became a Christian. All the bad things I did created the best thing for my mom. I believe that there are no accidents and that things happen for a reason.

"Becoming a Christian again was easy for me. I was tired of living my life the way I was – hurting the ones who loved me, being hurt by people who didn't care about me, not being able to trust anyone, being untrustworthy. Still, I had been a Christian once before and turned my back on God. I didn't know that I was allowed to become a Christian again. I went to church in Juvey at first just to get out of my room. A police officer who lived down the street from me came and talked with me every week. Also a pastor named Lou. I found out I could become a Christian again. I learned that the Lord is very loving. Not too long after that, my dad became a Christian too.

"God had a big impact on my going to Paradise Cove. My lawyer argued in court that the purpose of the juvenile court system is to rehabilitate not punish. He said that sending me to CYA or regular prison would be punishment not rehabilitation. My probation officer and the DA wanted me in CYA. My lawyer and mom had always tried to convince the judge to send me to rehab, but something always went wrong. Either the rehab center wouldn't accept me or the judge wouldn't accept rehab. Then a miracle happened! The day before my court date my lawyer found the program in Western Samoa! The DA and my probation officer were against sending me there, but I know that God wanted me here. The judge's exact words were, 'You're one lucky kid who has crapped on your parents' love numbers of times. But you will be going to Samoa. May the mosquitoes be big and the snakes be venomous!'

"So after four months in Juvenile Hall I was on my way to Samoa! I remember the trip very well. My probation officer came to Juvenile Hall. My mom and the pilot flying me were there. I was shackled and put in the car with the pilot. My mom drove to the airport to see me off. The pilot was nice enough to take my shackles off so I could hug my mom goodbye. She brought me some food from MacDonald's. I called my dad and grandma on the cell phone to say goodbye. When it was time to leave, I hugged mom one last time and gave her a kiss not knowing that it would be six months until I talked to her again."

Jessica's story resumed

"When he got arrested the last time, I was blind-sided. We'd had a wonderful time that weekend. I thought he was totally off drugs. He told me the only lie that would get him out of the house. He did a really good job of it this time! He was arrested for possession of drugs and firearms. He was caught with amphetamines, pot, LSD, I forget what all – but it was way more drugs than you need for personal use.

"Our family was pretty dysfunctional at that time. My husband was pretty angry. He was always for kicking Cary out. I kept rescuing him, even after he'd been kicked out of the house for several months.

"What really shocked me and hit me emotionally the hardest was when I learned that Cary had been practicing Satanism. Now, I wasn't a religious person, but I'd always considered myself a moral person. There was something about realizing that he had been performing Satanic rituals and inviting Satan into his life that made me realize the reality of the spiritual world. It was the most devastating and most glorious day of my life, because that was the day that I gave my life to the Lord in order to save my family, myself, and my son.

"Cary was in deep legal trouble. I started praying and I said, 'Lord, I do not know the right thing.' Part of me wanted him to go to CYA; part of me would have been happy if the gangs beat the shit out of him … maybe he'd learn; part of me still wanted to protect him; *but the biggest part of me wanted him to get better.* He wasn't the kind of kid who would easily survive the juvenile system. He wasn't violent. He was *impulsive.* Things he did, like throwing furniture, could have been called violent but he never directed his violence at people. He knew he couldn't hold his own in a fight. He also knew that being a small white boy in a prison wasn't a good thing. The judge ruled that Cary could go to a residential program if we could find an appropriate one and agreed to pay. So I started looking. I started to pray, 'Show me a program, Lord!'

"The first time I heard the word 'Samoa' I said, 'No way! I can't afford that!' But within two weeks of me hearing the word 'Samoa' he was there! My husband William wasn't playing a big role at this time. He wasn't non-supportive; he was actually visiting Cary in Juvenile Hall more than I was. But he wasn't actively supportive either."

katherine and kyle

Katherine: "One night, after he was back living with his dad, Anthony came into our house and yelled, 'I'm not staying at dad's anymore!' He grabbed a butcher knife, like his dad was going to come after him or something. I said, 'You stay here! We'll go talk to your father.' Well, I think his father was OK. Looking back, I think Anthony had been using drugs that night.

"After that, things got worse. He got in a fight that the school said was gang-related and they suspended him. This was only a couple of months into high school. Now, his low self-esteem took over. From then on he just tuned out. He hung out with kids that weren't going to school, that weren't doing anything themselves except getting into trouble.

"One night about midnight there was a knock on the door. It was a police officer. We didn't even know Anthony was out of the house! The officer said, 'I have your son here. It's a curfew violation. I didn't find anything on him but his pupils are dilated.' In my usual angry, passive self, I told Anthony to go to bed and stormed up and went to bed myself. When I got up the next morning Kyle had already gone off to work. I found that Anthony had vomited all over the place. I called Kyle who told me to get a specimen and take him to the hospital. He tested positive for marijuana. We restricted him a lot after that, took his phone away, forbade him to hang out with his friends, told him he had to go to Kyle's office after school and work. But that still didn't stop him. I'd drop him off at school but he wouldn't go to class. He'd go somewhere, get wasted, go to class for awhile, then go off campus during lunch and drink. After he'd come home from Kyle's office, he'd lock himself up in his bedroom. He wouldn't even come to dinner. And I said, 'Well, Kyle, I guess he's doing OK because he's not smoking marijuana.' Kyle had threatened that if he found any marijuana in the house he was going to turn it into the police.

"I'd been looking at the possibility of putting him into a program for about six months, collecting information about different options. In my heart I knew we weren't finished yet. I knew it was much worse. Mother's instinct. I would talk to Kyle about everything and he would want to give this or that one more try."

Kyle: "Well, it wasn't even that: I just wasn't supportive of a decision to put Anthony into a program. I was blind to what was going on. I just thought he was up in his room, didn't want to be with us, and withdrawn. Later we found out that he'd been sneaking out fairly routinely."

Katherine: "In April he decided he was going to go live with his dad again. I talked to my ex-husband and said, 'Elliot, he's had two tickets; he's hanging around with a bad crowd. This isn't good. What are we going to do?' And he said, 'OK, I'll take him for a while.' So, we gave Anthony a beeper and let him go. I said to Kyle, 'I give this three weeks to blow up.' And sure enough it did. They got into a big fight."

Kyle: "Anthony said he was going to go with his friends on Friday afternoon. His dad said, 'I want you with me tonight.' Anthony said, 'No, I'm leaving,' and he headed off to a park. His dad trailed him down there, found him, and they got into a physical fight, rolling around on the ground. Police broke it up. They let them go and they went over to his dad's store where Anthony locked his father in the basement and took off.

"Anthony was gone five days before we found him. At this point, we started making arrangements to have the escort service come. Up to now I had been kind of a non-believer, convincing myself that, 'Oh, everything's really going OK.' His running away jarred me, caused me to think that I'd really blown it, and made me realize that everything Katherine had been saying – which I had at some level denied – was true. By this time I was convinced that, if we went after him and got him back, he was only going to run again and run farther. So now I agreed: We had to do something. I had turned a corner from desperation to joining forces with Katherine. She had shown me literature about various programs. I'd looked at it but didn't really understand it. So now I began to intellectualize it and master the concepts of what we needed to do. But inside, my gut was going nuts realizing that we're going to send this kid that I love to a bunch of people whom we know nothing about. So now we're calling all the references to the Program we can locate. And I began to feel very positive about taking the action. But my blood pressure was rising to an all-time high and I was *acutely* anxious about how we were going to bring this off. To top it all off, I had to deal with Anthony's father. I mean, the divorce was fourteen years' history but the emotions behind it were *still* ignitable by a mere look between Katherine and her ex. There was still a lot of anger. So I got to deal with his dad and I was always anxious about having to do that."

Katherine: "But we succeeded. His father agreed to sign the papers to put him into the Program. Since they were fighting, he knew that Anthony was simply out of control. And I think that because of the fight, Anthony's father was afraid – afraid for both of them."

Kyle: "The escort people were *wonderful.* I sat down and talked with those guys when they arrived and after five minutes felt a great deal better about what we were doing.

"But I still felt anxious about how to coordinate the pick-up. Anthony was living with a girl friend. He sold drugs for her father who was himself a dealer. The plan was that my twenty-two-year-old daughter Kimberly would ride in the back seat of the escort car and call us on the cell phone when she saw him. We'd then call the police to pick up Anthony and turn him over to the escort. So she's sitting in the car near his apartment and Anthony is sitting outside on the balcony in front of a broken window. And there are about fifteen people coming in and out with beer bottles, throwing them out in the trash. So it must have been a big party. I get the call from Kimberly and call the PD. Three police cars come screeching up. Two officers detain Anthony, bring him out, and put him in the back of the squad car.

"Kimberly just lost it when she saw him hauled off. She said it was the hardest thing to watch her brother be hauled away. He looked horrible. His hair was so scraggly. She said that he must not have washed it in a week. He put up no fight. She ran away from the scene. That's her last vision of her brother. It's been real tough on her ever since. Anthony doesn't know that she helped in his capture; but *she* knows and it's been very, very hard on her. She was very angry at first, mad at us for sending her, for manipulating her into contributing. She initially said that he wasn't that bad, that we didn't need to send him. Later she agreed that he was in fact in bad enough shape that we did the right thing.

"So Anthony gets taken to the Police Department. I met them there and walked into a small room with the two policemen who'd brought him into custody and the two escorts. Anthony was sitting in a small chair. He was kind of slouched back. I made eye contact with him but couldn't read his expression. I expected him to be pretty upset, but he didn't seem to be hot. I said, 'Anthony, we love you, and we're never going to quit, we're never going to stop. And these two gentlemen want to talk to you.' He left with the two escorts. He walked away expressionless, but the overwhelming sense that I got from him was that of relieved acceptance. It wasn't confusion. It wasn't a question about what's happening to me.'"

Katherine: "What was going through his mind, we now know, was that he thought he was going to Juvenile Hall. The escort service had told us that they wouldn't tell Anthony where he was going until they got well on the road. They told us later that he was one of the calmest kids they'd encountered."

Shortly after he was headed for Samoa, Katherine went to Anthony's room and threw out all the Jim Morrison posters.

Jonathan's story resumed

As Jonathan continues his story, I'm struck by certain features of his personality. As I mentioned previously, he is a very likable young man. But he is also quite naïve. Both his story and the way he tells it reflect these traits. Also, I notice that Jonathan feels bad, or wrong. He does not project a feeling of health or well-being. He seems to have judged himself harshly – perhaps more harshly than anyone else.

"As time went along, I did a lot of wrong things that pulled my relationship with my parents apart, and it really damaged us. I really didn't do that many bad things. The things I did got me into jail, but the things I did weren't as bad as others I hear about, who were involved in gang activity and going around with weapons. I didn't do that. I'm lucky I didn't turn out that way.

"Before I came here, I had a very close relationship with an older man Scott, thirty-six years old. My mom used to do day care for this lady Kathy who lived on our block. I had a close relationship with her, like a mother/son relationship. Scott was her live-in boy friend. He started doing drugs, got into cocaine. Kathy never knew about it. He was a very smart man. He brought marijuana around me. I brought it to him, too. It was a partnership. I would steal stuff for him. Like one time he asked me to go steal him a starter off this pickup truck. I stole lots of stuff for him. He really loved me a lot and I loved him. He helped my family a lot. He built a computer for my mom.

"Then stuff really started going downhill. My mom and dad thought there was something wrong with Scott, that he was doing something behind the scenes that we didn't know about. But I'd say, 'No, mom. It's OK. Scott wouldn't do anything.' And I really believed that when I said it. When he started using, he got very agitated. He got fired from his job. All the time he was with Kathy he had another girlfriend in Oregon. He'd lie to Kathy, tell her he was going to Yakima to help out his father. But really he'd go to Oregon and screw this lady. He had a kid with her, then another one. Kathy would find out about him, but she'd always take him back. I'd say to myself, 'Scott's a good guy. He'll never do anything to hurt us.'"

Jonathan identified himself more as part of this couple's relationship than his own family. At his still tender age, Jonathan was drawn into a dysfunctional relationship between two individuals who themselves had important

85

personal problems. I imagined a young boy wanting nothing more than to be part of a family – just not the one he was given.

"One day I was over at his house when some undercover cops came. The night before I'd just stolen a bike for him. We got some bolt cutters and drove all over town just to steal a bicycle. I thought we were going to get caught when the police arrived. Scott said, 'Tell them I'm not here, that I've left.' Well, his truck was in the driveway! He ran in the bedroom and hid in the closet. I opened the door and they said, 'Is Scott _____ here?' I told them no. They kept asking me the same question and I kept telling them he wasn't there. They said, 'If he doesn't come out, we're going to have to get a search warrant.' I got really scared and I said, 'Hold on, let me see if he's here.' So I locked the front door and I went into the bedroom and asked him what I should do. He told me to be very quiet and tell them he's not here. And at that point, I got really scared. I didn't know what he had done. I was basically scared for myself, for my safety. Finally he came out and they arrested him.

"Scott kept calling me collect from jail. When my parents answered he hung up. One time he called and I said, 'Mom, it's Scott. May I please answer his call?' She said, 'No.' I did anyway because I really loved him. I had to be really quiet because my family was getting ready to go out. Scott seemed very worried about Kathy. 'Jonathan, what's Kathy doing?' he asked. He wanted to make really sure that she didn't get into his truck. So I agreed to keep her away from his truck.

"But Kathy had already been in his truck. One day she was looking for cigarettes, so she got into his truck to see if there were some there. She found cigarettes from Oregon, so she knew he'd been down there. She'd found other things there, though, receipts and credit cards he had ordered in her name. One of the receipts was from a pawnshop. Our computer had been stolen, the one he'd built for us! Mom and dad had of course already put two and two together, but I hadn't.

"The day the computer was stolen, my brother and I had gotten in this fight. It was really out of control and I had hit him on his back with a baseball bat. Scott was looking for me, supposedly to help. But I think it was then he got into our house and ripped off the computer. I found the pawn shop receipt and said, 'Kathy, he stole our computer!' But inside I was saying, 'No, no, Scott wouldn't do something like that!' I got really scared and finally realized it was him.

"Later on he called me up on the phone from jail again. By this time I was really pissed off at him. I was really hurt. I had this rage inside me that made me feel like I really had to get him back. He asked me what Kathy was doing. 'Is she going through the truck?' I said, 'Yeah, she sure is!' At this point, my mom told me to get off the phone. She realized I was talking to Scott. I said, 'Scott, where is my f---ing computer?' My mom took the phone and hung it up.

"Later, we found out about a lot of stuff he'd done. He'd charged about two thousand dollars on the bogus credit cards. He'd falsified some information and got a lot of money grams. He'd stolen from a lot of stores. There were warrants for his arrest in a lot of counties. What a con man!

"He pretended he loved me, and I think he sorta did. But it was a fake kind of love. And he was using me. He was using Kathy, too. He was more an older man who wanted nothing more than sex from her. Kathy would come home from work and he'd take her back in the back room and screw her while I was there. He was a man who wanted everything, you know. He used me to get what he wanted. At times, he got scared. He would tell me how he was feeling and I cried with him a lot, because I shared those feelings with him. He would leave and say he had to go away and that Kathy would never take him back. But she always would, even though he was down there in Oregon plunking this other woman. He was just a loser, you know.

"Him and Kathy was like a family I wished I had. I smoked ever since I was ten years old. They would allow me to smoke at their house. Every once in a while, Scott would allow me to drink, but never around Kathy. He was such a cool guy. I never knew he smoked marijuana until I started talking to him about it, you know, and then I started buying it and bringing it to him. And all along he had been doing this stuff, you know. And I'd find pipes in Kathy's car and I started to realize, 'Oh, Kathy does it too!' But I never did drugs with her, just with him.

"The reason I liked him was that he let me get away with things. It's like he supported the bad things that I did instead of the good. At first I thought he was a very good man. I always wanted to be over there. He'd do all these things to help me, but it was turning me in the wrong direction. He'd genuinely want to help me out when I was in trouble with my parents. He'd talk to me more as a father than a friend. There were times when I got into a scuffle with my mom, like when I'd grab her arm or something, and she'd call the police. And he said, 'Jonathan, if you ever get into any trouble, call me up.' And he really would come through. I went to stay with him and Kathy for a while because he intervened and the authorities let me go stay at their house. A part of me wanted to go back to my own home, because I knew this was not my home, but I was having so much fun being with them.

"So Scott was in jail. I got really put off by him being in jail. I missed him. I was in a lot of trouble myself. I felt like death. I wanted to die. I asked Kathy's kids, 'What's another way of killing yourself?' And they gave me ideas.

"One day I was home and my family was going to the Mariners game. Some trouble developed in the house. I carved the words 'f--- you' into my knuckles with a hot needle. Also, I cut on my arms with a knife, so there was a lot of blood. I wanted my parents to see that I was having a hard time. My dad got real mad. Mom decided to stay home with me. I said, 'No, I'm not staying here, I'm going!' I went out to my dad's truck and started to get in and my dad grabbed me and tried to hit me. I grabbed onto the truck as they were backing out of the driveway and tried to hang onto it.

"I was pretty desperate. I walked down the road. I saw the police coming. I realized that my mom had called them. They said, 'Robert, do you need some help?' And I said, 'Yeah I do.' So they took me to this psychiatric hospital for a seventy-two-hour stay. I told them I was OK; I wouldn't try to hurt myself anymore; I didn't want to die. They believed me.

"Then there was a court appearance to determine if I was going to be involuntarily confined there. I didn't want to be at the hospital. I was really angry with mom and rebellious, telling her to 'f--- off' and things like that. But the judge didn't confine me. My mom was frustrated and crying because she didn't even have a say and wasn't allowed to talk. She'd come to the end of her rope. After the hearing, she told me, 'You're not coming home. You're going to have to live in the streets.' I was filled with rage. My school counselor took me to the Department of Social and Health Services. She gave me a couple dollars and said, 'If you get hungry, you can get something to eat.'

"I road the metro bus home to get something. My plan was that I'd have mom bring me back to the Department. When I got home, she wasn't there. At that time I realized that my life had ended. My mom had locked all the windows and doors but I found a way to get in through my brother's window. As soon as I got in I said to myself, 'Where's the gun? I want to hurt myself.' I went downstairs and took the gun out of the gun room. My dad put the key for the safe above the door to the room. We used the guns mainly for hunting, like for deer and stuff. When I pulled the gun out I wasn't going to kill myself. I had a plan where I was going to shoot myself in the leg and just graze it enough where I could put the gun back, call the police, and say that someone broke into my house. That way, my parents would take care of me.

"There was only one shell. It was for a twenty-gauge lever-action shotgun. We've gone hunting and I've seen a twelve-gauge gun. You shoot a bird and even with a twelve-gauge sometimes the bird doesn't drop. And so I said to myself, 'Oh, this isn't going to hurt me.' I had changed into some old clothes. I was crying all this time. I was really scared. I tied a towel around my leg as a tourniquet to keep myself from bleeding to death. I was sitting on the floor with my legs out in front of me. I had the gun propped up next to me aimed at my leg. I was trying to think. 'What am I going to do? How is this going to happen? What am I going to do after it happens?' I had forgotten to bring a telephone next to me so I didn't have anything to get hold of the police with so I could get help. Our gun room is really a small room with not much space to maneuver. So realizing I needed to get the phone, I started to get up. The gun hit the wall and went off and blew out the calf of my left leg – about seven inches length and three inches wide.

"When it hit me I jumped right up, knowing I had to get outside. I didn't have a phone to call the police. I knew there was something serious wrong. I didn't have a chance to look down and see what happened. All's I heard was a ringing noise in my ear. I didn't hear the boom. I wasn't crying. I was yelling really loud, 'Help! Help! Call 9-1-1 please!'

"An old man down at the bottom of my driveway was going to get his mail. He couldn't hear me. Finally, I got his attention and he went to call the police. A lot of people saw what had happened. They ran into their houses to call for help. By this time Scott was out of jail and he was at Kathy's house. They heard me screaming. They thought it was my mom screaming and that I was hurting her. They didn't care.

"An officer came and pulled his gun out on me. I got really scared. He said, 'Jonathan, what did you do?' I said, 'I shot my f---ing self!' I started cussing at him and telling him to hurry up. I knew this guy. Sam was a policeman who also worked off-duty in security for the school I went to. He helped on Friday nights at a place for kids where, instead of getting into trouble, they could hang out at a place with no alcohol or drugs. I said, 'Sam, put away the gun!' He said, 'No, I can't – it's company policy.' He searched the house and made sure no one was there. All this time I was screaming. It wasn't actually hurting – I was just screaming. It felt my foot was asleep. I was in shock. The ambulance and fire came. They bandaged me up. I blacked out then regained consciousness. I was really hot, dehydrated. I was yelling, 'Get me to the f---ing hospital. I'm going to die!' I could feel my leg just pumping blood out.

"All the neighbors were lined up outside my house. I saw Kathy and I asked her to help me, please. She turned away because she couldn't stand the blood. Pretty soon she told me to just stop yelling and calm down. I tried to control my breathing. Sam got on the cell phone to call my mom who worked only a mile away. The ambulance got me up on the stretcher. They tried to question me and I yelled at them, 'Stop asking me questions – it hurts too much!'

"When my mom got there I saw her face. It was real sad. I saw her as she pulled up in the driveway and she was crying. That was the last thing I saw. I passed out.

"They took me to the trauma center and applied lots of ace wraps to stop the bleeding. When my dad arrived I said, 'Oh, man!' And he looked at me and said, 'God damn you! Look what you did to yourself!' And that really hurt me because I could see that I had really hurt my father. They unwrapped my leg. And my dad looked at it and he said, 'Oh my god!' And he started crying. And I was crying too. I said, 'Daddy, daddy, help me!' And he said, 'Son, you've really screwed yourself up this time.' He left the room for awhile. Then he came back and grabbed my hand and held it for a long time. It took forever to get into surgery, but finally I went in. I fell asleep. I was in surgery for a long time.

"When I got out of surgery and regained consciousness, I was really hungry. With the oxygen mask, my throat was really dry. I said, 'Mom, I need some-thing to eat and drink.' But I couldn't swallow because my throat and mouth were so dry. Mom stayed with me that night. I woke up the next morning. It was really hard on me, like living a dream. I said, 'Why am I in here?' Then I'd say, 'Well, I shot myself!' It was really hard for me to realize I'd shot myself – that it was *me* that had done this. A lot of people blamed themselves. My sister thought it was her fault because she wasn't at the house at the time. But really it was my fault.

"The things that led up to that – it was both myself and my parents. We didn't get along and all. I ended up shooting myself because I was in such a desperate situation, you know. One of the reasons was for sympathy, to get love from my parents. If I shot myself I'd come back home. I'd live with them. They'd love me a lot more. They'd know something was wrong in my life. I'd get that love from them I wanted. As I sat in the hospital I got so much attention from my mom and dad. It was a lot more attention than I thought I'd have. To be honest with you, I got tired of it after a while – I had so much. I felt like just amputating my leg. The doctor said, 'Let's not do that right now, though – let's wait a while and see what we can do.'

"After I got out of the hospital, I went into a psychiatric hospital for seven days. They wanted to be sure I was OK. I came home. We had so much love for each other, my parents and I. We really did. But we slowly pulled apart again. I'd walk on my leg when I wasn't supposed to and this would anger them. My parents were really worried for my leg – that I was going to damage it more. They'd say, 'The doctor's going to get mad at you because you're walking.' And I'd say, 'Oh no he won't. It's OK.' And I started walking with the crutches and put a little pressure on it. I continued until I didn't use crutches anymore – I just walked directly on the leg. I was supposed to wear a walking brace/cast.

"One day I was at home all alone. In our living room, we have a big fireplace that extends out from the wall. Earlier I had a fire going in the fireplace. There was this light bulb above the fireplace. The fire had gone out but the fireplace was still hot. I didn't check it to see if it was still hot. So, I noticed the light bulb was out and decided to change the light bulb, you know, to do something for my mom and dad. So I climbed up onto the fireplace. I was barefoot. I had one leg, my bad leg, on the fireplace and the other leg on something else. Of course, I couldn't feel anything with that leg because by this time my nerves were all gone and I had no feeling in that part of my leg. I realized I couldn't reach the light bulb, so I got down.

"Not knowing that I'd burned myself, I put on my duck slippers and went outside to get the ladder. After I changed the bulb, I laid down because I was really tired – I had been walking around a lot. I took my slipper off to lay down and noticed it was really wet on the bottom. It wasn't wet outside at all. I looked at my slipper. There was a bad smell to it. I looked at the bottom of my foot and saw a really bad blister and realized it was a really bad burn. I called my mom and said, 'Mom, mom, I've burned myself, I've burned myself, you need to come home!'

"I went back to the hospital for a week. I asked the doctors how they were going to get me fixed up again. The doctors brought up the possibility of amputation. I was really scared. It would take a lot of work and effort to fix the leg, they said. They had a plan but it would mean a lot of pain. I said, 'No, I don't want to go through all that pain.' I wanted to take the easy way out and have my leg amputated.

"So we set it up. It took a long time to get me to the hospital for the operation. I threatened to do it myself. My mom got really worried about me and put me back in the psychiatric hospital. I didn't leave the hospital until the day I had my leg amputated.

"At this point as I talk to you, I wish I'd never had my leg amputated. I'd be walking fine now. That really screwed my life up. I've had to deal with it here in the Program. I've been doing a very good job of dealing with it and accepting the fact that I did it. I've been walking now for about a year with this prosthetic device.

"There were so many things I could have done to prevent me from coming here! I didn't look at it as a big deal – you know, my *life*. I just really wish I'd taken a bigger look at the things I was doing to myself, to my life, and to others' lives. Basically, I just really screwed my life up."

Jonathan speaks quietly with a kind of fatality in his voice. It's almost as if his life is over. Then he'll bring up something in the future, about how good it will be to get back with his parents again one day.

Robert and Mary Beth resumed

Mary Beth: "The day he carved the letters on his knuckles he was taken to the county hospital. A mental health professional decided to keep him for a while. One professional there said to me, 'He's run away several times this summer but you keep letting him come home. That's your fault. Don't let him come home any more.' That seemed good advice to me. Meanwhile, we'd been trying to get him placed somewhere within the state system to get him out of the house. We weren't having very much luck. Later this same counselor told me to take him home. I said, 'You're kidding! You just told me *not* to take him home!' And she said, 'Well, I think he'll be fine. If anything happens, you just call the county mental health professional.' I thought that was the most ridiculous thing I'd ever heard! I argued back-and-forth for about an hour before she finally agreed to send Jonathan to his first psychiatric evaluation.

"He was placed on what was supposed to be a seventy-two-hour hold. It ended up being fifty-two hours. The hospital never contacted us and never talked to us. I had to make all the phone calls *to them*. They made this so-called psychiatric evaluation based on the input of a kid barely fifteen! The next day we were to have a court appearance. Jonathan had already been to juvenile hall three or four times prior. I knew that wasn't accomplishing anything. So that night I went to the hospital and said, 'Jonathan, you need to stay here, you need to get a full psychiatric evaluation.' He said to me, 'Mom, I'm not like these people, I don't need to be here, I can work this out at home.' I said, 'No, you need to stay here the full fourteen days and get a proper evaluation before you're allowed to come. If you leave beforehand, you're not to come home.'

"Finally he agreed. I was pretty hopeful. I went to court the next morning and the hospital official said they were going to release him because he was not a danger to himself or anyone. By this time, Jonathan actually *wanted* to stay on a voluntary basis. But they required an involuntary stay or nothing because that way he wouldn't just walk out.

"During the court hearing, I said, 'Jonathan, I have been the one to be by your side in everything, through all the crap you've pulled. I've always been there. I've never turned my back on you. But right now you're not choosing to help yourself, so I'm turning my back on you. You're on your own. I love you very much.' And I turned around and walked away. (Sobbing) *And an hour later he shot himself?*"

Robert: "We didn't want him home – because of the way he was abusing Mary Beth. He never hit her. But there were times when he'd get out of hand and she'd back him into his bedroom. He's bigger than her, but she never backed down from him. There were times she'd pushed him back in his bedroom. She would sit on him a couple of times until the police arrived. But he never hit her. He would push her. And that was enough for me. Who knows what would have happened with that gun, whether he would have done to us what he did to himself?"

Mary Beth: "When Jonathan got dropped off at the state placement office, he decided that he really did need help. He intended to come home and ask me to take him back. I was in touch with that office right after they had dropped him off. One moment he was sitting there, the next he had taken off. I *knew* he would come home. So I locked every door and barred every window I could think of. I tried to do everything I could to make it hard for him to get back into the house. The gun never even occurred to me because it was in a locked room in a locked safe. I left for work."

Robert: "He thought he'd hurt himself enough so we would take care of him and nurse him back to health and let him stay home. That way he wouldn't have to go to a foster home or a state shelter."

Mary Beth: "He was terrified to be away from home. I mean, this kid had slept under bridges and lived on the streets! Yet he was terrified to be away from home. He was determined not to be away from home. His plan was, even though it would hurt a little bit, he'd put a few BB's into his leg ..."

Robert: "... but it was a *twenty-guage shotgun*! ..."

Mary Beth: "... he'd call the police, say he'd been attacked, we'd feel sorry for him, and take him back. Somehow he would get it worked out and things would be better. He wasn't trying to kill himself."

Robert: "He had it planned out. He was going to shoot himself in the foot. He said to himself, well, if I do that I can't walk, so he put it up to the calf of his leg. With his ADD and all the problems we'd had, I could never trust him with a gun. So I never showed him how to use it. He just went in there without knowing what he was doing, put the shell in, and the gun was ready to go. There's no safety on it – it's just a hammer you have to let down by pulling the trigger, but he didn't know that. When I arrived at the emergency room, the first thing he said was, 'Dad, the gun doesn't do that to the birds!' And I said, 'Son, the birds are *thirty yards out* when I shoot them – and this was *point blank*!'"

Mary Beth: "That's the impulsivity. Kids like Jonathan honestly don't know what they're doing. They don't think of the implications, the outcome, of what they're doing. I always told him he had tunnel vision, that all he could see is right in front of him. I always said, 'You've got to look to the sides to understand what's going on around you.' I spent most of my life with this kid making analogies for him to understand. He's a very smart kid, a very mechanically-minded kid. He rebuilt the carburetor on his sister's car at fourteen years old!"

Jonathan's behavior did not improve after the amputation. Further experiences with social service and mental health professionals only produced more of the same results. Mary Beth attended a Discovery seminar to obtain information about Paradise Cove.

Mary Beth: "When I came home I found Jonathan passed out on the floor, lying next to four cans of aerosol. I dialed 9-1-1. That scared the hell out of me! We got him to the hospital. I prayed real hard to keep him alive until I could get could it together to put him into the Program. I was waiting for the school district to send him. It wasn't but about a week later, I got a call from the police saying he was suspected of breaking into someone's house. I said to Jonathan, 'That's it! You're gone! I can't do this!' I called Robert at work and said, 'That's it, I'm taking him!' I borrowed the money. The day I took my son to the Program, I had twenty dollars in my pocket. I cashed in my 401K. I borrowed money from family for our plane fare. I used a new Sears credit card to pay for the rental car. And it was done.

"Robert didn't argue about it, but I did it all. I feel like I've hurt our relationship because I've taken over, but Robert has always let me do it. So while I didn't like taking charge, I did it because he didn't. I think it had a lot to do with Robert's upbringing being so negative. Nothing would ever work – 'No, we can't do that, we can't do that!' And I said, 'Bullshit! We *can* make it happen!' And I made it happen. A week later Jonathan was in the Program voluntarily."

Robert: "We had Jonathan in just about every program we could come up with – lockup facilities, juvenile detention, counseling – everything to make an impact on his life. We knew that if it was up to the state, they'd just lock him up and forget about him. There's a lot of good things about Jonathan. He's a good kid, a smart kid. It's just that he's made some really bad choices."

Mary Beth: "I say to anyone, *'where there's a will there's a way!'* We are living proof! Again, I say it is not easy, but worth the fight. My child would not be here now had I not fought for him!"

Robert: "Yeah, that's the way it happened."

The main message Jonathan conveyed to me the day that I met him at Paradise Cove was, "I've still got a lot of issues to deal with yet." It's fascinating to me how completely *connected* we can be with others. Separated by thousands of miles, mom and dad had recently told me the same thing about themselves. I fell in love with my three new friends so quickly. Their warmth and feeling, their eagerness to please and figure it all out, their bewilderment and sadness concerning these events – I thought about them as I watched Jonathan limp down the path to the beach below. He turned around and waved goodbye to me another time. I'm pulling for my friends. I know this much: They want *more* out of life. But are they willing to give up whatever they have to give up to get it? They will answer that question.

A family sometimes runs slow like a river will. It takes the passage of many seasons for a river to change. And a river is profoundly affected by its surroundings. Melting snow from winter storms swells a river and uprooted trees become fallen limbs borne upon its back. The deepest part of a river knows of its burden and has a sense of its own direction, never running in a straight line, but snaking around and going where its destiny will take it. In its meandering a river bears the enormous weight of itself and everything it carries. And sometimes around a turn it damns up, unable to pass freely beyond a tangle of rocks and trees it has placed in its own path. It is in a river's nature to run free. And only the river knows how to break itself free. It possesses that kind of power. If it will use it.

Road not taken: Stan and Patrick

We do not need to send our children to a residential facility whenever our child develops a severe problem adjusting to life! Clearly, Jonathan needs a kind of intervention designed to get his attention and allow him to respond. Such a process of intervention may take a long time. But I do *not* contend that such measures are required for everyone. Responsible parents may explore several options (therapy, group processes such as ToughLove and Al-Anon, HMO-provided programs, school programs, etc.) before determining that a long-term, intensive program is needed.

But it is also important to recognize when neither you nor the actions you are taking are reaching your child. Does the story of Stan and Patrick illustrate such a case?

Just after the holiday season and not long after Patrick turned seventeen, Stan introduced himself to me. He is a large, powerful man whose obvious physical presence is matched by a powerfully decisive personality. Stan is a successful, hard-working businessman who manufactures computer peripherals. Stan knows what it takes to be a success in this life. He is an open, engaging individual, certain about things and equally certain about how things should be in the home. He wants to make quick decisions and take quick, decisive action – as if his domestic problems would yield to the same problem-solving approach of any common business problem.

Stan is concerned about Patrick's irresponsible behavior and outbursts of uncontrollable anger around the home. Stan and his ex-wife had adopted Patrick in his infancy. She apparently had severe emotional problems early on and Stan divorced her when the kids were still young, proceeding to raise the kids by himself. Patrick is the last of the brood.

After listening to Stan talk about his domestic situation, I develop a mental image of an immature young man in control of the household and a frustrated, opinionated, perhaps inflexible father unable to establish leverage with his son. Stan's frustration resulted from his true devotion to Patrick as well as his knowledge that he was unsuccessful at controlling him. In response to all of Stan's machinations, Patrick was recalcitrant and obdurate. Dad had done just about everything a father can do to lay down the law. And dad appeared to be a man who easily gave in to rage when he didn't get the results that he wanted from his son. Patrick simply dug in his heels, knowing the precise set of calculations required to get Stan's number every time without fail. In short, father and son were at stalemate, each a mirror of the highly controlling nature of the other.

Each week I saw Stan, he brought another description of the ongoing battle royal. Their warfare wasn't physical – it was a mental and psychological skirmish, a war of psychological and emotional control. The conflict was over a small set of domestic responsibilities – emptying the trash, cleaning up the common areas, and the presence of Patrick's girlfriend – under what circumstances she should be allowed in the house and when. In his drive to be a decisive and responsible father, Stan had overspent a parent's natural fund of authority and squandered all the do-this-or-else measures that a parent can get away with naturally. Stan was nearly out of leverage.

I saw myself so completely in Stan. It was like staring at myself in the mirror! I wanted to assist him so much, but I wasn't sure that he could see the connection between us.

Just like me, Stan seemed all locked up in his son's potential. Patrick showed great potential as a distance runner and had the possibility to attain a world class status and turn professional. The father wished very much for the boy to achieve his dream and funded his son's racing. He thought that this was the incentive that his son needed to make sensible decisions about his life and to cooperate around the house. And in fact the boy seemed to honor his father's dedication to his future by working very hard at his sport. His dream was to turn professional. He practiced daily and worked very hard at the conditioning required. Sure, he had stopped going to school. Sure, he talked about getting a job but a job never seemed to materialize. Nevertheless, there was always Patrick's *potential* to talk about …!

While Patrick understood that his father financed his racing, he absolutely believed that to be his father's parental obligation. He refused to obey house rules because he didn't believe that his father should have *any* say in his life. Besides, he concluded that his father was a hypocrite – a do-as-I-say-not-as-I-do type. Patrick told me, "Hey, if dad decides not to fund my racing, I'll just go out and get a sponsor."

Patrick's girlfriend was only fourteen. She practically lived at their house. Tina's age was terribly distressful to Stan. No fool, Stan knew that clearly the kids were sexually active. He talked with the girl's parents, sharing with them his concerns about their daughter. He asked them to refuse permission for their daughter to come over to his home when he himself was not present. But her parents did not seem to care. Instead of refusing their daughter, they refused to support Stan's position. Day after day, Tina continued coming to Stan's house anyway –while he was at the office, at night, on the weekends – she was always there. Stan decided that her parents would be no help whatsoever and considered taking legal action against them for being irresponsible and neglectful parents.

With great concern, Stan observed Patrick's domination and control over this young girl who barely had an identity of her own. Tina clung to Patrick like a child. She barely spoke except in whispers directly into her boyfriend's ear – words he alone could hear. "She's just a *baby*" I said to myself when I met her. She clung to her "man's" arm, refusing eye contact with anyone but him. It was like watching a Baby Barbie wearing makeup and a ruined self-concept and clinging to a selfish Ken! She deferred completely to her man in all matters. To make things worse on Stan, he saw it all very clearly. His son was abusive to the girl – playing psychological and mind control games with her. This concerned Stan deeply because, as a sensitive and caring man himself, it was never his intention to raise a son who would treat women disrespectfully or abuse them.

One day Stan came home early from work and found the son, just shy of eighteen, together with now fifteen-year-old Tina. Patrick was in the bathtub taking a bath; she was primping herself in the mirror. They stared blankly at Stan. "Well," their look at him seemed to say, "what are you going to *do* about it?!"

One Saturday in early July, Patrick had a race. Stan, ever the dutiful and doting father, attended this race like all the others. Afterwards, Stan accidentally left an expensive pair of running shoes he'd purchased for Patrick at the track. They drove off. Later after the discovery of the loss and a fruitless search, son screamed at father. His emotions completely out of control, Patrick verbally threatened his dad in a loud and angry voice. "I oughta *kill* you!" he yelled. This, over a mere pair of running shoes!

I suggested the possibility of a residential program and encouraged Stan to look into it. He had already given it some consideration but was not ready to consider that approach. His choice was to redouble his efforts at being tough around the house. He launched yet another campaign, in a continuous string of campaigns, to be the household authority, negotiate house rules, write home contracts, and regain control – despite the obvious reality that his son neither had reason to agree with his dad nor likely was capable of adhering to any agreement. Nevertheless, Stan continued to choose to do what he had always done, expecting a new campaign to work.

The issue to me was not so much whether Stan and Patrick worked out some sort of accommodation in their less-than-peaceful coexistence; the issue was that it's *only that* – coexistence! There was no conflict resolution. Patrick was getting away with thinking that he can get away with anything in life, run rough shod over people, and abuse authorities and women. He was getting by with thinking that it's all about winning and, hey, he *was* winning in the way he thought about it. He was manipulating better and what counted was: Who manipulates best, wins. Or so he thought.

Later I received a call from Stan. He was going through another rough time with his son. Stan seemed in denial of what looked to me like a very strong possibility of drug use, given the extreme outbursts of anger he described. Even if Patrick wasn't using, his behavior was clearly uncontrollable. At least it was worth drug testing Patrick to find out.

Stan had less than a year to create something totally new for his son; and he hadn't even given Patrick a drug test to know for sure if he was using! Instead Stan wanted others to suggest some magic trick to turn his son around. Every suggestion for action outside the confines of the home itself met with reasons why it wouldn't work or couldn't be considered now. There was *always* one reason after another why this or that wouldn't work. Stan opined that he "did not think" his son was using. For that reason, using tougher measures such as a residential program seemed extreme, he stated. "Besides, what will that do to his running career?" Stan wondered. I mentioned the possibility that Patrick might *still* have a career left after a year or so in a residential program! I saw how Stan was waiting for definitive proof just like I had been. He would not budge until he got it.

So ... again I gazed in the mirror which Stan held up to me. I saw in Stan my own closed mind. Not long ago I danced the same dance of illusion and denial. Not so long ago I felt I had to have all the answers and the perfect solution before I could take any meaningful action. I too searched for the magic button, some phantom trick to manipulate my son to make the critical changes I wanted him to make. It wasn't that long ago when I thought my false dreams were true. Despite the allure of tricks, techniques, and rule changes as a means for profoundly altering the course of my son's life, they were in the end but illusions I wanted to be true!

Perhaps wisdom includes learning to recognize what the universe provides us. You and I may not like what it says to us all the time, but the universe nevertheless speaks to us continuously. Stan was in frequent contact with parents no longer in illusion about their children's reality. They were available to assist him to open up a whole new possibility. Not just the possibility of helping his son turn his life around, but the possibility to heal their wounded relationship. But the ever-decisive Stan said he was "not ready for the extreme solution" of placing his kid in a residential program.

I've lost contact with Stan and his son. I'm not out to prove him wrong or right. I only report faithfully what I observed. One night after listening to another story of Patrick's behavior at home, I said to myself, "Tick-tock ... tick-tock ... tick-tock .... Patrick will be eighteen faster than Stan can spell Paradise Cove backwards!" As I drove home I thought of what a good teacher Stan was to me. He held up a mirror to me and showed me how easy it is to deny the possibility that the universe sets *squarely* in front of me. The universe is supportive. It uses time and space favorably. It puts us in close proximity to critical people at critical moments in our lives. I too need to be more attentive to the possibilities before me. "What am I overlooking at this moment? What is obvious that I do not see?" I wondered. I either open my eyes to reality or deception.

The story of Stan and Patrick is simply a story of a road not taken. Their story is not yet finished. I can choose to have a little empathy for their predicament. I can choose to learn from them, to drink from the cup of experience, and to be grateful for the cup itself. Life is open-ended. As father and son walk along the pathways of their lives, life will present them with other opportunities.

Crisis — a turning point

I believe that one of the most important and instructive personal outcomes of our participation in ToughLove was its guidance to parents in precipitating a "controlled crisis" in the lives of their recalcitrant children. To read about this in more depth, I suggest that any interested parent read David and Suzannah York's wonderful book *ToughLove*.

The ToughLove process taught me that I had a lot more power in my life than I knew. I walked into my first ToughLove meeting the way most parents do — feeling alone, a victim, and powerless!

With the support of fellow ToughLove travelers, I realized that I could discover my power as a parent or remain in the illusion that I had little or no power – an illusion that seemed altogether too easy and comfortable for me. I began to introspect a little more about my behavior at home. It didn't take long to realize that I had *never taken a stand* with regard to Jacob's behavior. I saw that the decision not to take a stand – and no decision *is* a decision! – was a choice I made. No one *forced* me to make it. I began to realize that there were lots of things I could do which I hadn't tried, even considered. I had so easily tricked myself into thinking that as a parent I was powerless. "Why did I do that?" I wondered. Good question.

Once my refusal to take a stand sank in, I realized there was still more to learn. To alter Jacob's negative attitude and behavior, I had *first* to create a crisis within myself before I could unleash any positive energy upon him! I had to become highly uncomfortable and dissatisfied with the status quo in my family and myself before I would choose to muster the internal strength to overcome my fear to act. Somehow through all of the negativity and stress in my family, I was *comfortable!* I realized that I was comfortable feeling powerless because I accepted it as a given. Once I realized that I actually *had a choice* of being powerful or powerless, I became disgusted with the choice I was making and terribly uncomfortable with myself.

Once we begin to change we *can* create a crisis for a loved one. Of course, how our loved one reacts to the crisis we precipitate is up to them. We can't control that. Yes, it may backfire. But the alternative is doing nothing and remaining powerless.

One of the activities that got me moving in a positive direction was to assign myself a presentation to my ToughLove group on the power of creating a controlled crisis. I immersed myself in the topic and committed a lot of energy to it. I looked up the word *crisis* in the dictionary. It comes from the Greek *krisis* which means "decision." "Yes," I thought, "making a *decision* is something I have been avoiding. I'm afraid of choosing incorrectly." My fear dragged me down into an endless "analysis paralysis," a ceaseless weighing of one alternative against another. Paralysis through endless thinking only resulted in inaction and more status quo. I was always dreaming up one incentive or consequence after another that would pull my son up from his downward spiral, but nothing was really changing as a result. Obviously, I was very comfortable with the thinking part but very uncomfortable with thinking "out of the box"!

One meaning of *crisis* as defined in Webster's Dictionary is "an unstable or crucial time or state of affairs whose outcome will make a decisive difference for better or worse." If I was serious about doing something, I was going to have to introduce instability into the situation with Jacob. "That's good," I concluded as I came to my senses, "because it's a situation that *needs* a little instability – a *lot of it*, in fact!" I was coming home to status quo day after day and didn't like it one damned bit!

But I also noted "for better or *worse!*" Ugh! I didn't like that "worse" part! Yet what did we have to lose? Where was Jacob going with his life? Only downhill, as far as we could tell. It looked to us like we only had something potentially wonderful to gain and not a lot to lose. Why not take the risk that he may never talk to us again? If he's ever going to talk to us again, let it not be out of more blame and anger, we decided!

Another important point stressed by the Yorks is the aspect of "controlled" crisis. The decision to place Jacob in a residential program turned into something we thought about carefully, discussed, and planned together. Although it was a very emotional experience for us, the process we initiated, from the initial decision to the escort, was not some out-of-control reaction. We took thoughtful, decisive, and courageous action that Jacob never thought we would take and we created a positive crisis in all our lives.

Lying to save a life

A lot of parents I have met who placed their kids in a residential program lied to their children to get them to a facility. Most of us struggled with the issue of being dishonest with our children. The mother of a teen in Paradise Cove, Lisa compared dealing with her son Craig to dealing with her mother-in-law:

> "Even when my mother-in-law started becoming quite debilitated with dementia, it was very hard for my husband and me to be anything short of totally honest with her. Time and time again we found ourselves in the middle of a big mess, because in our attempt to be honest and forthright we failed to realize that *she* could not handle the honesty. We were actually doing her a disservice by overloading her with too much information which inevitably ended in disaster. Instead of going on auto pilot with our expectation of complete honesty at all times, we saw that we needed to learn to watch *her* behavior and gauge our verbal input to her to match her present emotional state. Every two minutes, it seemed, she would ask, 'Now where am I, what is this place called? Etc.' Rather than trying to orient her to her surroundings every time, her caregiver taught us to distract her away from her anxiety and focus her attention on something more acceptable and pleasant for her. We had to give up the faulty belief that we *owed* our parent total honesty. What we *really owed her* was to learn quickly how to help her live less frightening days. What she needed most from us was to distort reality so that she could cope better minute to minute.

"I think that applies to our children also. Many of us bought into the false belief that our children were much more mature and self-reliant than their behaviors suggested. So we acted towards, and responded to, them in adult ways, expecting adult responses from them. I'd approach something from an adult position, but Craig would respond in a very childlike, immature, often hurtful way. I couldn't believe my ears! Then I'd proceed as if that childlike state was only a momentary glitch on the screen, instead of his predominant state of being! Time and again our conversations ended in a blow up. I simply couldn't figure out what I was doing wrong. (Notice I assumed that I was the one blowing it!)

"I now realize that I was handling Craig in the same unsuccessful way that Davis and I had been handling his mother. I kept trying the honest and forthright route with Craig and he couldn't cope with it. His behavior told me that he could not handle what he was insisting that he had the birthright to be given. Pulling rank as his parent and making a clear statement that he would go to Paradise Cove – no matter what it took – was truly for the greater good, even though it involved lying to make it happen. The bottom line is that Davis and I finally seized back control of our lives and put Craig in a safe place so he could regain control of *his*. When I take inventory of the enormous amount of lying that Craig did to us (and himself), deceiving him to get him to Paradise Cove seems like grounds for sainthood for us!

"Until my child is eighteen I have a legal, moral, and ethical responsibility to make decisions for him and, from time to time, to pull executive rank if I think it is in *his* best interest. When and if I make decisions thoughtfully and from a place of wisdom, instead of out of pure emotional reaction, it's much easier to understand and accept."

Saundra told this story after her son had been in Paradise Cove for a year:

"I can remember the pain like it was yesterday. When we sent Jason to Paradise Cove, I was at the airport sobbing because he had just gotten on a plane with his dad accompanying him. He had no idea where he was going and did not know that I wasn't going with him.

"I walked him to the plane. The last thing I said to him was, 'I love you son!'

"He looked at me. 'What, you're not going with me?' And then came the glare!

"We had totally tricked Jason because we were so desperate to get him help. He kept running away so we knew we had to lie to him to get him on that plane. It was, for sure, the hardest thing I have ever done in my life. I learned a lot that day. As I stood in the airport obviously in pain, so many people reached out to me! Complete strangers took the time to talk to me.

"One of the stewards from the plane asked, 'Who did you just put on the plane?'

"I sobbed, 'My son!'

"'How old is he?' I'm sure he was expecting me to say two years old.

"'Fifteen,' I replied.

"'Never been away from you before, huh!' This elicited even more sobbing! 'Well,' said this kind stranger, 'I'm going to go tell your son that you are in so much pain. Watch the plane because I will have him lower the shade up and down and then you will know that he's going to miss you too!'

"More big tears! 'Good luck!' I said through my tears. 'He's pretty mad at me!'

"So I watched the plane roll away. No shade was pulled up and down. It was the worst pain I could have experienced.

"Later my husband told me that they were seated on the other side of the plane and Jason *was* saying goodbye to me after all! Even though I was sending him away, even though I had tricked him, I knew that he still loved me and that some day he would thank me for saving his life."

The responsibility of parenting

When we take on the role of the parent, along with that role comes a great deal of responsibility. One father of a son recently placed in a residential program articulated the sense of responsibility as well as anyone.

"My decision to place my son in the Program was not about change as much as it is about restoration of a quality in my son's life that was totally lost. *What's been lost is his spirit!* He has to get it back if he's ever going to face the world as an adult. It feels to me like maybe his last chance to do that. He's never understood that what I want most for him simply is to be his own person. He couldn't see how marijuana and alcohol robbed him of the very thing he thought I wanted him *not* to have! It's a twisted thing he's gotten himself into. It will take all the strength I have to be sure he sticks it out until he is strong again. But that is *my* end of it."

One night not long after Jacob had arrived at Paradise Cove, we dined out with dear friends. Positive reports about Jacob were already coming back and we were sharing these promising tidings with our dinner companions. They seemed so very happy for us, that perhaps we had done something which would make a positive difference in his life. One of the couples, Kurt and Bonnie, have known Jacob since he was about five. Suddenly, Bonnie began to speak with very deep feeling.

"I wish we had done that with Brandon," she said.

Their son Brandon was now serving at San Quentin. We all shared a concern that maybe one term wouldn't be his last in a state with a three-strike law. But the good news was that Brandon had come under the influence of a lifer who became a very positive mentor to Brandon before he was released. The lifer taught Brandon how much he had to live for and how much he was wasting his time in prison with such a family as he had waiting for him with open arms at home.

Brandon was always a handful. Once Kurt left eight-year-old Brandon in my charge for a weekend. Well, that was a joke! Brandon was in complete charge *of me!* By Sunday evening I was completely exhausted. By comparison my boys were so quiet and docile. Year after year passed by and Brandon brought ever more drama into Kurt and Bonnie's lives. Their marriage suffered. Somehow they stuck it out.

"At one point," Bonnie said, "we considered putting Brandon in a program. They seemed so expensive. We just didn't think we could do that."

I've always known and respected Bonnie for her complete honesty and openness. "But we ended up spending probably just about as much paying for his long trips to Juvenile Hall, to the California Youth Authority, for lawyers, for prison expenses, and the like, as you will end up paying for Jacob at Paradise Cove. But think how much Jacob is going to learn there about himself that Brandon was never able to learn behind bars. I wish we had done what you did!"

Not long after he was released and back home living with parents hoping that he had changed his life, Brandon was back for a second term. Strike two. Brandon is out again now. He's a *neat kid* – a kid who needs assistance more than punishment. I'm rooting for him. I've always liked him. As my grandmother would have said had she known him, "He would charm the socks off of you!" Perhaps it will all work out for Brandon now. I hope so for his sake and for the sake of his long-suffering and loving parents. As I write about this family I know and love so much, I think of them surrounded by a peaceful and radiant light. I send my friends this vision of peace and happiness – a vision they deserve very much to have and to live. I know in my heart that, with such love for their son, my friends did the best they could do at the time. One road was taken, another not. Our three friends walk this particular path for a reason none of us may ever understand. Other opportunities await them.

And life, the ever-giving river, flows on.

JOURNEY

*I*slands Apart is focused on the dimensions of individual and family breakdown and on their journey towards healing, not on a specific residential program or on residential programs in general. However, I need to explain how the Paradise Cove program in Western Samoa works in order that key portions of the remainder of this book are meaningful. The mechanics and philosophy of the Program serve as backdrop to an inner journey awaiting the children and parents involved.

Paradise Cove is privately-owned and participates as a member of the World Wide Association of Specialty Programs, an umbrella organization which coordinates the operation of several independent residential facilities located in the United States and abroad. Some facilities are for girls, some (like Paradise Cove) for boys, and some are co-educational.

The structure and characteristics of the programs associated with the World Wide organization are continuously changing in an effort to make a greater impact on the kids and families. The Program has changed considerably even as I wrote this book and the one I describe here will no doubt evolve.

Escort service

Except in rare cases, most teens do not elect to place themselves in a residential program even when aware that they are making life-threatening choices. When teens are incapable of making life-saving or life-enhancing choices, some parents choose to intervene as Sandy and I did. Employing the services of an escort service is one means of intervention. Legally authorized in writing by a parental authority, an escort service provides personnel to locate, pick up, and transport your child, willingly or unwillingly, to a residential facility of your choice. The World Wide Association of Specialty Programs works with several professional escort services to provide a safe journey from the home to the appropriate facility.

As we discovered, some so-called "parent unfriendly states" (such as California) do not allow parents to place their children in a residential facility for longer than seventy-two hours without then asking the child's permission to stay. Clearly, kids afflicted by the kinds of childhood disorders of the children in this book (e.g., heavy influence of drugs and peers, opposi-tional-defiant behavior, uncontrollable anger and rage, low self-esteem, dropping out of school, etc.) seldom have the maturity and insight into themselves to make responsible decisions. Three days is *hardly* long enough to undo root causes of problems taking years to develop, let alone the ef-fects of intensive drug use and destructive peer influence. Three days is not nearly enough time to free up a child from "stinkin' thinkin'" to make a responsible *and free* decisions. However even in parent unfriendly states, it is legal for parents to use a service to transport a child to a residential program located in a "parent friendly" state. Facilities located in these states or abroad can enforce a teenager's stay indefinitely with parental consent.

Despite physical maturity, teens are inwardly still children – especially when their emotional development has been stunted by prolonged drug use and a negative peer influence. Children cannot necessarily see their lives objec-tively or make life-enhancing choices for themselves.

One of life's disturbing and not very well-understood realities is that there are many forms of self-destruction or suicide. Those forms are becoming increasingly varied and available in a culture that seems ever ready to pro-vide the necessary tools. Among the young of our Western culture the urge to self-destruct may be stronger than perhaps ever before. Some forms of self-destruction are sudden and dramatic while others, such as drug addic-tion, are prolonged. Alert parents notice a self-destructive impulse in their children and register it as a "wake-up call" to take responsibility. Self-destructive acts may be dramatic appeals for assistance rather than an actual urge to die. But cries for assistance, no matter what form they take, can al-ways be understood to be a clear message that the child feels helpless. The challenge of growing up is learning to live consciously. A self-destructive child is being pulled by dark forces inside and around him. While his lan-guage and behavior may completely say otherwise, a child needs and truly wants the assistance of his loved ones. It is easy to underestimate the hope-lessness of others and to be blind *especially* to those closest to us.

Despite popular thinking, *parents continue to have an important role in a teen's life* even though the teen (and often parents themselves) may not share that view. A parent is obligated to see the reality of a child's life as clearly as possible. Parenting entails an awesome responsibility. Our blindness as par-ents is a sure measure of our own unconsciousness. Awareness of our chil-dren's state of being is a critical part of our parental obligation. When we signed up to become parents we volunteered not merely to feed, clothe, shelter, and provide education, opportunities, a supportive environment, and fun! (As if that isn't a long enough list!) Our obligation is to see our children clearly and respond creatively to what we see. This demands that we rise above our own emotion and often deep conditioning to view our children as objectively as possible – to rise *above* a conflict of which we are most likely an integral part. This demands *our* consciousness! Parents have life-saving choices to make when the quality of a child's life is threatened. *One of those choices may be to intervene in a teen's life against his will in order to save him from poor choices.* It ain't easy, folks! But as the therapist once said to the patient, "I never promised you a rose garden!"

Paradise Cove — a beach far away

The Paradise Cove program is "specifically designed to help Teens replace inappropriate attitudes and behaviors with new, productive ones," according to its Web page. It is a beach facility located on the southeastern shore of the South Pacific Island of Western Samoa. Located approximately 4,800 miles from the West Coast of the United States and mid-way between the United States and New Zealand, Western Samoa is a small Polynesian island with a pace of living far different from the frenetic pace here in the states.

The beach setting is comprised of three separate beaches, each housing a separate facility: Singalele (pronounced "sing-a-lay-lee"), Fagalele ("fung-a-lay-lee"), and Faga ("fung-a"). When Jacob first arrived at Paradise Cove he was placed not at the beach but at a mountain facility called *Le Tiara*. This facility was later closed. All boys now live on the beaches.

A tranquil, slower-paced island culture affords adolescents an opportunity to reflect, assess their lives, make new decisions, and get a new start. The island setting is beautiful, calm, gentle, and quiet. In a sense, time almost stops in Western Samoa.

The island retains the imprint of a tribal culture that existed before it was "civilized" by European contact beginning in the early 1700s. The Samoan culture is well known for its strong family emphasis, respect for authority, and genuine care for others. The Paradise Cove Program is heavily influenced by these attributes. Teens are exposed to an entirely new perspective.

Teens are far removed from negative influences back home. Without drugs and destructive peer influences, kids are free to think independently and make powerful new choices. By intervening in their children's lives and sending them to a remote island in the Pacific, parents send a strong message to their child: *In our best judgment as your parents, your life is not working!*

It takes a family

Life at Paradise Cove is organized into the "family" unit. A family consists of ten-fifteen boys led by a family leader and assistant family leader. Family leaders are "upper level" boys. (More about levels later.) The family is recognized as the basic unit of cooperation and living. Families have a purpose, an authority structure, and ground rules. Like all families everywhere, a Paradise Cove family is bound together or torn apart by the level of cooperation, commitment, honesty, trust, love, and consciousness that family members contribute. Everyone from family leader on down is evaluated by the effectiveness of his family and his own contribution to results.

Each family is joined by a native Samoan man on the staff who is addressed as "father" by the boys. The father's role is to serve as an authority if matters get out of hand and to be an example to the boys. However, the family leader (i.e., an upper level boy) is charged with exercising the real authority in the family. On being appointed family leader, one of the leader's initial tasks is to develop a good relationship with his father. In ideal circumstances, father and family leader work harmoniously together, thus emulating the role of parents in an American family. Whenever problems arise in the family, the family leader must work toward problem resolution with the father as well as the student family members involved.

A young man thrust into the role of family leader is expected to lead by example. Boys are therefore not asked to be leaders unless their own behavior has taken a dramatic turn for the better. Family leaders are themselves organized into groups and routinely receive feedback on the results they are obtaining in their families and their own personal behavior. Family leaders often consult with each other, as well as with staff, to obtain advice on how to deal with challenging situations.

When rules are broken, trust violated, etc., the family leader gives consequences to the offending boys. This responsibility is normally very challenging to a young man learning to lead. Only months before, he likely was acting the same way as the peer he is now obliged to discipline. This is a stern introduction to the uncertain world of parenting itself. When do I reward? When do I punish? Do my actions match my words? Suddenly, a young man is required to take the larger view – the very view he scorned only months before. He is challenged to be peer counselor, leader, authority, and role model. It is the family leader's job to figure out what to do in complex situations. He must sort out for himself when to hold the line and when to bend. If he continually allows the boys in his family to push him around, his own progress will be jeopardized. If he continually comes across to the boys as a by-the-book authoritarian, he will never enroll them

108

in accepting his leadership. Becoming family leader is one of the most valuable components of the training.

A key to success at Paradise Cove is its reliance on peer counseling. Kids learn from each other. Any desperate parent can tell horrifying stories of the negative impact of peers upon each other. So, imagine what can happen when a child's peer group changes from one that teaches how *not* to succeed in life to one that teaches to *succeed?* Whom you surround yourself with *does* matter. Mary Pipher in *Reviving Ophelia* asserts that teens want to belong to a community. Since there is not much community in today's American culture, they turn to gangs for it, she reports. Paradise Cove creates a constructive (if temporary) community much healthier than the alternative.

Families perform all basic activities together – playing, studying, eating, socializing, and dealing with conflict. Relationships within the family are key. Families members are expected to give honest feedback to each other. Boys learn how to provide this feedback in personal growth seminars, which I'll describe below. Feedback is one member's honest appraisal of what he sees is working or not working in another member. Members challenge each other on issues of honesty, trust, blame, and so on. Learning to deliver and receive honest feedback is a basic ongoing activity of the family unit.

Families are frequently disbanded and reorganized, preventing boys from developing overly close attachments. This is not about establishing a high comfort level! The emphasis is on giving and getting honest feedback and working on the issues that sent the boy to Paradise Cove to begin with.

A family lives in an authentic grass hut right on the beach. The Samoan word for this hut is *fale* (pronounced "folly"). Fales are the dominant structural unit on the entire island. As I drove down island roads, I passed by fale after fale. Each village has a village fale where disputes are resolved and ceremonies performed. The fale provides the family a place to sleep, store personal items, congregate, study, etc.

The setting is primitive. Fales are open air. Boys sleep on mats just as the Samoan people do. Students wear the traditional *lava lava* tied about their waste and eat the bland food customary to the island and prepared by local staff. Living in this primitive condition gives a boy an opportunity to appreciate material privileges he most likely took for granted back home. The simple lifestyle of a peasant reduces distraction and helps teens focus on the elemental things in life and on changes they wish to make in their lives. Jacob learned to appreciate and love the lifestyle and Samoan people. These were among the most powerful aspects of his experience at Paradise Cove.

Daily structure

Every day has a scheduled structure of individual and group activities. Boys participate in emotional growth and personal development exercises each day, from listening to motivational tapes, to family group discussion, to attending and staffing seminars.

In addition to time spent on attitude and behavior modification, boys work on academics through an accredited individual study course. Boys are tutored and, if they elect, can earn credits on an accelerated basis. Mastery of the subject matter is rewarded and emphasized, while the lack of performance has consequences. Internal growth and maturation have a slightly higher priority than academics because without them a student is not really ready to be educated. A student's internal condition determines and shapes his attitude towards education, achievement, life-goals, and relationships.

Fun and recreation are an important part of life at Paradise Cove, an apt name for this tropical island setting which resembles Maui in beauty. The clean, translucent tropical water and beach create opportunities for a variety of water and beach sports – swimming, snorkeling, spear fishing, and beach volleyball. There is also ample time for hiking. When I visited Paradise Cove some boys were having fun on the beach while others were engaged in work projects – cleaning and building. When I visited, I watched boys do laundry, clean fales, swim, and play volleyball. The ethic of hard work and hard play offers a distinct contrast to artificial experiences back home – an indulgent, often brooding and violent world of drugs, MTV, video games, hanging out, and gangs. In contrast, the difficult challenge of spearing a fish is a *real* experience providing food for an evening meal and a great story to tell the folks back home!

The daily structure, combined with the basic rules of program life, provide opportunities to learn to deal with life constructively. Most of the boys who earn a trip to Paradise Cove have difficulty with rules, structure, and authority. Most kids arrive with little respect for legal, educational, religious, and family institutions. Most are unwilling to follow even simple house rules – even when created in fairly democratic conditions by loving and supportive parents. At Paradise Cove, inappropriate attitudes and behaviors are challenged and discussed. Because the Program is rule-based, opportunities for surfacing and dealing with these issues are abundant. An authority problem at home doesn't hack it here.

Visitors are often struck by student respect and politeness demonstrated at the facilities. These student characteristics certainly stood out in my mind as I met the young men at Paradise Cove. "What? Kids actually asking permission and saying 'thank you'?" I wondered if I had been beamed to the

110

wrong planet! What a contrast their behavior was to the mainstream behavior of youth back home. It became very clear to me which norm I preferred. I'd much rather hang out with upper level boys at Paradise Cove than with kids at most high schools.

The game plan

Students progress through a promotional system of "levels." A student arrives on Level One, a status affording few privileges. A Level One student has earned simply the right to be there and the basics of subsistence: food, shelter, clothing, and participation in family life. At Level Six, the highest level, a student has achieved the advanced status and responsibility of leadership and is about to be reunited with his real family back home.

But levels are at best only an external reflection of what is hopefully an internal shift in the lives of these youngsters. The daily structure provides an opportunity to learn positive habits to replace the negative ones formed even at this still early age in their lives. Positive habits lead to success that in turn creates a positive self-image. The emphasis is on true inner change, not simply outer compliance. David Gilcrease, leader of the seminar program, identifies four stages of internal change:

Resistance. At first, teens are typically resistant. It is their resistance to responsibility, honesty, and the process of maturation that earned their passage to Paradise Cove. However, a student will respond to his environment simply to earn privileges. Level One ain't fun!

Open. As a student progresses, he recognizes that he is not succeeding in life – *on his own terms and by his own definition of success*. He becomes open to the possibility of personal change. This is the beginning of honest self-assessment.

Initial. When a student actually begins to make life changes, he begins to think and act differently. The environment around him responds.

Internalization. Given enough time to "work the program," a teen begins to internalize a way of life leading to greater rewards. Once internalization begins, a kid starts living constructively – not for external approval but because he really *wants* to steer his life in a positive, constructive direction of his own creation. A boy declares an end to the war he has been waging against society and family. Family healing now becomes possible because he is internally receptive to family back home and their differences.

Internalization is a critical concept for parents to understand. Change in any of us can be superficial and short-lived or long and lasting. Internalization is critical to a kid's success – especially kids with deep-seated problems. Even if the observable behavior that bought a kid his ticket to Paradise Cove suddenly appeared in a short period of time, the underlying cause of his problems took *much* longer to develop. To undo those problems and to internalize change so deeply that it becomes lasting change *takes time. Internalization is not a quick fix!* Parents are encouraged to leave their kids in the Program until the Program says that they have internalized change.

Movement through stages of change is of course not necessarily an orderly linear progression. Students are tested at every level of experience. Falling back into old patterns is a frequent occurrence. Each student has a different pace of change – a unique timing in his life.

A critical turning point is when a student begins to change not because someone else wants it of him and not even because it's "the morally right thing to do," but because he sees that it works beneficially for himself and others. This creates a new way of seeing and acting in the world. Suddenly, the Big Battle begins to end and a new task is created – building a new track record of success so that he can return home confident, healed, and committed to a healthy life with self, family, and others.

Operating for our own benefit is not necessarily selfish. It *can* be of course, but it does not *have* to be. If I create a win for me but a loss for others, I create results that do not *work* in the long term. There may be short-term gratification – which most of these kids are already experts in pursuing! – but long-term failure. A focal point of the behavioral training is that winning for myself at the cost of others is not really winning at all. Kids learn powerful lessons by misunderstanding this important point and realizing through experience how crucial a win-win strategy is to his life and family.

❖

Brainwashing?

Many parents and relatives who learn about the Program express immediate concerns about brainwashing. Not surprisingly, these questions occur particularly in adults who have experienced, or continue to experience, significant issues with authority in their own lives. I was certainly one of those! As a so-called "child of the sixties," I had a lot of difficulty with the entire notion of being an authority to my children – and of course this played no small part in our difficulties with both our sons.

In 1967 I read an article by David Harris about an exciting new youth culture emerging quickly in San Francisco. I quickly determined that I wanted to "join the revolution" and drove my '58 Chevy from Idaho to San Francisco just in time for the Summer of Love. As a flower child with substance abuse and authority issues of my own, I had a long journey to be able to face up to the responsibilities of living and parenting in the Eighties and Nineties. Some things stuck with me from those early days. I would *never* allow my child to be brainwashed! I had to satisfy myself that brainwashing would *not* be involved in any structured living situation for my son. One of the first questions I asked when inquiring about Paradise Cove was how those in charge keep their own power in check. It was not until I had answered that question satisfactorily for myself – by talking with experienced parents and program graduates – that I sent Jacob to Samoa.

I soon learned that the point of the Program is *not* to teach a kid to obey authority blindly but actually to assist them in developing their own authentic inner voice of authority. The plain truth is that most boys who arrive at the facility have *already* been brainwashed to hate authority and resist their parents by the street culture, media, and "friends." At Paradise Cove, Jacob was given a chance to free himself from brainwashing.

I remember the first time I walked onto the campus of San Francisco State University in 1967. I was struck by how *uniform* the campus culture was! Here was a culture purportedly objecting (as I was) to the "uniforms" of the middle class business man – the Italian suit, tie, closely-cropped hair, and Florsheim shoes. However, all my peers and I wore long hair, facial hair, tie-dyed tee-shirts, bell-bottomed pants – i.e., a uniform of the counterculture! "How unconsciously one set of beliefs can be replaced with another," I thought then. How important peer pressure *is* in our lives. It is one of the most powerful forms of brainwashing because most of us want approval of our peers far more than we would care to admit!

Peer pressure exists at Paradise Cove just as it does everywhere. But the pressure exerted at the facility encourages kids to find their own unique, yet constructive and cooperative, way in this world.

The Program and in particular the personal growth seminars foster an educational process which teaches an individual to consider whether or not the outcomes he is achieving in his life are *working* for him or not. The language of *good*, *bad*, *right*, and *wrong* is put aside. These kids have heard these words all their lives yet here they are at Paradise Cove. So for the time being, these words are set aside and the words *working* and *non-working* are substituted. These more congenial words shift a kid's focus from the load of guilt, righteousness, and judgment embedded in words like *right* or *wrong* to whether or not he is getting the kind of results he wants in his life. The question, "Did my behavior *work* for me?" is a powerful question and focuses kids on tangible behaviors and attitudes. Not until the student truly internalizes that his life is indeed *not* working – which is why he is at Paradise Cove in the first place! – that real progress begins. And it is not until a young man freely chooses to live differently, on terms satisfactory both to himself and society, that a real *internal shift* is made.

Seminars

Much of the internal shift comes within the context of day-to-day life in a facility like Paradise Cove. Many programs today teach primarily through daily structure and behavior modification. However, the programs participating in the World Wide Association of Speciality Programs add a series of powerful personal growth seminars. All youth in all participating programs are required to successfully complete a sequence of specially-designed and tailored seminars aimed at enhancing self-esteem, honesty, accountability, integrity, trust, leadership, communication, self-knowledge, and responsible decision-making. The seminar series teaches a kid how to deal with anger, peer pressure, and self-limiting beliefs. A similar series of seminars are available to parents and other members of the families and are held in major cities in the U.S. The seminar experience unfolds in the following sequence:

1. Discovery Seminar. Discovery is a seminar usually attended by the child within the first couple of months of his arrival in the Program. It requires teens to deal directly and honestly with the issues that have earned their ticket into the Program. Kids learn that they are not *bad* kids. They begin to assess whether their behavior is working or not. Before moving onto the next seminar, the student must complete Discovery. It is not uncommon that a child is booted out of the seminar for non-cooperation more than once before he successfully completes it. All parents and family members back home are strongly encouraged to complete Discovery as well, which closely matches the seminar that their children attend.

2. Focus Seminar. A student attends Focus within a couple of months after completing Discovery. Focus centers on critical life experiences and self-limiting beliefs that have created low self-esteem and inappropriate behavior. The student begins to make new choices. The focus is shifted to "what *works* in my life." This requires the risk of giving up an old image and belief system. Before moving onto the next seminar, the child has to complete Focus. Back home, families are strongly encouraged to complete Focus. It is a necessary and key part of the parent's individual journey.

3. Accountability Seminar. Within another couple of months, teens attend the Accountability seminar, which stresses being accountable for life choices and making responsible decisions. This is a high-impact, very challenging seminar designed to challenge teens regarding overall results. Are they walking the talk? They work on interactions with family, school, and authorities and deal with anger and sticking to agreements. Before moving onto the next seminar, the child has to complete Accountability.

4. Keys to Success Seminar. This is an ongoing monthly seminar for upper-level teens in leadership. The purpose is to develop practical use of the tools developed in the previous three seminars, including skills that enhance family and peer relationships such as communication, coaching, and responsible decision-making. Eligible students attend Keys within two months of completing Accountability.

5. Parent/Child I Seminar. "P/C I" is a critical seminar attended by parent and child together. All attendees must have attended at least Discovery seminar. A student has to be recommended by the Program to attend P/C I. It is not uncommon for parents to greet a child at the airport and head directly to P/C I. This seminar definitely "rocks the family boat" and surfaces most important issues lying under the surface. It is an opportunity to spend a few days together as a family again, to focus on past issues, to strengthen family ties, and to start the family reunification process. P/C I is a major opportunity for parents and child to work in a guided environment towards family healing. During the seminar students work on home contracts (i.e., agreements with their parents about how they will live in the home when they return) and adults intensify their process of creating a home environment that will support their child. P/C I is available only to those involved in the World Wide program.

Upon completion of the P/C I seminar, the child enters the Internalization Phase of the program. This is the final stage of the Program when typically the child is within four to six months of returning home – whatever is necessary to achieve success. Work on the home contract continues during this phase as does ongoing resolution of issues that hamper completion of the contract and relating to family members successfully. During Internalization a teen will visit home at least one or two times. Much is learned during these "trial runs" which leads to home contract revision and further work on family and personal issues. A home visit allows the family to "live" what has been learned while in the Program

6. Parent/Child II Seminar. After completing Parent/Child I and meeting several prerequisites, families are invited to attend the Parent/Child II seminar coinciding often with a student's formal exit from the Program. P/C II solidifies the home contract, provides more personal growth experiences, and celebrates the family in the creation of new value for themselves. P/C II is available only to those involved in the World Wide program.

7. Visions Seminar. The Visions seminar is offered to parents. Its focus is on achieving personal results in alignment with an inner sense of personal purpose and vision. Visions continues the personal growth initiated in Discovery and Focus. The purpose of Visions is to implement the training principles into a participant's life, not to add something on top of the life. The seminar engages participants in sustained activities over an eight-week period bounded by two training weekends. An important part of the training is developing a support network consisting of others committed to assisting you in achieving your highest potential. Visions is a critical part of the parent's personal growth process.

Staffing. A key component of internalization is seminar "staffing" – i.e., assisting in seminars for others. Kids in the Program have opportunities to staff seminars as do family members have back home. Through staffing you see others grappling with issues similar to yours. For example, a mother staffing Discovery and overly attached to her child might observe another mother struggling with the same issue. We learn from each other. A staffing experience can sometimes be more powerful than actually going through the seminar yourself. Silent observation coupled with active, supportive participation and service are powerful and rewarding teaching devices. Assisting others drives home the question: Am I dealing with my own issues? Staffing builds compassion, empathy, understanding, personal power, and commitment.

❖

Ongoing Family Support

The World Wide Association of Specialty Programs offers monthly, facilitated support group meetings in several major cities in the United States. These meetings are designed to assist families in an ongoing process of family healing even after the bills are all paid and the kids are back home with their families. They have two half-day monthly segments led by experienced parents who have been involved in the Program for a long time.

One segment, *In Program*, is for families with kids still in the Program – from those who may have just arrived at a facility to those in the final stages of internalization. The purpose of the In Program meeting is to facilitate individual readiness for the eventual return of the child, encourage seminar attendance, and foster internal growth and awareness. Siblings and grandparents are welcome.

An *After Care* segment is for families whose kids have completed Parent/Child I and II and have returned home to live with their families. The purpose of these support group meeting is to assist families with the reintegration process, strengthen and solidify family relationships, and further the learning and internal growth processes.

116

❖

Cult?

The seminars no doubt *challenge* individuals. Nothing less would get through to highly resistant adolescents! But it is a mistake to think that kids are the only ones stuck in stickin' thinkin'! I have yet to meet a parent with a hand resting firmly on the book of total wisdom! Most parents have much to learn not only about being a parent but about being themselves. Too often, parents have illusions that only their child has problems – "if only *my kid* would straighten out, then I'd be fine!" This is both simplistic and convenient. Open-minded parents discover that many dimensions of *their own lives are not working either* – in ways contributing to family breakdown.

Occasionally, a disenchanted seminar participant will leave a seminar in anger or concern, claiming that the seminars are brainwashing, too rough, or mean-spirited. Some individuals who have not participated at all and thus can have no idea what they're talking about have made equal claims. I can only share my experience. I have participated in and staffed many seminars. They are hardly the arm of some cult designed by a mastermind to emotionally flog people into the android service of a Vulcan mind meld! Seminars assist people in *opening* their minds further to possibilities and in making conscious, free choices. In contrast to shutting minds down, these seminars are about *opening minds up!* That entails challenging entrenched ways of thinking and seeing – with honesty.

My experience is that *being deeply honest* is a profound challenge to me and, frankly, most of us. We human beings are *ingenious* in our ability to hide from honesty with ourselves and in our relationships. Many of us spend entire marriages, watch our children grow, and live our entire lives without honesty. But when a person reaches deep into his/her raw core of being – and this includes our wayward children – there is normally a deep thirst for honesty. Our true nature is to know ourselves and each other as we are.

One way to hide is to dismiss a process for honest self-discovery on your own terms as a "cult." I have a great concern for the few who feel this way. My concern is for their relationship with their children, not with the label they attach. By this time, I have experienced many children involved in one way or another with this Program. No matter how deeply they are buried beneath black-eye shadow and painted fingernails, eyes half-closed from the sleep of intoxication, or images of toughness – in their hearts, they all want our honesty. The least we can give is our open minds, willing to learn and explore alongside them.

A lifetime process?

Pursuit of personal growth and discovery can be a lifetime pursuit. Because of the difficult issues facing families and because of the dramatic nature of intervention, most people come to the seminars willing to look at least some aspects of their lives with new clarity and honesty. For many adults and teens alike these seminars, coming as they do at a crisis point in their lives, are highly impactful. Some of the issues surfaced directly impact the family – e.g., relationships with spouse and children. Other issues are more directly personal – e.g., self-limiting beliefs. Many participants find that important untapped portions of their lives surface, demanding sudden attention. Many decide to engage lifelong problems for the first time and see new vistas of life possibility opening up before them. Children generally are inspired when they see their moms and dads "working *their own* program" and getting in touch with their inner selves. Children are challenged by parents who are evolving. Likewise, parents are inspired when they experience their children maturing. Family healing is built upon personal healing. This business of healing *can* become an infectious journey of a lifetime.

The game plan for parents

Parents play a crucial role in a process seemingly centered on the child. In fact, the process is centered on *the family*. Parents are equal partners in the process. By our actions we parents show our children who we are and what we stand for. Parents can participate in a process of healing in several ways.

One of the most important things a parent can do is to keep a child in the Program until recommended home by the staff. Time and again, I have heard parents tell stories of bringing a child home too soon, or "taking the cake out of the oven before it is done." My experience of parents who have pulled their child out early is often one of regret. Internalization of change is no easy feat! Short-term gain often seems so real. I learned early on that better results come from total commitment.

Sometimes parents get discouraged about time. "Jared has been there for a year and he's only on Level One," lamented one parent. Instead of focusing on how much it was costing her, she concentrated on the results she wanted for her child. She stuck with the process, realizing that it might take Jared a long time even to begin a true process of change, let alone internalize change deeply. Sometimes what a child needs from us more than anything is for us to hold for his highest possibility.

118

Our commitment was to allow the Program to decide when Jacob was ready to come home rather than to make that decision ourselves. Despite the fact that our techniques with Jacob hadn't worked, I found it initially difficult to give power to people I hadn't even met. The illusion that I knew best proved to be one of many self-deceptions. But I learned to frame this issue another way. My power, I learned, lay in aligning my efforts with people who dealt with kids like Jacob all the time but who were not emotionally entangled in his life. I delegated to them the responsibility to deal with my son for a time. But I never relinquished the authority of being his parent.

Our role was to participate in the process with all our available energy. Participation became part of our overall game plan. Participation meant attending and staffing the seminars, participating in support group meetings, and undertaking a daily program of inner discovery. Our responsibility included getting to know the staff who worked with our son and listening to their wise observations and counsel.

Our role was also to cooperate with the Program. It is potentially destructive to a child's progress to manipulate the staff into creating exceptions for him, to rescue him from afar, to talk negatively about the Program to him, to object to a change in the rules or the structure of the Program, etc. Parents who spent vital energy in these directions seem to benefit less because they have less energy to devote to the challenge of inner change.

Another role we had was to support Jacob in his hard-won gains. This support came in several forms – e.g., not overreacting to his confession of past misdeeds, taking the home contract he wrote seriously, and so forth.

We learned that our experience was not about putting our son in a Program so much as it was getting started as individuals and family in an inner journey together. As we progressed on this journey, we realized that in contrast to the general myth that parents of teens are powerless, we have much more power than we realize! Understanding what real power is and claiming it for our lives is one of the central themes of this book.

Our most important task during this time, aside from healing ourselves, was to heal our relationship as husband and wife. Joshua, one of Jacob's best friends at Paradise Cove told us once. "Once I figured out that my parents were no longer divided, I knew that my little game was up. I knew that there was no fooling around any more. I knew I had to get to work."

The right to family healing

In November, 1997, two men from an escort service hired by Jim and Sue Van Blarigan visited their home in Oakland, California, and left with their son David, aged sixteen. David was soon flown to the Tranquility Bay facility in Jamaica to begin his journey. While still in the airport ingenious David broke free and called the Van Blarigans' neighbor Neil Aschemeyer.

A retired administrative court judge and sympathetic friend, Aschemeyer swallowed David's claims of mistreatment – allegations since disproved and disputed publicly by David himself. Aschemeyer in turn called to inform a former colleague, Deputy District Attorney Robert Hutchins, an eighteen-year veteran of child-abduction cases, who brought charges against the Van Blarigans.

Hutchins claimed that "when [the Van Blarigans] had David ripped out of his bed ... they were stripping him of his civil rights." He claimed that this was a case of good parental intention going too far. Hutchins relied on two main arguments: (1) Parents don't have the right to award custody to a third party and (2) children fourteen and over have the right to refuse certain kinds of treatment. Hutchins accused the Van Blarigans of being "aiders and abettors" in their son's kidnapping and false imprisonment, thus "stripping [David] of his civil rights." Hutchins asked Superior Court Judge Ken Kawaichi to set legal precedent by ordering the boy's immediate return to Oakland to have him testify about his experiences in order to ascertain whether he was in a fit place.

Hutchins' argument proved specious and weakly assembled. First of all, the Van Blarigans never gave up legal custody of their son – they simply paid for services to be performed on their behalf. Throughout the hearing, Hutchins alluded to potential physical and psychological harm to "kids in these camps" yet failed to present one detail of evidence that harm had been done to David.

Attorney Dan Koller, arguing on behalf of the Van Blarigans, pointed out the logical absurdity of following Hutchins' line of reasoning: "Would parents have to ask their children's permission to be sent to summer camp or private school?" he asked. "That's ridiculous!"

The media circled about the hearing like sharks, pressuring the Van Blarigans to grant interviews. Media focus was twofold: the abduction and the trial. Most attempts to arrange media interviews of children and families who had been through the Program and seminars, and had rebuilt their families, were ignored. One night approximately twenty-five parents and program graduates gathered at a hotel in Oakland, California, to meet with the film crew of the national television news magazine, Dateline. At last, it appeared that a media vehicle of stature and credibility would seek to hear what our *real* experiences were. But Dateline cancelled. "The Van Blarigans and the trial are the story," the producer said. Clearly, family healing was *not*.

It did not take long for Judge Kawaichi to throw the case out of court. The legal issue was not whether the Van Blarigans made the right choice for their son. The issue came down to whether they could *make choices like these for their son at all*. Kawaichi was not about to strip away parental rights. Had Hutchins' argument prevailed, parents would have little if any authority left to manage defiant children. Carried to Hutchin's extreme, parental judgment would count for nothing. Parental authority – at least in Alameda County – would be history. Childrearing could be held hostage to the opinions of any neighbor and subjected to arbitrary legal scrutiny.

At stake was the right of parents to heal a wounded member of their family. In Sue and Jim's *best judgment* David needed a strong helping hand which they were unable to provide in any other way.

An unfortunate personal outcome of the Van Blarigan case was that Jim's own parents and brother aligned themselves with prosecutor Hutchins. They joined in the legal action against Jim and Sue and continued to make attempts to get David returned even after the hearing's conclusion. I find it difficult to imagine the pain that the Van Blarigans must have gone through during this ordeal! On placing David in the Program, they experienced many of the same emotions we did – guilt, relief, shock, and embarrassment. Like us, they shed many tears. But their name and honor were trampled by a media police with little or no feeling and a legal system that apparently can attack without any evidence other than someone's opinion about right and wrong. And then ... at precisely the hour when they needed it the most, Jim and Sue were denied the support and love of their own family as well.

Our own family was a complete contrast. Sandy and I felt love and support coming from the family members we needed to talk to and cry with. I remember the kind assurances from our loved ones that they understood that what we had done was out of love for Jacob. They acknowledged us as loving and caring parents, not as people who had done something wrong. They told us that they stood behind us. They supported our right to act and affirmed us for caring enough *to* act. Rather than opposing us, they asked us how they could support us in our hour of darkness. With their loving support, we were able to turn our energies immediately and without distraction to the critical business of repairing ourselves so that one day we might reunite as a whole family again.

❖

Obligation of parent and village

Young Christine Corrigan was thirteen years old on November 19, 1996, when she died weighing 680 pounds. Her body, scarred with bedsores, was found lying in a bed soiled from her own waste, dead from apparent heart failure.

Christine lived in El Cerrito in the *same county* as David Van Blarigan. Authorities from *the same District Attorney's office* that charged the Van Blarigans with abuse charged Christine's mother Marlene with neglect, claiming that she failed to care for her daughter. Defense lawyers contended that Christine had Prader-Willi syndrome, characterized by an insatiable appetite and slow metabolism. Christine was taken care of by an HMO from birth onwards. She saw a registered dietitian for thirty visits when she was nine years old and weighed about 300 pounds. Christine's school district rebuffed her mother's attempts to get help for her daughter. The system was failing Christine and obviously her mother didn't know what to do.

The judge who ordered Marlene to stand trial said she was shocked by photos of Christine's body. Corrigan neglected "the basic duty for a parent to look out for her child," she said. The girl's massive weight "should have been a signal to do whatever it took" to improve her health, said Municipal Court Judge Laurel Lindenbaum.

After a five-day nonjury trial, Marlene was convicted on January 9, 1998, of misdemeanor child abuse rather than the felony charge (sought by the prosecution) that could have sent her to prison for six years. She was placed on three years' probation, including counseling and serving 240 hours as a community volunteer.

Neither you nor I have lived in the house of Marlene Corrigan or Jim and Sue Van Blarigan. We have not had to walk in their shoes. Clearly, their children brought challenges into their lives for which they were unprepared. Therefore, what was their responsibility?

We are a culture very confused about parental responsibility. Parents who raise their children permissively but fail to take all preventive measures required to sustain their children's health are accused of neglect. However, "authoritarian" parents who insist on defining limits for their children and who take a strong and powerful stand against their child's self-destruction are accused of abuse.

In its rush to judgment, the media and D.A. overlooked basic factors in the Van Blarigan case that ultimately Judge Kawaichi did not. Parents and society have a collective social obligation to be *responsive* to their children's needs. I have the privilege to know Jim and Sue Van Blarigan. Far from being abusive parents, they are *parents who cared enough* to intervene in their son's life which, in their best judgment as the responsible people living with David, was reeling out of control. By far the parents I have met who have placed their children in a rehabilitation program are parents who care enough to take a stand and intervene – often at great personal cost.

Parents who choose to intervene are parents who refuse to see their daughters sell their bodies or allow their sons to steal to pay for their latest "bag." They are the parents who refuse to see their children threaten school authorities with knives. They refuse to see their children become statistics in an overworked and under-funded juvenile system which will house and feed them (at cost) but will not provide them the care they need to grow inside as individuals. There is no undertaking *the journey* behind bars.

I do not deny that serious parental abuse exists. Of course it does! But so does neglect. And there is a large middle ground we must not turn away from and ignore. Even normal children pass through stages where their problems are multifaceted and complex – problems that do not always yield to easy solutions. As parents we must create an environment for our children that is *responsive*, neither permissive nor depriving but enabling, where we nurture, but also set limits. And if we cannot ourselves make an impact on our children's lives, we must seek those who can, and intervene for our children's sake, if not for society's as a whole.

Letter from a mother

"Dear Friends,

"With all the publicity over putting our kids in the Program, I hear a theme over and over. Who has the right to take a child in the middle of the night and put him in a Program that doesn't even meet USA standards, especially if the family hasn't exhausted every last avenue first? Well, last Thursday night while we were watching a *48 Hours* show on the Program, a good friend of mine wasn't as lucky. We had met while getting our nursing degrees five years ago. At that time she brought her then sixteen-year-old son to the hospital so we could look at his arm infected from a tattoo he had carved into himself. As time wore on, he got into drugs and alcohol. My friend continued to deny that dramatic intervention was needed, but now her son is twenty-one and his brain is fried. They tried to find help for him, because he was always very violent and on some type of drug. Authorities told them repeatedly that nothing could be done until he showed that he is a threat to society. Last Thursday he proved it.

His step-father woke up from sleep because he felt something pressing on his eyelid. It was a gun barrel held by his stoned son! Now the authorities say they can do something. The kid is sitting in jail waiting for prison or commitment. The parents look like death warmed over.

"I have a really hard time listening to the professionals say what's right or wrong or say that nothing can be done. Lives are at stake."

Journey

In a dream I stand beside my son on a meadow at the base of a mountain range. Threading the meadow is an enticing, but somewhat intimidating, trail that runs through the rocky meadow and quickly disappears into rugged mountains beyond. This trail will challenge and demand much of us. Yet it leads to unknown possibility and promise. It awaits but our willingness to explore and discover.

But my son is already weary and resistant, unaccustomed as he is to the struggle of mountainous terrain. I have perhaps protected him too much. Certainly, I have spoiled him. I consider that I have never taken him into such rugged country before or truly challenged him to make great demands of himself. Now it is time, I sense, for him. And for me. Past time. It is a moment when we must become, together, more than we have been up to this moment. It is a defining moment – a time to become all that we *are*.

At first I suggest that we take this journey together. But he resists. Realizing the importance of the journey to his life and mine, I increase my attempts. Finally when I insist he protests, kicking wildly and violently, swearing at me in a strange language I do not understand. Who is this child – this child who abuses not only me but himself as well? For a time I fall back into an all-too-familiar uncertainty wondering what to do. I love my son. But suddenly he is a stranger – to us both.

I know in my heart that he and I were born for this moment. I notice that I have that kind of knowing built right in, if I will consult it. I know what my child needs even though he does not know it himself. I have a choice – to stand for what I know or deny it. I decide. We *will* take this path together. I will do my job. And we will not be the same for it. We begin.

124

AWAKENING

Time Warp

*I*nterminable months of hoping, looking for a sign, and wondering what to do were over. Sometimes I couldn't believe what we had done. It seemed so drastic, like something I might read about in *People* magazine. I'd feel sorry for the family – but thank God nothing that weird would ever happen to *us!*

In a sense, one form of waiting was simply supplanted by another. Now we would wait and pray that the Program had some magic to perform. The day after Jacob left, I went to work. At least work took my mind off things a little. But not much. We waited for the one chance we would have to talk to Jacob (at the intake facility) before he would be transported to Paradise Cove in Western Samoa. How angry would he be? What would he say to us? What would we say to him?

Although I knew that we were not allowed to talk with Jacob until then, we could talk with the staff. I called every day to see how he was doing. What a doting father! (As if doting had ever worked!) I spoke mostly with a man named Cameron who spoke to me calmly and reassuringly. Jacob was doing fine, he assured. He gave me a sense of what Jacob was doing and how he was handling it. My learning process had already begun: perhaps it was time for me to calm down a little, I thought. After all, this would be a long haul. I got the feeling that Cameron had met parents like me before! With the passage of days, I began to relax and come to terms with what we had done.

Sandy and I decided that Sunday would be our once-a-week letter-writing day and our first letters were written on Sunday, March 24, 1996.

> Dear Jake,
>
> The other morning when I got up, the cupboards were open. I thought you were home again. It's the little things I miss. Dirty dishes in the sink. The cereal box left out on the table. The quiet. We do miss you. But it sounds like such a good place for you. You can choose now to use this experience to make a difference in your life, and you said that you wanted to quit smoking. I hear you have your sense of smell and taste again. You get some exercise and do your

school work. Aunt Vickie and Roxie both send you their love. They cried for us and you – it is such a drastic step – but I'm still so glad it has begun for you. ...

... I miss you so much and cry when I realize that most of your junior year will be there and not at home. But you'd be in such trouble here, maybe jail. So it's better where you are. All the rest of your life you will know how to structure and pace yourself for something you wish to accomplish. ...

Love you, Mom

Dear Jake,

There is probably not a waking hour that passes by when I don't think of you, of how you are doing, of how you are dealing with this. As you probably know, I call just about every day to see how things are going – something I will not be able to do when you are in Samoa. ... I pray for you, for me, for Mom. ... I miss you, being near to you. It was a sacrifice of the highest order for me to choose to put you in this program because now I cannot see you and be with you. Even though I did not approve of your behavior, I have always loved you, and always will.

Love, Dad

One week after Jacob had been escorted from our home, our therapist wrote to him.

My experience of you last week was that you were ready for some help. You were so open and willing to share with your parents and me. I hadn't experienced you that accessible before, and I really appreciated your ability to participate in the good spirit in that room last week. When you acknowledged your pain and talked about how awful school was for you, I could really understand why you were dropping out.

Now it sounds like you have a safe structure in which to finish high school, clear up the confused thoughts and beliefs, and really get to know and love yourself. I truly hope all of this happens for you. I remember telling you that you can't transcend (go above) the laws until you thoroughly understand them and know how to be totally obedient. Where you are now may give you that foundation. I have every faith that you will cooperate with the program and benefit greatly from learning accountability and personal responsibility.

This was such a hard thing to do for your parents. They obviously love you a lot to put themselves in such pain! And I know that you know that too!

The next weekend I sat down to balance the checkbook and noticed that the pile of processed checks was unnaturally thick. Curiosity aroused, I shuffled through the thick pile and there they were – check after check forged by that same Jacob who "was just about to get his life together."

Although short a sum of money, I was actually grateful. Discovering the bad checks verified the extent of Jacob's desperation. Sandy knew it more intuitively than I; I always seemed to need some kind of "proof." Well, I had all the proof I needed. Jacob *had earned* his way into this Program. He had chosen this path. Increasingly, his actions had been a loud and desperate cry for help. I began to come to terms with our choice to put him into the Program and leave behind the initial guilt I felt. I could now accept my own actions – actions I *never* would have considered before, such as having my own son spirited out of his own bedroom by strangers! I could now begin to prepare myself for the work at hand – unfinished business that had to do more with myself than anyone else.

We had little knowledge of Jacob's day-to-day activities. The program staff didn't call us. We would call *them*, we learned. They would put most of their energy into working with Jacob and, if there had to be a trade-off, that was an easy choice! While initially frustrating, I began to realize right away that there was a kind of beauty in the design of this purposeful separation and what, in a business relationship, I might term "poor communication." I began to realize how intensely I was "tuned in" to Jacob and how I was preoccupied inordinately with his life. Not only did Jacob need a clean break from his life at home, but we needed a separation from him. If we used our time wisely, we could at least recuperate from the turmoil of the past few months, and let staff who dealt with kids like Jacob every day to care for him. We didn't need a whole lot of communication – save maybe with ourselves.

Later on I was to find out that, while at the intake facility, Jacob had already begun to his express accumulated emotions about home, parents, and everything else. During one of the sessions he talked longingly about a poster of Jim Morrison of the The Doors hanging in his room at home. "I'll kill my parents if they destroy my poster, man!" he said, probably not paying attention to his words. He went on about how important that poster was to him and how much Morrison's music and poetry meant to him. After listening to him for awhile Cameron observed, "You know, Jacob, you love your poster more than you love your parents." Jacob told me later, "Dad, I flipped out then because I knew that it was true and I didn't want to hear it. I was ashamed." Accepting the truth is an early step on the path toward awakening.

A few days passed and the phone rang. It was a difficult, tearful conversation. By that time, Jacob seemed to be accepting his fate. He sobbed and several times said, "I'm sorry, Mom and Dad." To his credit, he did not ask to come home; something inside him was calling. He worried about how much this would cost us. "No price is too much," we answered. Finally he said, "By the way, Dad, you'll find some checks I wrote …."

I was prepared. "Yeah, I know," I said. "I found them this past weekend when I balanced the checkbook. So what I have to say to you, Jacob, is that

you should be very thankful that you are where you can get the help that
you need, because if you weren't there, you'd be in jail right now. We would
have brought charges against you. I want you home again, because I love
you. But not until you can live responsibly."

Jacob continued to say he was sorry. Through our tears we said our last
words to each other for several months. The next day Jacob was flown to a
new life in Western Samoa.

There were clear signs that he was ready for a change in his life. Later on,
Jacob told me a story about being driven across the Nevada desert to the
Las Vegas airport to catch a plane for Western Samoa. "While driving, we
spotted a camel alongside the road. Someone in the area apparently owned
a camel – right there in the desert of Southern Utah! The driver stopped the
van and we got out to look at the camel." I asked Jacob, "Well, why didn't
you just run away? You're a fast runner!" He thought for a moment and
said, "By that time, I *wanted* to go to Samoa. I liked the sound of it. I was
tired of fighting. I was tired of the stress."

Several days later, his first letter arrived. We learned immediately that communicating by phone calls and letters would create a kind of *time warp*. The
letters would reflect a thought written perhaps two or three weeks ago.
Meanwhile we might have more recent information by phone from the
staff. Written in an angry scrawl the day after he left, his first letter home
reflected intense initial feelings of betrayal. It mentioned the barbecue we
had in our home that night the escort service paid him a visit.

> Mom Dad
> Send me
> Harmonica
> Pirate shirt
> my bell-bottom pants
> boxer shorts I only have one pair
> More pants more shirts
> Not so much *Ugly stuff*
>
> > Bob Marley t-shirt
> > Bob Dylan t-shirt
> >
> > > pictures of me
> > > with long hair the night
> > > before I left
>
> > Jake
>
> > Understand the note you left
> > ("Jake, we're having a barbecue at eight, you're invited")
> > I gave my *heart*
> > I thought I was *accepted*

I hope you read the rules before you sent me hear and visited it
which you obviously did not. I love you yes but I hate you MORE
than my new haircut.
Jake Ethan Flood

But this attitude was soon to change. His second letter, written while he was at an intake facility waiting to leave for Samoa, reflected this new feeling.

Dear Mom, Dad

I've been thinking a lot. That's all you can really do in here. I suppose that's what you're supposed to do. It's really sad in here. Sometimes like right now I heard that you called and sent your love. I'd give anything to talk to you for five minutes. There are some things I need to tell you. It seems that everyone talks to their parents but me. The majority of the time I'm happy. I see how good sobriety would, and does, work in my life. I've learned a lot real quick. Stuff about perception and how much it helps. It's *all* in your perception. If you go in with a positive and moving attitude, you come out with positive and moving things. I've thought about the rotten choices I made while stoned. Sure I wrote some cool poems but it didn't get me to LA. It got me here. I cry a lot and think about home, not as much as I think about my issues. I'm a smart kid, an *extremely* fortunate kid, *very* self-centered. But I can sure move my peers. I'd give anything for a second chance but I don't think of it as a possibility. I'm eager to start my life, and I'm really stuck on Samoa and how L-O-N-G I'm going to be there. But when I go I shall not whine. I shall go and get all I can. ... Things I've said to you I never, ever meant. Except I love you *more* than listening and playing music, acting, the world. I'm doing good here. ... I've also learned about me and how easy it is for me to jump outside and look at myself, to see what I'm doing and if there's movement in it. I honestly think I've learned as much as the kids who leave Samoa learn. I've heard what they've learned and thank my higher power I've already got that. So I'm going for more. I'll always go for more (except drugs). I'll never stop learning. ... When I'm sober I'm alive, I'm creative, I'm energetic, I'm me. My level of perception is scary. I feel what others go through.

Well, I love all

and I really love you.

Love,

your constantly growing son

Jake

P.S.: Send me my harmonica.

Well, it looked like we were off to a good start. We didn't believe that this would be a quick fix like his letter suggested it *might* be! It took many years to get to this point; it would take at least several months to get to a new place – where *internally* he would be different.

Back home I was wondering what would be different for me. I hoped that this would perhaps make a difference in my life as well. I decided I would hold nothing back from Jacob and began to pour my heart out to him.

Dear Jake,

... When I first held you, newly born, in my arms, I knew how much I loved you. You were a son and you were perfect for me because I always wanted sons. I knew that you had spunk and heart the instant I held you. I knew that you were unique and special. I knew that you had a strong soul. I felt that there was a powerful bond between us that could never be torn. That feeling is with me now as I write you. I didn't "sign up" to be your father for life; I fell in love forever. I feel as though I'm with you right now even though the great expanse of the Pacific lies between us. You're sleeping at this moment on a beach across a vast ocean but our spirits, yours and mine, know no boundaries, make no distinctions about being awake or asleep, care not about distances or time. We are family. Your unique and bright spirit is with me at this moment in this small room, next to me as I type into this computer.

You are an odd source of strength to me, Jake. ... You have been the crisis which has changed my life. You have taught me, through the problems you posed for us as parents, to be a stronger person and father. You have taught me to stand for something for the first time in my life, Jake. I can now say that I take a stand against drugs, against self-destruction, against dishonesty in any disguise, against abuse in any form. Up until now, I have always waffled. I now have a strength I never had before. This is your gift to me and I'm grateful for it, although it has been at no small cost to all of us.

I've decided that my stand against all these issues must equally apply to myself. Take honesty, for example. I catch myself saying I'm sorry to your Mom when I'm not – not really. For a long time, I said to you and Mom that I was against drugs but I wasn't – not really. Now I am, *really*, but I see the dishonesty that I had. It must have been confusing to you because I'm sure that you saw it.

Confessions of a father. One day you may have confessions of your own to make to a child.

So here I am, Jake. I love you and I'm learning to be me and learning on new levels what love really is. I suppose that, across the winds, we are united in the same struggle, you and I, albeit we are unique, each struggling with our own issues. ...

Love forever, Dad.

Jacob's story

The initial drama was now behind us. Now came the slow part – adjustment to a life apart with little information about the daily events in our son's life. We were comforted somewhat by knowing that, had Jacob been here at home, we would have had about the same amount of information with *a lot* less comfort about his circumstances! For Jacob, the drama continued – after all, he was going to a tropical island!

"So I was on the plane headed for Samoa and I was actually *stoked* about the trip. I was excited! I'd heard a lot of great stuff about the program and I thought I could play volleyball everyday and kind of hang out. I had this great picture of me in my one remaining hippie shirt, kicking it on the beach, wearing one of the lava lavas, playing harmonica, and just max'ing out and speaking my philosophical BS and having people pretending to look up to me. I was in a good mood. I was somewhat relieved to get away from all the stuff back home and not have to worry about all I worried about, all I had to take care of, all that crap, so I was actually in an all right place ... but not the best place.

"I was relieved to get away from the family life and the pressure, and in a sense I was relieved that I did not have to worry about drugs anymore. I just was not thinking about it anymore. I had already ruled it out as a possibility for awhile.

"I really didn't know what kind of time frame I was looking at. I heard it was a long-term program. Actually I had about six months in my head, because this guy back in the hospital said you could do it in six months and then I had a goal, like I want to get out by Christmas. It was BS at the time. I wanted to fake it and get out by Christmas.

"My goal was to do just what I needed to do to get out. I'd done the program deal before, so I was just going to do it again. I was just going to bust another fake and speak that I was a changed guy again.

"The flight over sucked because I was stuck between two *obnoxious* kids trying to get me to buy in on their pity stories, which I didn't. We finally arrived in Western Samoa and were picked up by the driver. We thought we were going to the beautiful beach, to play volleyball and all this stuff.

"But my whole view of the Program changed within an instant. We're driving up this old dirt road, up in the boondocks, up in the mountainous part of the island. And we drive up to this chain link fence and I see this Samoan guy coming down to unlock the fence. And going through my mind was, "All right, we're picking up some Samoan guy and then we're heading down to the beach." This place looked like a little military place. Then I see about ten white kids standing in a line doing a head count. The exact words that went through my mind were "*Oh, shit! We are screwed!*" I heard the Freedom Family head count, the kids counting off "twelve, eleven, ten, ..." and that's the family I ended up being in. The school teacher greeted us, "Well, boys, welcome home." I'm thinking, "You're *kidding* me, right?!" That's all I kept saying until we went in, were given tubs to store our few possessions, and were shown around. They called this place "La Tiera." Then a Samoan man by the name of Tau came and basically recruited me into the Freedom Family.

133

"So I went into his family and I *faked* it. I knew a girl back in the intake facility who had already been to the Program and was back for a return visit. So I had watched her in intake and picked up on all of her moves and how she gave feedback to others and how that was what was considered cool. I picked up on how she'd say to another girl, "I experience you as a wallflower," and I'm saying to myself, "OK, cool no problem." So here I am in the Freedom Family and I'm saying, "Yeah, I went through this big transition in intake, blah, blah, blah." And I see the guys who are slacking in the family, and I would just be in the gang, and I'd start nailing them with feedback, and I always gave good feedback, so it was not a problem. It was just a game.

"And the first day I got up and played my harmonica and sang in front of everybody, so then I had everybody under my heel. They were all saying, "Yeah, look at him taking a risk the first day," and all that stuff, so automatically I was the hottest Level One in the family from Day One. I didn't consciously say, "OK, I'm going to play the Program now." It was just so routine for me from all the other programs I'd been in that it's just the routine I fell into.

"I didn't consciously think about trying to manipulate you and Mom to get myself out of the Program. I just figured I was there for a while.

"After a month or so I went to the Discovery seminar, and I came to some realizations about myself. I realized that I was *fake*. In Discovery I got all my anger out. I mean I let go; I *went off!* I *completely* let go of my resentments of everything and it was just like I used to be able to do in an acting class back home. I saw the opportunity to deal with some serious issues in my life. Whenever I'd get a free space to vent my anger, I'd do it. And that's what I do in my acting classes all the time. I mean, I'd let go of everything. Basically, I was on a high. I had figured out that I was being fake and that I was manipulating people. I said to myself, "OK, I'll just come back to my family and come clean with these guys. And who knows, back then in my head I might have been playing the same manipulation game unconsciously, only a little better. I don't know. Anyway, I came back to the family where I'd been doing good for a month, and said, "Hey guys, I'm a *fake*. I was faking you guys. I knew what you wanted so I gave it to you. Now I'd just like a new clean slate and a new start." And everyone said, "Well, you got it. We think you were doing sweet in the first place." And then like about two days later I got put up to Level Two.

"I never had huge resentments against you and Mom like some of the kids had against theirs. I was just pissed off at you. I didn't have a daddy who never came to my baseball games, for example. I didn't have anything specific against you. I just had anger towards you. I just *didn't like* you guys. I don't think you were bad parents. I think mainly it was me. You might have had some anger and some control stuff, but not that I could look back upon and say, "Oh, he was doing *that* to me and I hate him for it." I think it was ninety-nine-percent my stuff. But of course my stuff brought up a lot of crap in you and you both had *your own crap* too, and you reacted. Basically, I just didn't like you because you wouldn't leave me the hell alone. I thought you were just interfering where you shouldn't be, like with *my life*. I thought you should just shut up and give me money …! So in Discovery I let go of my anger towards you for that.

"There was another point where I got out my anger towards my brother. I had a lot of resentments against Mac, too. Basically because sometimes I felt *less than* – and that whole trip. I had said, "My brother is smarter than me; my brother is better than me." Psychologically, I don't know if that is why I took the path I did, but I know I had those feelings."

Jacob went to Discovery seminar in mid April, 1996, and wrote the following report on this experience:

Dear Mom and Dad,

Well, I'm at the first day back on my regular schedule. I've been in a seminar called "Discovery" for three days, and let me tell you it was intense! … It was all about me and the games I play. So here goes. Here's what I told myself for a long time.

I thought that Mac was more important than me. I felt like I wasn't getting the attention I deserved, more or less wanted. So I felt like I had to prove something to both of you. I felt unloved and uncared for. Remember, this was just my experience – just the way I felt. I felt Mac was getting all the attention, when we visited the Shrink and I was only allowed in for half the session. I didn't know Mac was going through some real problems about suicide, self-esteem, self-worth, etc. So in order to get the love and attention I tried to become, and did become, president of fifth grade, I tried out for school plays, I played my butt off in sports – all the things Mac couldn't do. I was a real acceptance and attention suck! So, for a majority of my childhood I was trying to get your acceptance, which, now that I look back on it, was always there. You just did what you felt was right. I agree with this. Mac was going through some real hard times. He needed the help. He got the attention. So he got everything handled, got his life together, and went to college. Then it seemed like, now that Mac was gone, you guess you could focus on me. I felt like I was your Second Favorite Son. When you didn't tell me that Mac tried to kill himself, that really hurt. So I (and I repeat *I myself*) built up anger and hate and pointed the finger at you two instead of the cause of this anger: me. I did this until the day I left Discovery seminar. I've stopped it now. This is no cry to bring me home. It's just to say that I take accountability for my actions and the feelings I put on them. I didn't seem to get your full attention so what would you hate more, how could I get you back, for all the *pain* you caused me? That's what I thought! I caused myself pain. Dad, I created you thirty years earlier [i.e., the hippie image I adorned back in the Sixties] just to piss you off, just for your attention, positive or negative. I just wanted attention, short-term pleasure, long-term pain. So that's just a few of the insights I had. I just want you to know *I really love you!*

Your constantly growing son

Jake

P.S.: I was using marijuana and cheating on the pee tests.

P.S.S.: I understand why you sent me here. I don't feel like you didn't want me. I know it was hard to send me here and I want to thank you wholeheartedly for doing it. I love you all. Mom, Dad: Jake loves you!

Later on I wrote the following in response to my "constantly growing son." I loved the way he concluded every letter with that reminder.

… You wrote that "I created you thirty years earlier just to piss you off, just for your attention, positive or negative." First of all, you succeeded in pissing me off, that's for sure!!! Second, I want you to know that your image acted as a mirror-like reflection back to me. You showed me my own fuzzy thinking, my own excuses, my own unsatisfactory conclusion to my drug experiences, the weakness of my belief structure, etc. That was a large part of my anger back to you. I now see that I had experiences as a young man that I have not really assimilated. I have not absorbed the lessons from them into my system, so to speak. So you have shown me my weakness.

After Jacob's experience in Discovery, he began to make a lot of internal and external shifts. He wrote about anger and particularly how it had been focused on us:

I'm much more aware of it and what it does to me, which is nothing. I made a commitment to constantly ask myself the question, Is there positive movement in my being angry? If there's not, I drop it. I notice that there's no positive movement in my frustration and anger. I'm more able to accept things.

He wrote about how anger overwhelmed other emotions, such as sadness, sorrow, guilt, and pain. He singled out how he's been quick to talk and a good talker but shy on following through. He wrote more about how all he went for was acceptance "from my peers, my parents, basically anyone but myself." He described viewing "things from a positive rather than negative perspective" and began to visualize himself working in positive ways. He wrote about focusing not on getting to the upper levels of the program but on "personal progress and growth." He described how he abused "beautiful things and gifts that my parents gave me and all I did was take more." He talked about how "I'd *really* like to make it up to them" and "how I'd like to talk to my parents not yell at them." He expressed "gratitude for all the privileges and good things in life." A recurring theme in his letters was honesty: "I've told so many stories sometimes I can't decipher between a lie and the truth, but I'm definitely becoming more truthful." He wrote about learning to love, like, and be himself rather than some hippie image. He observed feeling sorry for himself and how that had influenced his life. Sometimes he wrote confessions, like the time he stole the Caravan and how he cheated on the drug tests.

"After Discovery I went back into my family and started really *ripping* it up, because I had this little high going and I was *stoked on life*. I was happy for once; I was not carrying around all the baggage and I didn't have to worry about needing to get high or getting high. If I had done the Discovery seminar outside the program, it would not have helped. I would've just faked it through again and then I would've gone out and done the same thing again and then I would have just had the need for another seminar.

"The upper levels liked what I was doing, complimented me a lot, told me to keep going. Getting to Level Three was going to be hard. Back then Level Three was the hardest level to get. I knew kids who were working *hard* four, five months to get to Level Three. I got Three in a month. I was *wailing*, like *no holds barred!*

"Then I went through the Focus seminar where things *really* came into effect for me. The whole thing I dealt with in Focus was that I was still playing the game. I was not consciously faking it, but I just was doing what I needed to do to get by – just because that was what I knew how to do. I knew how to play the game the best. The seminar leader Duane ripped me to pieces. If I've ever had a spiritual experience, it was *then*. My whole vision went black and I almost fainted. I got hot, sweaty, and I could not see anything anymore. It was just black. All I could hear was Duane's voice just echoing in my head. I can barely remember what he was talking about. It was just stuff like, 'You're fake; you're playing the game.' Stuff like that. But Duane hit me just so hard with his words. I didn't deny it, or get mad at him, and say, 'No, you are full of crap, Duane.' Because for the first time it was like reality is right *there*. Why would I want to possibly deny it? His words hit me in a way, not that I would get defensive, but in a way that I was just like, 'Oh, whoops.' It was real dramatic. I was bawling. The guy *notched* me. He knew my game. I was a manipulator. I'm sure my game was just like his own shucking and jiving game in *his* earlier life growing up in a black ghetto. So he hit me in a place where I could not come back. I just could not come *back* to him. I was looking to – but actually I couldn't; I was just knocked over. He *clocked* me, and I couldn't hang with it any more.

"Somewhere along the line in that seminar I discovered who I really am and what I'm about. I am a powerful, passionate, peaceful, glowing, and radiant man. So when I came out I said, 'Screw this – I'm ripping it up for *myself*.'"

Jacob sent a letter home to Sandy for Mother's Day, 1996.

Dear Mom,

Well, in case ya didn't know, I'm here in Samoa (joke). Well, I must commend you on your decision to send me to this island of change. This place is really what you make it – basically like anything else in life. I've made it a place for personal growth and change. You're a beautiful woman and, mother, I love you with all my heart and then some. You're a very special person in my life and always have been. You're an inspiration of change. I want you to know I'm smiling a lot here – a lot more than I was at home. You took the step in this to get me away from drugs and make me work on my acceptance and negative thinking. I hope that, although I'm far away, this is the nicest Mother's Day you ever had. Just know that your son is changing for the better. I thank you for giving me all the chances you've given me and especially the beautiful chance of life. I love you and I just wanted you to know. I don't believe in wrong or right, but you were right in sending me here. Happy Mother's Day!

Love,

Your constantly growing son

Jake

Another letter reflected his new mood of excitement and optimism for life, as well as a new-found feeling about his parents.

Dear Mom and Dad,

… The other day me and everybody laughed at my old hippie image. Me, I never laughed so hard in my whole life! I do not regret the things I did to my body, to you two, the way I dressed. There's no movement in regret. I learned from that very large mistake and look for the growth in it. I love you two very dearly. … I'm glad you're proud of me for Level Two but I'm more proud of myself. *I'm going somewhere in my life!* Thank you for sending me here. … Mom, your letters are beautiful. I'm not so much interested in the garden or school. I'm sorry, I'm interested in *you* – in how you feel, if you hate me. I know you don't. Your feelings are what I want. Here are mine. Mother, you brought me into this world. You are the most beautiful woman in the world. I cry when I think of your hug, the look in your eyes when you talked about Mac that one day when we lay on the bed watching t.v. and you told me of his attempted suicide. I knew of your love, its power and capability, right then and there. I love you with every piece of my heart and a little more. Dad, you are a gorgeous man unafraid of the emotions you feel, able to express yourself, a funny guy – you've always been funny. And loving – always there to give your love through supporting me in baseball, watching me on stage, or sending me to Samoa. Just don't keep me here through *next* Mother's Day … ha, ha! I love you both. This is my little care package. I have no chocolates or candies, but *I got love, baby!* *Weeee ha!* I love life! Life is to love! As I once wrote you, there are two choices on the road to life – you may walk or run. Me, baby, I'm *flying*!

Please send me two big containers of baby powder for my rash and five bars of Dove ASAP.

Love

Your constantly growing son

Jake

Jacob moved quickly in the Program. Too quickly, a worried mom and dad felt back home. We called his case manager, Rita, every week and his counselor, Sonja, once a month. For several weeks running I never failed to remind Rita that Jacob was professionally trained as an actor. "Watch out that he's not just charming you, Rita!" I warned. But we underestimated her as much as we underestimated Jacob. Both were working hard. Rita held Jake to his promise to work hard. After a while we began to believe that perhaps a miracle was occurring, that he was truly engaged and not passing everything off with some fake participation. One day Rita said to us, "I think he's doing this for himself." Sonja reinforced this view over time. Hearing words of assurance helped us trust in the process. But trusting the process was one thing. Trusting Jacob was quite another. At a deep level I had very little trust that he was capable of serious inner work. My letters to Jacob slipped easily from dealing with my own issues to lecturing my far-away son.

I still wondered about our decision, questioning whether it was the right thing to do, all the while knowing that it was the one viable course we could have taken. We were also dealing with strangers whom we were paying for a service we couldn't see. I privately hoped these people were effective with Jacob. We voiced many doubts and questions to ourselves. But as we became acquainted with Rita through our weekly calls, we developed both a respect and fondness for this soft-spoken, gentle, confident Polynesian woman with laughter in her voice and a giving spirit. Sonja had less occasion to deal with our son and so knew less about him. But Jacob managed to stand out to her. In contrast to Rita's warmth, Sonja seemed a very bottom-line person, astute, hard-nosed, not easily won over. When she said that Jacob was making progress, it seemed ever more possible. We soon developed a very open, honest relationship with both women.

Rita told us endearing things about our son. She passed messages along to us, making up a little for the reality that Jacob would not earn the right to talk with us by phone for quite a while. Was this *really* our son she told us about? She reported her experiences with a kid who was kind, caring, polite, cooperative, obedient, laughing, a leader, eager to please and work hard – a kid who missed his parents and had a renewed appreciation for family. The boy she described possessed a sincerity, a willingness, and a power which he had kept quite hidden from our view. *Wow!* It had been so long since Jacob had done anything that could endear us to him, this boy seemed even less known to us than the stranger we sent away. However, the young man she spoke of reminded us a lot of the spirited youngster we took to Little League games. *This* was the kid we wanted to know again intensely! Later, he told us ....

> "After the Focus seminar there was no stopping me. I took a different approach in giving feedback. I didn't just slam people anymore. I'd give them feedback in a caring way. And I started seeing a lot of fake-ness in the upper level guys above me who, I thought to a certain extent, were still playing the game. And I didn't want to be that. Now I did not go out and tell them this, but

I had some words with them about it. I was probably making up most of it in my head.

"At this time there was a mold of a way to be a leader in the Program. It was a slam, in-your-face, way of doing things, an 'I-am-a-strong-powerful-determined-man' way of doing things. But I did not think that was *me*. I'm not James Dean. It was more me if I just came from my heart. I saw some other guys doing it differently too and they were on Level Four. So I decided, 'I'm going my own way here.' I wanted to be Level Four – don't get me wrong. But I had been trying so hard to get to Level Two and Three. Now I didn't even ask or talk to anybody about levels and I just figured that when I got them, I got them. So I did my own thing after Focus and *that's* when things started to roll. And that is also when the movement in the levels stopped for me for awhile."

While all of these positives were occurring in our lives, one of our greatest challenges was dealing with our fear. Sandy and I wondered if the news about Jacob was a short-lived, transitory phase and whether we'd hear that he had crashed and burned. We worried about what would happen when he returned home to live with us. Jacob in turn worried about coming home and doing drugs again. We began to deal with these fears in our letters and in the different processes each of us was engaged in.

Soon he reached Level Three. The first phone call home was scheduled through Rita. At the time there was no phone on site for the boys to use. (I once asked Rita about e-mail. She laughed and said, "E-*what?!* I think you don't realize that this is a Third World country!") The boys would be driven into Apia, a one-hour trip, and use a pay phone for the collect call home. Three days passed about as slowly as three days can pass until at last the day came. Morning dragged on as we waited around the house. No phone call. Every time the phone rang we thought, "Well, this is Jake calling," only it would be someone else. I could hear the anxiety and fear in my voice. Afternoon came and went. No phone call. Evening. Still no call. Well, maybe it would be tomorrow. But no call then either. Had he been dropped from Level Three? Was there an accident on the way into town? Was there a problem with the phone system? Had we been outside in the back yard when the phone rang? We could do little other than accept the uncertainty of the situation and deal with fear and anxiety. In our weekly call Rita explained that Jacob had not paid attention and missed the call for his ride into town. We would wait *another month*.

It was a lesson for him and for us. By this time, we all wanted to talk together as a family again very badly. Jacob learned to be a little more heads up; Mom and Dad learned to let go. We all had fears about the conversation and how it would go. There was no accident this had happened. We weren't ready yet. So there was another month of waiting, another month of letting go.

When the call finally occurred, it was a beautiful moment. Each of us cried a lot. Not much – and everything – was said in a satellite-delayed exchange of beautiful, healing words. Jacob told us how much he loved and missed us. He thanked us for putting him in the Program and told us that he was not ready to come home. He said that the only thing he regretted was how much this was costing us, but he said how much he liked this time in his life. He enjoyed assisting the other kids. He was polite and loving. He thanked us for being supportive to him by attending the seminars and acknowledged us for the growth he could see in us from afar. He even asked us about our lives. It was beautiful to hear. It was everything we had hoped for. But was this our son?

Over time and succeeding phone calls, an apprehensive mother and father began to appreciate the emergence of the genuine and real young man – sincere, engaging, and appreciative. He retained his sense of humor and his natural independence – a relief to me since it dispelled any lingering fears that he was being brainwashed. We gained a deep respect for our son because it was obvious how intelligent and caring he was. As he described what he was learning about himself and how he was progressing, he revealed a wisdom developed through experience in dealing with young men exactly like him and a structure which would hold him accountable.

In our phone calls and letters, each of us acknowledged our apprehension about the time ahead of us when one day we would be together again. We shared feelings of ambivalence – a desire to reunite mixed with a fear of how being together again might affect us. But Sandy and I discovered that we could talk with Jacob on a wholly new depth and level of honesty. It was more like talking with an understanding friend. We did not judge each other. We were supportive of each other and were open in expressing our deep feelings and fears.

"I saw others move into leadership positions around me. After a while I'm saying, 'Oh come on, where is my chance here?' And then finally I got my chance and they moved me to Faga beach to be family leader of Courage Family, a family that was just *bombing*. It was the hardest family to work with, out of all the families, I think. This was a family that had been failing for months. Courage Family had, like, one kid doing good or something like that.

"I had some problems in the first week, but after that I started rolling. I went in and tried to be a family leader like my former family leader had been. Which does not work. Because he is different. He is all motivational stuff. So I just started being *me* and earned my respect from the family right off the bat. I just went in there and had confidence basically. Once I knew I could do it, I just did it. I didn't give a funk about nothing. It was all Focus seminar for me, and after Focus I didn't give a crap as long as I was doing my thing – being happy and being positive. And then I just fit it within the confines of the Program. So I

141

went back to being me and I went back to the basics and that is when things started rolling in my family. And the old family leader, who they put on probation had a huge resentment against me for coming into the family and taking over his family. He ended up going home and I know that he is back to his old crap. I don't even have to ask. I think that he played a major part in bringing that family down. It was weird. But I moved beyond that. I got some players on my side, and I just enrolled people one by one, one *on* one. I'd enroll one guy, enroll the next, enroll the next, until I got the majority of the family on a team and then we would get everybody and we would just rock it. That's how it works, baby.

"So that was cool and I ripped it up on Level Three for three months. I *worked my ass off*. I mean *every day* I worked hard. Two months in a row I got an award for the hottest person on the beach. This was out of like about 120 kids or so. I was stoked about this. There were some really powerful people on the beach that I thought were really ripping it up and out of all those guys the upper levels thought I was doing the hottest for a *long* time. I was *constant*. It was like an MVP award, an honor. It had been a long time since I'd gotten an honor. It felt good.

"Then they gave Level Four to me. That was a big thing for me because that day, when I got it, they gave a lot of people Level Four who I did not feel deserved it, who in my eyes did not work as hard as I worked. Now you know, that is probably my own thing but I mean I was almost like *offended*, being the little punk I am. But mostly I was into getting the *old* me back again. I was getting back to the basics of being me. When I started dealing with life through the old me again, then the fact that this other kid got moved up a level ahead of me and I thought I deserved it more than he did – well, that didn't bother me as much. So I just focused on rocking my own boat.

"As far as my relationship with my parents during this time, I was mainly focused on myself and what I needed to be doing. But when I did think about them, I dug what they did. I dug how they took a stand against what I was doing. All I could see was that I was in a good place and they had put me there, so that was cool. I wanted to get back to mend and have a nice relationship for once."

Our son learned a lot as he moved into leadership.

"You were *the man* on Four. So now I'm pimping around the beach going, 'What's up, what's up, what's up.' Four was cool. You'd spend one week in the La Tiera facility basically being a family leader of Level Ones and then you'd spend a week at the beach maxin' and relaxin'. On-the beach, you'd have to do family stuff, but you were not *in* a family as a Level Four. That was sweet. I'd go out swimming in the cove and I had freedom for once. I was stoked.

"I think the most change for me was when I became Level Four and was assigned to the Faith family. There were three families bombing at La Tiera. I had two fathers, Pepe and Lima. Lima's Samoan name was Al Lima, and everybody just called him Lima. No Samoan fathers really had an impact on me, except this guy. He was just this huge guy, this *rock*, and he was like a *man*, but he just had *the biggest heart* I had ever seen in my life. He'd never hit a soul; he was just the most loving guy I've ever known. We hit it off instantly and he called me 'Jacopo, Jacopo,' which is Samoan for Jake. We were buddies. While the Level Ones were doing tapes or something, me and Lima would talk. We were a team and that was good because a lot of Level Fours had problems with their Samoan fathers and, you know, that showed through in the family, and then they could not work with the family because they would not be together.

"I spent a lot of time thinking of things I could do to help the Level Ones, and right off the bat I earned their respect. I didn't screw around. What I did was I enrolled them in me, which helped them enroll in their possibility of themselves – get what I am saying? It was like, 'Well, if Flood can do it, *I* can do it. So let's do it.'

"I took a lot of advice from my friend Dave and from some other guys who basically told me to lay the law down, to make sure they know who's in charge, because the whole thing with Level Fours is that I could give consequences now. So I took their advice, which was really good advice, and I laid down the law. I'd say, 'Hey, that is not cool; you got a warning.' I'd show them that they could not screw around and that, for example, there really is no side talking.

"So I'd say the first two or three weeks I was pretty gung ho and I was a *jerk*. I was, like, 'You got a warning for this,' or 'you got a warning for that,' right, and I power tripped, basically. I took the power that they gave me and I wanted to do *good* with it, but I just power tripped all over kids. So as a result I just made enemies. They hated me. They thought I was a jerk, because I *was* being a jerk. I thought that I had to be firm. No, not *be* a certain way; I'd already evolved past that. But I thought that, in order for me to work successfully, I needed to give a lot of consequences or something like that, because I had that impression from some upper levels of what they did in their families when they were Level Fours. So I went and just did *that*, but they had been basically just *showing off* in front of me, saying in effect, 'I am a cool Level Four here.' So I just slowly said to myself, 'All right. This *ain't* working.' So I made buddies with the guys and I said, 'All right, let's kick back and do the real deal.' I put myself on the line, I could have gotten in trouble a lot of times. I would say, 'Hey, you don't have to do, like, dumb stuff that you know you are not going to do at home.' For example, one rule was if you pass gas you get a warning or something like that, unless you ask permission or go outside. I said, 'Man, just fart and claim it!' Basically, what I would do was I showed them that I was hip and that I could hang, that I was not just a hard ass. Then they are thinking, 'This man is cool, this guy is not bad.' I showed them that side where I was easy going and I was having fun, but at the same time I was *doing* something different with my life. I was *working* the Program on my terms. This is where I really got that respect. I got that whole family because I worked the Program, I was *honest* with them, I was friends with them, I joked around with them, I played with them, I would get down and dirty with them, and I'd tell them what's up if they were doing something dumb.

143

"Once a father trusted me I could do anything. At first Lima would say, 'Jacopo, what are you doing?' thinking that was I was hurting a kid by what I was doing. So once I basically told Lima what was up, there came a point where he saw the effects that I saw in the kids. And he was there for the same reason I was – for the kids, to help them out. So he goes, 'OK, Jacopo, you go, you go.' And he trusted me. And if I would go, 'Hey, Lima, help me out here!' he would just jump right in. And so that's how we worked it. So, things started rolling. There were things that I could have gotten in trouble for that I thought were better for the kids, that they would not let me do, but I still did them. Like I would talk to them after shutdown. The kids would lay down to sleep and I'd tell them about the day, like what went on with me, how I experienced people during the day. I'd do this at night because my shutdown was not for an hour later. Or if they did good I would tell them a ghost story or something and I'd just tell them my views on life. And they'd dig that because then they really got to know who I was. We were advised to keep a *professional* distance, which is BS, which did not work, and which I tried in the first three weeks. But it didn't work. So I showed them *myself* and then pretty soon I had them all enrolled in me and when I enrolled them into me, that is when they moved to, 'Let's *do* it; we can do it our own way here.'

"I had these two kids in my family, Anthony and Dusty. They were the hard asses in my family. I remember one day they were just going off, *spitting* and kicking chairs down. They wanted to start a little revolution inside La Tiera. So I said, 'All right, it's walking time.' Level Ones used to have to walk. You stand in a line and you walk back and forth. No destination, particularly. You just walk. It is not fun on Level One, really. Purposeless marching. But I made it purposeful: I would talk. It was just fitness; it was basically a thing to show the kids that it would be good to get off Level One. So anyway, it was a fun time to squeeze stuff in – while walking, during educational video, *anytime*. I will tell you straight up: I bent the rules, I didn't break them. There was no set rule that you couldn't take a kid out of the schedule, but they didn't want you to unless he was going through some emotional thing, which they were constantly. So while they were watching a movie, I'd pull a kid to the side and we'd talk and I'd say, 'What's up? 'What are you doing? Are you having fun? No? Well, all right, change it!' Stuff like that. That's how I ruled the hard asses in my family. They were doing this little revolt, spitting and putting their feet on the table, you know, big stuff there. Anthony would go into his old, 'screw all this stuff' mode and then I'd have a conversation with him. I'd tell him, 'Hey, what you are doing is just not *happening*.' I actually became friends with Anthony. But I was pissed off at him because he wouldn't do anything in the Program. He said, 'I don't want to be fake.' And I said, 'You don't *have* to be fake!' And I told him there was a way to align the two roads into one, your road and the Program road, to make them both work, because that is what I had found, basically.

"As for me, I saw my potential as limitless in any direction in my life."

Sandy's story

Sandy and I are driving in our car when I ask her to recall painful days now behind us. As I listen to her I am often reminded of the beautiful girl I met long ago and see now as she talks to me. As I listen to her tell her story I remember falling in love. And even as she recalls the deeply painful moments in our relationship, it feels like we've fallen in love all over again. Only this time with the experience of years together.

"I was a good kid in my childhood. I wanted to please and did everything I could to please. I kept trying harder and harder to please. *Everything* I did was about pleasing. I was totally focused on how to succeed so that others would think highly of me and approve of me.

"Fortunately, I had success in school and college. But I also had to work really hard. It always ticked me off because I had to work a lot harder than my smart girlfriend who never studied and for whom school was always so easy. But I had to work and work for everything I got. *Nothing* came easy. Now I realize that it was a good thing because when I got to college I knew how to study.

"I wasn't disciplined as a child. If I did something wrong I would get talked to. I didn't lose privileges; I never got grounded. My parents were older and my siblings were several years older than me. I was left a lot to raise myself, and I did. I was never a bad kid. I seemed to be self-regulating and oriented in a positive direction.

"So when I had a 'bad kid,' I really did not know what to do. I couldn't believe that he didn't want to please like I did. And I didn't understand why he didn't want to try to succeed in school – he just didn't seem to care whether he succeeded or not. Now I realize that he *did* care, but school didn't come easy for him and he was unwilling to let anybody else help him. He was looking for approval but when he didn't think he could get it through the conventional ways, he just wouldn't try.

"He'd try other ways to get approval. Jake didn't have a small high school nor was he raised with any particular feeling of community – not even in our family. He went outside and looked to his peers for his community, support, and approval. The only peers he felt successful around were the peers doing drugs. And that's what he was all about.

"Bottom line, it was really hard for me to understand why Jake didn't want to be the 'good kid' I was. I never saw him as a bad kid. He's always had a good heart; he just got mixed up along the way and made bad choices. I did notice that he lied and exaggerated a lot when he was young. I didn't call it lying then. When he lied I didn't make a big deal out of it or react because I thought that when he got older he would not do it any more.

"I felt sorry for him – because he had trouble learning and listening and because he didn't have any desire to complete anything. If it didn't come easy to

145

him, he seemed to say, 'Why bother?' I identified a little bit with his learning disability and I was big into rescuing people. What I realize now is that I was communicating to him that he couldn't do things himself and that I needed to do them for him. I was continuing a pattern handed down to me by my mother who always rescued me and sent me the message that I had to have someone do things for me. I remember 4-H. I had to sew a dress for the upcoming county fair. It was really hard for me to sew and I didn't want to do it because I hated sewing. Plus, I hated the 4-H teacher because she yelled at us. I wasn't particularly good at sewing, nor was my mother. But I had to have the dress done so I could get a ribbon for sewing. So my mother finished the dress for me! I remember feeling so guilty. And she sent the message that she didn't think I could finish it. She didn't want me to be disappointed and unable to attend the 4-H event. If she'd let me suffer the consequences of not finishing the dress, I would have had a wholly different experience. *I* chose not to finish! My mother was allowing me to enter her work as my work. The message I got was, 'It's OK to be dishonest in order to look good. *Anything* to look good!' Well, I did the same thing with Jake. He had a first grade project to write a report on a ground hog. I did the whole thing for him. And he was supposed to make a cake in boy scouts. I wouldn't let him decorate it. He won a prize, but it wasn't his. I did it! It was *my* prize! So I think I was always giving him the message that he wasn't capable and that I had to do it for him.

"In Discovery I realized that I didn't look at all to other people what I thought I looked like. I thought I looked like this helping, loving, kind, and thoughtful person who would never say anything negative to anybody. And people saw that, yes, because that is part of me. But what they also saw was that I was full of hurt, pain, and resentment.

"The other thing I saw was how angry Tim was at me – furiously angry. I was shut off to him because I was so tired of trying to please him, and unable to do it anyway. I was just *disgusted* with him. I was shut down and depressed, and I didn't want to have a relationship with him. I basically wanted him to go away. And Jake wanted *us* to go away. 'Go away! Leave me alone!' he'd say. All of us were closing doors to each other. We were floating on the same sea but miles apart and no life boats available.

"I didn't really want Tim to leave me because it was kind of convenient to have him around. And I *did* love him. But I was tired of trying to please Tim and I was sick of being controlled by him. And then he blasted me at a certain point in the seminar and I realized that he wasn't just angry with me, he was *furious* with me. I just didn't want to live with that anymore. You know, you can sort of live with quiet disgust; but this was *fury!* So, then I thought, 'We've got to change something here. This is not going to work.'

"Tim and I would change roles in response to all the problems that our kids would have. We would fight. One time he'd rescue and I'd be the tough, firm (bad) guy. The next time, he'd be the bad guy and *I'd* rescue. So one of our kids would do something, but we'd disagree what to do. So our kids got completely off the hook, since we were totally into our own fight. This was especially

146

true with Jake. He would just sort of get us going and then he'd sneak off and do whatever he pleased. So that was the dynamic between us.

"Me, I felt like a failure. Here I was supposed to be this great mother, caretaker, and teacher. But my son had a learning disability and wouldn't even let me help him. What kind of a mother was I that my kid had to resort to drugs and couldn't even stay in school? I realized in Discovery seminar what a total failure I felt like. In the Focus seminar I realized that I was so depressed, so *numb*, that I really didn't even want to live. And I also realized that all this time I thought it was *Tim's* fault that I felt this way. Focus helped me realize that, sure he'd contributed to it, but *I had made these decisions for myself.* Tim just happened to be convenient. I realized I'd been blaming it all on him and, if only he'd change, and Jake too, then I'd feel better about myself. But what I realized was that it wasn't up to them or other people or our therapist or the pills I was taking. It was totally up to me to do something about my life. This was a big, big deal for me. I knew at that point that I had to make a shift if I was going to survive and be healthy.

"But I really didn't know *how* to make that shift. When I was depressed I'd eat a lot to feel better, sort of an instant gratification. I was way overweight. And then I'd hate how I looked and I was mad about that. And then I'd blame other people: If only they'd treat me differently, then I'd be better. So here I had this knowledge about my blame, but I didn't quite know what to do.

Sandy's depression remained for yet a few more months. The seminars came and went, providing her insights. But I could tell that inside she did not feel much different than before. Then in her own good time, her wings unfolded and she flew.

"Soon after Focus we had opportunities to staff and I took advantage of them. I'd sit in those seminars and listen to people talk about their lives. This enabled me to see myself in other people. I'd keep hearing myself. I would see men angry with their wives or people around them and I'd say to myself, 'Oh there's another jerk trying to change his wife when he needs to change himself.' And I saw the women just shutting down. They seemed emotionally dead. I saw them numbing out in different ways like I did – some of them overeating, some feeling guilty about the choices their kids had made – as if *they themselves* had forced their kids into these decisions. I saw a lot of depressed women like me. I found myself pulling for the women to stand up for themselves and to focus on themselves and get their focus off their husbands and children.

"Also I observed people who naturally wanted their children to succeed in life but who were trying to control all their kids' decisions. I saw that they were making their kids out to be much worse than they actually were. And I saw that they were too focused on their kids' lives and that I too was overly focused on the lives of my children. I needed to shift the focus onto myself.

"Seeing others who were just like me made me want to change my life even more. I saw how judgmental I was. I saw that I was just as judgmental as my husband whom I hated *for his judgment.* I realized that I hated people who were judgmental and who were always doing things for me because I felt that they were telling me, 'Well, you either can't do it or do it well, so I'd better do it *for you*.' And it made me so furious. And then I realized that I was doing this myself and that's why they made me so angry – because *they were just like me*.

"And I realized that I didn't want Jake to come home to me in this state – that I really needed to change. And it just wasn't Jake – I didn't want to be a rescuer any more – I didn't want to be a rescuer to the people I worked with, to the kids I taught. I was just so sick of being a rescuer. Who did I think I was – that I would think I knew what everyone else needed in their lives? I would see this rescuing tendency in people I staffed with. Sometimes I'd find myself hanging back and letting others do something for me. Then I'd see myself resenting them when they rescued me. So ... it was kind of funny when I stopped to take a look at it. I started to be able to laugh at myself and say, 'Oh, there I go again.' And I found out I could stop it.

"Another thing I realized was how much I live for the future or the past but not the present tense. I saw how I wasn't dealing with what was going on right now. I was always fearful about what might happen. I caught myself talking to others about what I feared might happen. One seminar leader we assisted wouldn't tell us staff what was going to happen next in the seminar, yet here we were his staff and we were supposed to assist him. He was expecting us to respond to the needs of the seminar in the moment and use our intuition more. And that just drove me *nuts!* And finally I said to myself, 'OK, I can *do* this.' I allowed myself to feel freer and not be completely bound up in having to know what was going to happen and have all these expectations. I would just *trust* that whatever happened was supposed to happen and that it would be the best thing that was supposed to happen at that moment. I could just live in, and enjoy, that moment. Once I could release myself and be in the moment, I felt so free. I didn't feel resentful. I didn't dwell on my expectations or think about what everyone else was supposed to do and get in a big snit over everything.

"I started catching myself in my day-to-day life. I began to expect more out of my students in my classroom. I asked more of them. I asked more of myself too. But if what I asked didn't happen, then I was OK with it because I was not attached to my expected outcome.

"Letting go and living more in the moment assisted me in my family life. If Tim started some tirade about why didn't I do something this way or that way, I said to myself, 'OK, what am I going to do about this right now? What's going to work for me right at this moment?' That seemed to really work well for me.

"One day a woman who had her son in the same Program started talking to me about this book called *The 12 Steps – A Way Out: A Spiritual Process for Healing Damaged Emotions*. She showed me the book and suggested that we form a co-dependency group together. Another friend of ours also with a son in the Program had actually done the Twelve Steps of Codependence before. We formed a group of seven women and met in my house every Monday night. We finished the whole book. It was so hard and yet so *wonderful* because it enabled us to connect with a Higher Power. It helped me see that, if I could "Let Go and

Let God," as they say in the Twelve Step process, I could really live my life more in the moment. I could really trust that what was going to happen in the moment was simply what was intended. My will was really getting in the way and I needed simply to get out of the way. That was really good for me.

"As I went through the Twelve Step process, I realized that I really wanted to look physically better – because I felt better about myself now. I had taken myself off anti-depressants. The medication made me feel better short-term. It brought me up. But when it wore off I'd go down and have these cravings (like chocolate or anything that would bring me up) and I'd want carbohydrates and I'd stuff myself and binge. Once I stopped taking anti-depressants, I seemed more evened out. I realized that I was in a habit of binge-eating. So I decided to pay for a weight loss program. I've been doing that ever since. I got into a habit of eating protein rather than carbohydrates. I started to feel so much better about myself because I wasn't binge-ing any more and I was exercising. I lost about forty pounds and really liked the way I looked. I looked *good*! My outside matched my inside. I notice today that the minute I feel empty inside I want to eat. I want to make other choices – like deal with the emptiness.

"The Twelve Step process and the seminars really had a powerful impact on my family relationships because, if I could let go of what I expected and just trust that whatever was going to happen would happen and keep the focus on myself, things may not always turn out the way I wanted, but they would turn out for the best."

I watched as Sandy went through a remarkable transformation. She began to take care of herself in a variety of ways. She rose early to exercise. She dieted and eventually weighed nearly what she weighed when we began dating in college! She spent more time gardening and brought beautiful flowers into the house. Everywhere I went people told me how wonderful Sandy looked. She busied herself with staffing and supporting others. There wasn't enough time to spend long, depressing hours in bed. To me, the most remarkable change was in her face. She no longer looked like someone in pain from depression. Instead, she seemed happy and healthy, bright and more assured. I fell in love all over again, a love that was returned gladly.

Of course we had our moments of conflict. But something was different now because we seemed to be able to work our way out of these conflicts. Thanks to what we learned from therapy, from the seminars, from other parents with kids in the program, and from our spiritual processes, we had better tools to deal with conflict.

My story

With MacLean away at college and the turbulence of a teen in crisis far away in another land, the house was quiet. The time was at hand to face the fact that we were a *family* in crisis. One day hopefully, the Jacob we once knew, with a spark of life and humor in his eyes, would return. But would we be any different?

I seemed to be two different people. One was a good-time guy, fun to be around, open, a risk taker, witty, interesting, thoughtful, a team player, a leader. The other was unhappy, depressive, lonely, angry, judgmental, at war. I could not reconcile myself to myself. I did not "add up." I did not know who I was. Neither one of the two faces I showed to the world was necessarily the real me. I was simply putting on contradictory masks for show. Who was *really* inside me? Did I even know?

While I was beginning to look inward and at my own part in our family breakdown, the temptation to diagnose the problems of the other family contributors was great. I succumbed to it regularly. Our therapist Joan, along with Sandy, had begun to help me become more aware of the influence of judgment and control in my life. But my focus remained external. I was vocal about what I saw, bringing their shortcomings to the attention of my loved ones. This only resulted in hurting the people I loved, but I did not understand how severely.

Raising two challenging boys and neglecting important internal and relationship needs had exacted a steep price from Sandy and me. We were separated by a deep reservoir of barely suppressed emotion. One evening in therapy I uttered one too many judgmental pronouncements about Sandy, and she *exploded!* Of course, in twenty-seven years of marriage it wasn't the first time my wife had been angry with me, but I was surprised and dismayed by an intensity of feeling I had never seen before. This was serious! She left the session in a fury that I didn't know how to handle. All I understood is that I had better look seriously at what I was doing.

When I opened my eyes, even slightly, to look at a picture of what I was creating in my family, this is what I saw: For starters, I had a kid strung out on drugs, now in rehab in Western Samoa. By that measure alone, things certainly weren't perfect in my life! But it hardly ended there. Whenever MacLean was home to visit, he couldn't wait to get away from me, from us, from what Sandy and I were creating together. He practically *fled* back to school. One day he screamed in frustration, "It's just not *worth* it being here!" and headed back for school before the term began. When I wasn't angry with Jacob, I seemed to be upset with MacLean. When I wasn't focused on my sons, Sandy became the beneficiary of my focused attention. I seemed always to be *fixing* the people I lived with, my fingers on the control nobs trying to make adjustments to *their* lives. I manipulated and staged, blamed and controlled. I perceived many things accurately but I did not hold myself in focus long enough to see that my playing God, sometimes subtle, most of the time blatant, hurt the people I loved and drove them away. Inside I was driven by fear – fear that the fabric of our family life might come unraveled completely. My unconscious strategy to orchestrate change in everyone else in order to save the family was backfiring badly, bringing on the very result I most feared. The more I controlled and judged, the more the fabric came undone. Now that our boys were away my strategy had remained the same: Change the person around me to save the family. Sandy was the only one left. When Jacob returned, yes, things *would* have to be different between us – but usually what I meant by that was that *Sandy* would have to be different, not me! The result? The door to our room was often closed and along with it the door to Sandy's heart.

Life was clearly letting me know that things were not necessarily as I wanted them to be! And I would get really self-involved and think that I was the cause of everything. I would feel as if I held three delicate and fragile lives in my hands. Without malice, I had somehow managed to break each fragile life. Sandy was the latest to crack. While each broke of his own accord, I had not assisted with support and love, only criticism and correction. Everyone was angry with me. I had played a part in their breaking. I blamed myself. What could I have done to change their outcome?

Or ... I would think I had nothing to do with any of it. Maybe it was just "all their stuff." Now *there* was a tempting line of reasoning! Of course, I could walk away from it all. It happens in families every day. But I wondered what would become of me if I bailed out now? Was there not some *reason* this was happening to me? The simple truth is that I loved Mac, Jacob, and Sandy with a deep heart feeling that burned and ached in bad times and sang with joy in good times. More than anything, I was afraid of *losing* them. My heart ached for relationship not war. I wanted back the simple, primary things: Closeness. Affection. Love. Sharing. Fun. Trust. Warmth. The *goodies*. All the goodies we once had now seemed lost. Perhaps forever, I feared. They had been replaced somehow with a kind of *separation* in our lives. We were *islands apart*. Our lives had devolved into a kind of living hell together, a life of anger and strife. And the people I loved, the people I most wanted to be with, seemed to have concluded that maybe we were better off apart. And so they escaped – Jacob took drugs and dropped out; MacLean buried himself in a flurry of projects and year-round college attendance; Sandy shut the door and lay in bed depressed. Had I escaped too? All I understood is that I held an important piece to the puzzle. I knew

I had to do my part – whatever it was. I now understood that I *was* part of the problem not outside and above it. I was *motivated* to begin.

While we were fairly smooth in the outer world and concealed much of our nastiness from others, in the mud pit of therapy the *real* feelings came out. At first, I only experienced being attacked by Sandy. But gradually, I began to focus on myself. Instead of verbalizing my feelings about her and her attack, I began to describe how I felt inside *about me and my life*. The more I looked honestly at myself, the more bleak was the picture I saw.

The truth was that I judged my life a failure. I felt ill-equipped to deal with this world – inferior and incomplete. I felt mistreated, a victim in an un-friendly and hostile world. I felt unfulfilled, burned out, dry, enervated. As I appraised the topography of my inner landscape I saw no color, no life, no magic and fun any more. And instead of doing something about it, I turned my vision outward, seeing fault in others. It was the easiest thing to do. To avoid the pain of examining my own life, I shined a light on everyone else's imperfections. Sandy always seemed available to take the punishment. Until now. Either I would deal with my own inner turmoil and get some control over my life, she told me, or I'd get the hell out. And she meant it.

I had wanted to believe that my turmoil began and ended with family rela-tionships. But it wasn't that simple. Darker, malevolent influences com-pletely determined my life from deep within. Joan our therapist pushed me to explore. Why the judgment? Why the control? Why the preoccupation with everyone else? What was I afraid of? At last I began to reveal the desolate country of inner feeling I saw when I looked within. I saw nothing but an arid wasteland. I felt all dead inside. "I feel over fifty and all dried up," I said one day. I could no longer feel a life force beating within my heart. All I could feel was the hurt of living. I felt alone and lonely in an indifferent universe. Somewhere along the way I had turned my back on a *living part of me* – a healthy, living center once vital now turned to dust. I wanted Sandy's companionship, yet how could she be my companion in these circumstances? I realized that I missed the vitality of a connection with something bigger than me – a context for living, an oasis in the desert, a life energy. I realized that *I* had chosen my inner isolation. *I* had chosen this arid land. No human companion could ever give me what I was looking for. I would only torment everyone around me until I found it again.

Joan suggested that it might be better for me to see her alone. I understood the nature of the workout ahead. I was ready to begin the plunge into my-self – seriously. I felt bad, *real bad*. As soon as I let go, an inner voice I seemed to have no control over began to whisper to me, "*You* are the sick one! *You* are the source of the problems in your family. *You* are the wounded one, unfit as husband and father. *You* have let them down. *You* ...

are not fit for this world." Was I insane? I would sit alone at night in the dark. I was being dragged down, way down, to the lowest place in a black inner lake of night. I was weightless yet sinking, a vectored contradiction, slipping down a channel to my own deep, where energy seemed pointless, where there seemed no center and no creator – just me and a voice and endless sinking.

I wrote a poem about how I felt and everything the voice told me. I *hated* myself for having these stupid, pitiful laments! After reading the poem to Joan, I shrieked, "Jesus Christ! I'm fifty years old and writing poetry like a college kid! I'm embarrassed and ashamed!"

Joan looked at me. "Why?" she asked. "Everyone has these feelings from time to time."

"But at my age I should be above that. I haven't written a poem in years and now I see why. It's *stupid!*"

Joan regarded me thoughtfully for a moment and asked, "Tim, why don't you feel *compassion* for yourself? Perhaps you spend a lot of energy denying that it's OK to *have* these dark emotions. Perhaps you don't write poetry because you don't want to reveal yourself *to* yourself. Perhaps," she continued, "coming to terms with the dark part of you will release your power and give you back the vitality you long for."

Intellectually, I understood and agreed. But intellectual understanding alone does not change a life lived. I kept judging myself as an immature man, inadequate husband and father, and – bad poet! I could no longer express even the merest thought without self-loathing and criticism – all to be projected out upon someone close to me when I could no longer live with the accusation I heaped upon myself. I was stuck in a vicious cycle of attack on self, attack on others, attack on self ....

Joan interrupted one of my litanies of self-abuse. "Listen to me! If you heard another man read that very same poem, wouldn't you have compassion *for him?*"

I caught my breath and let the air out long and slow. It took me a long time to answer. "Of course ... of course, I would," I acknowledged slowly. I felt a tear find it's way down my cheek. It was so simple! The first step I needed to take was *to accept myself as human!* Maybe if I could accept myself, I could begin to accept humanity around me.

The next weekend Sandy and I attended the Discovery Seminar. There were a lot of group processes. I spent a lot of energy trying to hide out, to look cool and in control. But Discovery proved to be an uncomfortable, unsettling experience out in the open, a public place where I could not easily hide. I soon learned to my great discomfort that I fooled no one. Ordinary people with no prior knowledge of me could easily tell me all kinds of things I thought I successfully concealed. Ouch! I didn't like being visible when I spent so much energy trying to look good! I was like a walking large-print book. Several readers were giving me a *book report!* The feedback I received could be sorted into three piles: One pile contained perceptions about the good things – intelligence, insight, stuff like that. Another pile contained several observations that I seemed arrogant, righteous, judgmental, full of blame and anger. The last pile contained observations that I seemed all broken up inside. Well, no news here – but wow! I wasn't hiding anything, was I?

Ironically, I felt rather grateful to receive the feedback. I was exposed. Now I could focus on the truth. Only by honesty can we see ourselves clearly. But my seminar was not over yet. There was more to come.

At one point I had a chance to give Sandy feedback about what I saw working and not working in her life. Instead of assisting her with caring and compassion, as I had been coached to do, I *attacked her* with full force, like an animal sensing a vulnerable prey. I justified to myself that I was doing the right thing. But I was paying her back for all the anger I'd experienced from her over the past few months. My "feedback" was only spitefulness and revenge. I went for the kill and hit the mark.

Within a few moments of finishing, a brief spark of awareness flickered and I realized what I had done. No one except Sandy had heard. It was between her and me. Later that evening we went to our hotel room. I told her I was sorry. She would not accept my apology. I could see the profound hurt in her eyes. I spent a tormented, sleepless night. The next day I tearfully confessed to the seminar what I had done. I knew I would either change or lose my family.

But after Discovery seminar nothing changed. Oh, I tried hard. I talked to Joan about what had happened and said that I knew that I needed to be "vigilant" – on a constant watch for the judgments and resentments. And I *was* vigilant. I worked very hard to observe and retrain myself. My outer behavior gradually improved. I bit my tongue and caught words before they were expressed. But often I wouldn't catch myself and the damage was done. Inside I was still the same – angry and hurting.

Beneath a '69 Chevy Pickup

A month later we went to the Focus Seminar. I dreaded attending and *hated* it when it began. For the first day-and-a-half I burned with a kind of white heat. I wasn't hiding any more – no way! I was pissed at the seminar leaders and their stupid processes; I judged everyone in sight; I was compressed tight into an intense fireball. I went through the exercises in complete anger until one very powerful experience revealed a dimension of me I didn't want to see: I was so angry that I simply did not want to live! I realized that this game reflected my life back to me as in a mirror. I suddenly awoke, as if from a long sleep. I rose from my body and looked back down upon myself in the seminar. It was late at night; everyone was tired. And there I was – checked out, sitting on the floor as close to the exit and as far away from the seminar leader as I could get. I had my head down between my hands. An angry frown marked by forehead. My teeth were clenched as tightly as my fists. I was Fury. I was preparing to leave – leave the seminar, leave the family, leave life, looking to escape the truth about myself, hiding out, in a rage over a process designed to get me to care enough about myself to live again – to *really live.*

I have come to appreciate a kind of grace, a built-in benevolence, in the universe quite beyond and above the meager limitations of my understanding. Because in that moment something – some life energy serene and beautiful and powerful – intervened in my life. It appeared in the form of a new inner voice to replace the sinister, dark voice of the prior weeks, a voice which said simply and calmly, *"This is not you!"* I wanted the real me to come out of the shadow, to live again. Unexpectedly, I surrendered. I felt a kind of trembling relief. I stood up and began to talk. I didn't understand why. I had no idea what to say. But in contrast to my normally contrived, planned personality, I was willing to be incoherent and unprepared, simply to stand there and be me for a moment. No act this time. I started to talk about the first thing that came to my mind. And I began ....

"Something happened to me two weeks ago. I can't get it out of my head. My older son Mac came home from college. No sooner was he home than he bought this ugly old '69 Chevy pickup and parked it in front of our house. God, is that thing ugly! It's got, like, rusted out pock marks on its hood and fenders, it's dirty, and you can't even tell what *color* this contraption is anymore. So right away Mac decides that he's got to fix the engine. 'Oh shit!' I'm telling myself. 'This is going to be something to watch! Another freakin' obsession!' So I kept out of it – *way* out of it. Mac has a job and every night he comes home from work and gets out his tools and works underneath this dead pickup. I don't even know what he's doing and I don't care, except that it's an awful mess and there's oil leaking all over the street and big parts dangling down from underneath the chassis and lying on the pavement. And here this mess is sitting square in front of our house and one of the neighbors calls the police complaining about the mess. So I'm telling Mac to hurry up and he's pissed at me because, 'Well, can't you see this is a complicated job, for Christ's sake?'

"So one night I come home from work to the same scene. Mac is working underneath his pickup. And I'm in a foul mood about this mess – because I always have to have *something* to be in a foul mood about, you see. And Sandy and Mac are pissed at me like they always are. Now, for the past several months we've had this long-time family friend living with us. So Pete comes up to me in the hallway and whispers to me, 'Tim, I happen to know that Mac would *really* like you to help him out with the pickup.' I looked at him and said, 'No, Pete! There's *no way* I'm getting involved with this. It'll take forever. Mac is probably way over his head in whatever he's doing. He knows I don't know a damned thing about car engines. He'll just use it as a way to make me feel stupid and put me down. No freakin' way!'

"And I walked away. And I don't think I took three steps down the hall before it hit me. My son whom I love *has to go through an intermediary to tell me that he wants to be loved!*'

And as I'm telling this to the group I began to break down and sob because of all the humiliation in it and because of all the relief it was *to tell* it. Remarkably, the other people in the seminar were crying too, because they are *human.* They seemed to have great empathy with my unhappiness and compassion for my being, after all, only human.

"Well, it wasn't five minutes before I had my good clothes off and my grungie clothes on and I was out peering under the pickup asking Mac if maybe he could use some help from an old fart who doesn't know shit about automobile engine repair. 'Sure!' he said, and he seemed kind of *excited* about it. And that kind of *excited me too.* I decided right then and there that I would be in this for the long haul – I didn't care how long it took. I'd do whatever I could to help him with this project.

"Pretty soon he's got me under the truck handing him tools. And we're laughing because I don't know one stupid tool from another – and we just decided to *laugh* about it instead of make some big federal case out everything. Mostly all I could do is loosen or tighten bolts, run the jack, help him lift things, hand him tools – you know, all the simple stuff. And I'm a klutz, so I'm dropping the tools. And it isn't long before I'm getting dirty and he's making jokes about it being my first time and all. And pretty soon he's trying to teach me about this thing he's replacing – the transfer case – and he's telling me about his life, and shit! we're having *fun* together! For the first time in *a long time*! And that's how I spent the last several nights – underneath a pickup with my son. And I guess the reason I'm telling you this story now is that ..."

And I really began to sob now.

"...*this is the man I want to be! This is who I was born to be! I don't want to live in judgment and anger anymore. I am a loving, caring, and giving man!*"

By now I was sobbing and shaking convulsively. But I had reached a turning point and in true turning points you lose all inhibitions. I didn't care how I looked or who saw me. I think it must have been a beautiful sight in all its ugliness. It's a beautiful thing not to worry about appearances and who's watching and what people may be thinking. *I was getting my life back and that's all that mattered.* Soon everyone surrounded me and gave me one of the most peaceful moments I've ever experienced in my life.

I realized that all I want is to love and be loved. I had a vision of soaring high above the world and looking down upon myself and all the people I knew – no longer with condescension but with love. I saw that we are all born the same – beautiful, whole, and pure. I had heard that sentiment expressed many times before, but in the end it was only someone else's thought, not mine. In all my actions I acted upon a fixed view of the world – in which all people appear as separate islands cut off from one another, forever strangers, alone and abandoned. But from my vantage point, high and serene, above the world, I both saw and *felt* the world anew. I saw that we do not have to be separate, that we are all made of the same clay, and that underneath our fear we all long to be who we are, to fulfill our true possibility. I saw that I had not been alone in choosing to live in fear. And I realized that elsewhere in the world a few people are having similar awakenings and choosing differently. What another is capable of doing, so am I, I thought. And for the first time, the vision was mine.

My life transformed in a moment of sweat, uncontrollable shaking, and tears, when I lost track of time and let go of everything I was protecting. I didn't become a different person; I merely rediscovered the beautiful man I had stopped becoming sometime in my youth. The beautiful man had got derailed somewhere along the way, wounded by the accidents of living. He had been buried beneath countless "nos," "you can'ts," and "you're no goods" – mostly said by him to himself. I had kept him locked away within a darkened prison built from the mortar and steel of my own fear. This beautiful man had been replaced by a pretender, a walking and talking mask of image and surface pretence, who held himself aloof, apart, and small with his cynicism, judgment, anger, and self-depreciation. But the magnificent man who is, and always had been, me was still there … waiting!

Suddenly, I couldn't wait to live my life! I couldn't wait to return to Joan and share with her my experience. She rejoiced with me. It was a goal we had been working on together for quite a while; it only needed this defining moment to happen. When my moment came, I rose to the occasion and broke through to the other side. Nothing magic happened. I simply remembered my basic, inborn nature. And I was *motivated* by that discovery to create a new life for myself, a life lived from love rather than fear, anger, and separation. I changed what I lived for, with a renewed hunger to live. The motivation to be the loving and caring man I truly am would create positive results in my family. However long it would take for them to see a difference in me – well, that's how long I would wait.

Big things from small

I can measure the direction my life has taken by looking closely at little, ordinary moments. Just as a long track is laid down with many small spikes holding it in place, the direction of a life lived is created from many small decisions laid out in a pattern along the days of our living. About a month after the excitement of the seminar had worn off, Sandy and I put together a package she would mail to Jacob in Samoa that weekend. By Monday it remained by the front door. By Tuesday too. Wednesday arrived: Sandy went to work but the package went nowhere. An obsession was born! Wherever I went a picture of the unmailed package lying there by the door projected itself uninvited onto the screen of my inner sight. I wouldn't put it aside. Of course, the picture elicited a mental process and the thoughts entailed judgment and emotion. "How could she just *leave* it there day after day?!" I railed. "The package contains things that Jacob *needs*, for God's sake! He'll think we've abandoned him!" Things went on this way for a few more days – the intruding obsession completely replacing the vision of love I had gained during the seminar.

Then quite unexpectedly a miracle occurred. I awoke as if from a dream. I saw that I did not take responsibility to mail a package that was important to me. Suddenly, I could *see* the dream I had been dreaming. There was another existence *outside* of the dream – the one I was experiencing now! From my new vantage point, I began to observe myself in the dream and to ask the dreamer questions. If he was bothered by the package, why wasn't he doing anything about it? Why had the package turned into an obsession? How much energy was he expending in the dream? As I asked myself these questions I began to see that only from outside the dream was it possible to *think* clearly – perhaps to think *at all!* The dreamer thought that *"Sandy should"* mail the package and had arranged it accordingly, knowing that it might take days before a busy school teacher would free herself up to get to the post office. It was I who had suggested to an unenthusiastic wife that she mail the package. As I reviewed the situation more clearly, I saw that, since I had mailed all the other letters and packages, hell, I thought she *owed it to me to mail this one!* Viewed in this unflattering but honest light, an unmailed package was a completely predictable result.

Curiously at the same time, the dreamer was desperate to get the package to his son. In a dream within a dream, the dreamer's nightmare was an imagined look of disappointment on poor Jacob's face when, day after day, no package arrived. The dreamer was desperate to make everything perfect for a young man who had violated most of the standards of the household, prompting an expensive trip across the world for treatment. Yet the dreamer was desperate to avoid hurting his son's feelings – frantic that his son know that he was loved, not abandoned.

How badly I wanted to purchase my son's love and approval through demonstrations of kindness. But in the objective light of consciousness, I knew that I could not alter anything within his heart. He would have to find out for himself – if he did not otherwise know – that we loved him in countless ways.

As I gradually awoke from this dream. I began to catch myself dreaming again. And then again. I began to develop a skill in watching myself. I became both observer and observed. I could see more possibilities inherent in every moment.

I began to laugh at myself and see how outrageously small I can be towards others, taking offense at their merest peccadillos. Laughter in turn elicited my *humanity* and dissipated the dark, heavy cloud of feeling separate from others. I began to see beyond external events to the deeper, internal events occurring within. I saw how I used the external to avoid seeing my inside. I read myself as I might read a character in a book. One day I exchanged a look of love with this funny little man looking back at me in the mirror. I realized that I loved him, pettiness and all. And I loved him for his dignity too, because he looked back at me with directness, honesty, and a fearless capacity and hunger for self-knowing. He was an explorer who had somewhat lost his way but who possessed an exciting capacity to recover and get on with his journey. His path, *my path*, lay at my feet. I could not contain my excitement about living – just for the adventure of it all!

One summer night I had dinner with MacLean in an Italian restaurant he liked. We talked about many things. It reminded me of the long talks I had in college with friends. Suddenly, I realized that I had changed my perspective. I did not see a bundle of faults. Sitting before me engaged in lively conversation was a wonderful young man I had once known only as a problem. I was even finding ways to communicate my love and a newly found respect for him. And he was changing too. He *felt* differently. He was accepting me too and enjoying my company. We were both coming together as adults drawn to each other.

As my own world widened so did the world around me. I began to start each day willing myself to live in a world of love and possibility, rather than a world of fear, anger, and blame. The world I lived in would be the world I created for myself each day. In the early morning hours I spent quiet moments giving thanks for the world that had always been there, giving thanks for my family, my job, my friends. I began to feel surrounded by precious gifts intended to enhance my continuous unfolding and becoming. I opened my eyes to see, as if for the first time, the magnificent woman who graced my days and who loved me still. I began to see my sons no longer as burdens but gifts, for it was through *them*, my young teachers, that I was learning to see for the first time. I realized what a profound gift my family was.

After this, I was on my way. Although I stumbled often, I never turned back. One day I looked out upon the inner landscape upon which an endless desert had stretched. It had become a living garden with branches green and tender.

It was then that I began to play and have fun again. Slowly my crazy sense of humor returned. I began to laugh and laugh. Sandy I went dancing and took a trip to Carmel with our good friends Shirley and James, whose son Joshua was close to Jacob at Paradise Cove. We dined out frequently. We snuggled in front of the fireplace with Kyle and Katherine at their cabin, had long talks, and healed ourselves with a tonic of tears and laughter.

And as I watched my garden grow and marvelled at how my family was transforming too, I looked around me and saw that others were creating equal miracles for themselves. I began to understand how we create miracles in our lives. Following are a few illustrations of miracles others were creating for themselves.

Ryan

"Even though I tried to avoid going into the Program, I knew the night I was escorted that I needed something. Any kind of program would be better than my life. I knew something had to change. But I didn't stop and do anything with that for a long time, really. It wasn't until I got dropped from Level Three. I got dropped because I traded an adaptor for some medication. About that time I realized I better do something with my life. Later, I got dropped again.

"My journey through the Program was like being turned inside out and being raw again. It's a beautiful process, no matter what it looks like. It's like if you live your life only in nighttime because it's dark and you want to hide things. No one can get a full picture of you. Everything's hazy. You're lost and no one can see you. And then you have the courage to set down the moon and bring up the sun and not try to hide everything, and just come out with it, you know. It's beautiful.

"I learned that I was OK just being myself. At the time, I wanted people to know that about me. In Focus seminar I wrote a letter to myself and I want to share it with you.

June 18th, 1995. Sunday

Dear Ryan,

We have made it past Focus seminar. You can do anything. You know that now. Don't ever lose sight of that. Remember all the times you were down or blue, remember all the great accomplishments you have made and many miracles and all the great relationships. Mainly remember the love. Not for others but for you. Ryan, this is a special something you have always looked for. You have created it. Hold on to it, Ryan. Also remember how much of a beautiful person you are. You are the most special person I know. You are such a beautiful and powerful leader. Don't forget it, Ryan. Don't let up one bit on your goals and dreams. You can do anything. You've proved it. Keep it up and hold on to your magical child. Spread your love to him.

I love you,

Ryan

P.S.: Don't forget who you are: confident, positive, loving, and forgiving.

"I learned in the seminars about all the positive and negative feelings I had towards my family. Abandonment. It was really hurtful. I just wanted to go crazy. So I did. I was overwhelmed by the thin line of love and anger I had towards them. At that time, I didn't know whether I hated them or loved them, but at the end of the process, I knew that I loved them and that I wanted to hold them and tell them I loved them.

"As I staffed seminars I learned about my power. Not to back down from it. Just *be* it. That's what's effective, what works for me. I had a lot of issues with myself and I had to learn to be OK with myself.

"As I progressed in leadership I learned how to be effective and to communicate. I constantly learned. I learned I was happy being a working person. I wasn't scared of success anymore. Leadership gave me an opportunity to be a hypocrite. I did a lot of right/wrong stuff. I got dropped. I had to work my way back up. Got up to Level Four, did a lot of the same thing again, got dropped, and worked my way back up again. Getting dropped was a big factor in my success. It was very helpful to me. A Samoan guy Lafi said, 'Be nice to the people on the way up the ladder because you're going to see them on the way down!' So I did. I learned a lot of respect for people. That meant a lot for me.

"But Tim, a lot of the times I wasn't happy because I didn't feel I had control over my life – like when the Program would change the rules or its structure. And that was a thing I had to accept. Or I could choose to have a fit about it. I learned a lot of patience and self-acceptance. To accept structure and understand it rather than fight it."

❖

Kyle and Katherine

Kyle: "I had been so focused on what's going on with Anthony that I experienced a big sense of relief after he left. The more I heard about his initial experiences in Samoa, the more I felt he was in the right place. So internally, I think I put the whole situation aside and said to myself, 'OK. Anthony's in a good place. Now I don't have to worry about anything associated with that and I can go on about my life.' I was real interested in what was going on with Anthony, his progress and all, but I didn't look here, inside me, at all. After he was gone I looked at the seminar materials but it didn't occur to me for a second that we were part of this. I began to get swept up in my medical practice again. We started building our new house about a month after he left."

Katherine: "I was devastated. Very depressed. I was relieved but I really didn't know much about the Program then. Then Jessica, who lived about an hour away and had a kid in the Program, called me one day. This was my first contact with another parent. It was so important to me. I immediately began to feel better. We decided to form a support group. We found out about the San Francisco Bay Area support group and attended that as well. Finally, I could talk to people. It helped me feel a lot better.

"One day a woman in one of the support group meetings said that, like me, she had been living almost in a state of mourning after she had placed her son in the Program. She observed to her older son that because of her younger son's drug use they could have been paying for his funeral. Her older challenged her head on and said, *'Mom, Joshua is not dead – get with it!'* That really hit me, how true it was of me. I'd been playing Poor Pitiful Me, feeling devastated and sorry for myself. *I decided it was time for me to get out of this game!* I decided it's time for me to look within and get accountable for myself, rather than looking for the Program to provide me all the information I need. I could take the initiative myself to find out the information I wanted to have!"

Kyle: "When we came to the Bay Area Support Group, I was *really* impressed by the people that I met there, by the feelings and emotions expressed, by the state of being of the parents. At that point I began to look forward to attending the seminars. But it took going to the Discovery seminar for me to get really in touch with the significance of this development in our family to me."

Katherine: "I was also very touched by the support group meeting, by that candlelight ceremony we had, and I was really looking forward to the seminar."

Katherine and Kyle described Anthony's father as a man without the tools to be an effective and emotionally present father. Anthony had been in Paradise Cove eleven months with only one communication from his dad. Katherine said that, while Anthony seemed still focused on his anger toward her, it was the *men* in his life that he had to face.

Katherine: "I think it has been very hard for Anthony to make a relationship with Kyle too, even though Kyle has brought a lot of stability to his life. He's trying to figure out where Kyle is in his life."

Kyle: "I have to take accountability for that, though. I had a certain way I wanted him to act – certain, perhaps unfair, limitations I wanted to impose – a certain image of him. A lot of that comes from my own perfection issue –

which really equates to major dissatisfaction with my own life, a feeling that I've always got to prove myself, I've always got to get better. I mean, I just *transmitted* that to my kids. And it isn't because I think I'm perfect or even successful. Actually, I'm beginning *only now* to feel successful, but in a different way than I thought I should. During the formative years with the kids I was driven to find success not in relationships but in how many patients I could see in a day."

Katherine: "And Kyle and I were raised a lot alike. I was never allowed to say a cuss word. I adopted the role of being the perfect child. I never let my parents down in any way. And here I have this kid doing all the things he was doing and I couldn't understand. Why is he doing what he's doing? 'Why do you want to be that way?' I'd ask. 'But Mom, I'm not *like* you!' he'd reply. 'Well yes, but you can go so much further in life if you're nice to people, Anthony.'"

"He's taught us a lot, really! We've learned so much from him, in combination with the seminars. I've written that to him – that if he hadn't done what he's done, we wouldn't have learned all these things about ourselves, about how this issue of being good and perfect and successful really pushes us around. I've told him what a blessing he's been, to reveal me to me, and then to give me an opportunity to discover my *true* self and who I want to be ... wow! So now I'm able to understand the things he writes to me in a wholly different way. We've had to go this deep, the three of us, to get to the bottom of our issues. If he'd said things to me before that he writes me now in his letters, I'd just have dismissed him as being disrespectful. Because I was always raised that a kid doesn't tell parents how they come across. *No way!* As a kid you're supposed to shut up and be obedient – that's what I was taught. And that was the conditioning I brought into my relationship with Anthony. So, he's had a real rough go of it and he's never been able to open up and say how he really felt."

Kyle: "Anthony was real confused, and part of his confusion was ours. He's a kid who's really bright but who didn't find a place in life. He never found a place he was comfortable until he found a group of derelict druggies. And they wanted him because they could manipulate him."

Katherine: "That's where a lot of really bright kids go – into the crowd of misfits. They become between-the-crack kind of people. He knew things weren't right, that he was trapped. At one point he had talked about the need to get out of his current environment and go someplace else to a different high school, to get a fresh start, to try to find a place for himself. So he knew he needed some kind of change. He's a good kid who was trapped in a no-escape situation with his peers and must not have known how to extricate himself from the course he'd taken."

Kyle: "He's an impulsive kid who had let his impulsiveness get him into the situation he was in."

Katherine: "A good example of this was at Le Tiara. A bunch of boys were standing around a staff car parked there. This situation was described to me by your son, Jake, who was Anthony's family leader at the time. Well, Anthony spit on the car for some reason. Jake said to him, 'OK, you're going to come and clean up the car or you're going to go into detention and it's not going to be pleasant and you're going to have to do essays.' And Anthony said, 'Fine. I'm not going to clean this car.' That's what I mean. He acts impulsively and then defiantly in terms of a consequence. He's always been impulsive.

In the first grade he ran out in front of a car. His best friend saved him. I really do feel that he was very unhappy, but his friend said that Anthony did it on purpose. Anthony was experiencing pain from very early on. People ask me, 'Why he isn't moving through the Program faster?' I say that Anthony's problems didn't spring up overnight. He isn't a kid who got into drugs because of a sudden change in his life. He has problems that run very deep and were always there. He stumbled into drugs as a way to seemingly cope. He acted impulsively out of desperation to find solutions to deep problems he wasn't really facing. He's not going to get over those problems really fast."

Kyle: "In my life I've had my bouts with drinking and working like crazy. In one sense I've always been a really solid individual; in another not. I've established a great reputation in my field. I established a professional standards committee, chaired it for eight years, facilitated the committee through several difficult decisions. I didn't realize it at the time, but that was mostly a manifestation of the image that I've had about *being right*. I went to Discovery for Anthony, to get in touch with what they were doing for him. I didn't realize that I needed to change here (pointing to his heart). Even after Discovery I was out to change everybody else – me too, of course – but I was still focused in an outer direction. However, the seminar had a *really* powerful effect on me. It caused me to look at how I play the right-wrong game *with everyone.* I had to acknowledge the truth about myself – 'Yep, that's me!' Win or lose, be right or wrong – that's been my life. That's the way we were raised. I had a brother one year ahead of me in school – same medical school, same residency program. We both became orthopedists and both became chief of staff of our respective facilities. Now twenty-two years later I realize *that's* how competitive we were and *that's* what I've been living my life for! I was still a little brother trying to prove I was just as good as my big brother – no, *better!* Our competition was never admitted or discussed. But I was always telling myself, 'You're doing good, but you can do even better!' Well, I have to say that it has been an enormous benefit to realize that about myself and to realize that I can change it."

Katherine: "Now we're wondering how much that influenced the way we dealt with Anthony and what he felt like inside being around this drive to success."

Kyle: "Or did he even know that we *cared* about him? This competitive thing must have affected everyone we cared about! I imposed that kind of value system upon all my kids – where the value is not the feeling, or the touching, or the holding, or the loving, but it's how successful you are, and that's all."

Katherine: "And now we're questioning what *is* success? Tim, as I watched you and your sons earlier this afternoon cuddling on our couch. You were rubbing Jake's back and touching Mac's hair – *that's* what life is about! Who *cares* about the other stuff?! It's nice that we have this new house. We're fortunate to have it. But I said to Kyle, 'There's nothing to this house unless there's love in it.

Materialistic things are nothing. It's not what life is about.' Tim, when you cried earlier in our living room and Mac put his hand on your knee, that was so neat – it showed that he's *there* for you. The more life goes on the more I realize that there's *so* much more than …. I want to have *real* contact with someone, I want to live from my heart, I want to have feelings for people. We've been over and over this with our older kids, talking about how we'd like to change. I said to Kyle, 'We're not living in honesty.' We've got to connect. It's got to come from here (pointing to her heart)."

Kyle: "You see, there's a lot of perfectionism and alcoholism in both our family backgrounds. Probably the only non-alcoholic in our families is my own mother. My dad was a so-called functional alcoholic. He practiced medicine for forty years but he'd come home and have a couple of quarts of beer at night – *every* night. Without exception. My experience was that there was a lack of intimacy and trust, a lot of coexistence. You check out when you get home after your first or second glass of beer. There was no conversation. I didn't think about it then. But now I think about what my parents handed to me – that kind of driven, Irish Catholic, total structure, guilt kind of stuff that says, 'If you step over the line, you will go to hell without doubt.' What did my dad hand to me? Precisely what I handed to my own kids. 'The sins of the fathers will be visited upon the sons.' *Until now.* After the seminar I couldn't wait to talk to my kids and tell them how I want to change my life."

Katherine: "And in my background, both parents were alcoholics. I was the oldest of four kids. I parented my siblings. I developed big-time codependency issues. I tried so hard to prevent my son from going through what I'd been through. I was so fearful that genetically I had created a substance abuser. Perfectionism – oh we weren't allowed to be imperfect! One time I said 'Damn!' and got the belt for it. I was talking about an actual dam, not using the expression. It was that bad. I wasn't allowed to step out of line. My father could not accept that his first-born was a girl. I was left-handed. He tried to change me to right-handed in the first grade. I wouldn't change for him. I wasn't defiant like Anthony was, but I tuned my father out. It was the silent kind of defiance. I got acceptance from other people. But Anthony took the approach of, 'You don't tell me what to do and I don't care who you are!' I've written him about that and how much we're alike. He wrote me back and said that we both have anger issues. It's true."

Kyle: "We were both raised with conditional love – we'll love you *if* …. We're going to break that family pattern *now*.

"Our patterns, our issues, are long-standing and it's going to be a challenge to rise above them. I remember Anthony's first grade teacher – how she was impatient with him. She gave happy smiles, or frowns. Most of the time she gave Anthony frowns. Anthony would come up to her and then she'd say 'No, go away!' He would stand over in the corner. He felt shamed. Katherine was getting on her case about the smiles and frowns. So one day she took out her anger at Katherine on Anthony and said to him, 'You'll never succeed in life!' Just the other day Anthony told his case manager, 'I'll never forget that happened to me. Until this day I still believed it!' Ten years of thinking that he would never succeed – from six to sixteen! At last, Anthony seems to be choosing something different."

❖

Afraid of Big Brother

When Paul arrived at Paradise Cove his goal was to "cut everything off" emotionally. He told himself that he didn't want to feel anything. In his first letter to his mother Melissa he informed her that he would never write or talk to her again. While he gradually softened, for a while his letters to Melissa were, as she described them, "cold and distant." "But at least he was writing to me!" she exclaimed with natural good humor.

In contrast to Jacob, Paul's progress was so slow: two steps forward, one step back. Then after this torturous pace, he would fall all the way back – to Level One. Then he would begin another slow ascent. But with every step forward and backward, Paul was learning. Inside him an accumulation of knowledge and experience was building. I learned quickly to respect this young man. Like his mother, he sought to know and understand. He would not rest until he figured things out for himself.

The evening before I interviewed Paul he had just received a strong warning with consequences called a "Category Two" for leaving his sandals outside his fale.

> "Last night I got a Category Two for leaving my sandals outside. I was awake still when I was informed and I lay there thinking about it. And I said to myself, 'No! It's the Program's fault! It's the stupid rule!' And then I'd say, 'Screw the Program … why are you doing this?' Another side of me would say, 'Well, let's take a logical look at this. Why did you leave your sandals outside? What can you do about this in the future? Why can't you just learn from it?' After a while, I just stopped and said to myself, 'Wait a minute! I'm not feeling very good right now. Aside from the victim and the logistics of it all, I'm just not feeling very good.' I feel that it's all about balance for me. I think if I get a Cat Two in the future and I can just accept it better and still feel good about myself, then I'll be happier."

As Paul continued to emerge from his personal isolation ward, he began to desire leadership. One day he was appointed family leader.

> "I was real authoritarian, real tight on the rules. I'd have a job to get done and I'd have twenty people to do it with, and I'd get it done. I got a lot of support from some of the other boys in leadership. But in terms of the emotional side of whatever we had to do, I could not take care of that side, because I had done nothing in terms of the emotional side of *my own* life. I didn't even *understand* it then. All I'd do is get real clear about the rules.

166

"So I got moved to a different family. I didn't do good there, and I got put on probation. I felt a whole lot inside but I didn't show it. I blocked my feelings. Everyone tried to get me to deal with my emotions and I'd sit there and think, 'No, I'm not going to let them break me.'

"One day after lunch, one of the leaders sat down with me and said, 'I'm not leaving you until you start dealing with your emotions.' When I was confronted a lot, I'd have this fear thing, fear that I'd break down. And there would always be the secret thing I didn't want to talk about. 'Why do you feel that way?' someone would ask. 'Because I don't love myself,' would always be the thought that would pop into my head. But I felt I couldn't say that out loud because it sounded bad."

At his core, Paul had a certain view of the world that bore examination.

"One of the core things I've learned is that I do a lot of stuff because other people want me to do it. Then I resented it. I resented being forced to go to school and do homework by my mom. My dad, he turned me onto computers – and it was something I liked and all. Computers became something I did because I liked them. But it had started out as something that he wanted and so I did it. So that became a core thing for me – doing what other people want me to do. And the core question was always, 'What does Paul want to do?'

"So then people here would try to get through to me and ask me questions. I'd just stonewall them. They'd ask, 'Why do you feel this way?' and I'd look down and just refuse to answer, trying to get away from my emotions. I thought that if I let them in, if I didn't protect my mind in a certain way, then I'd break down. My goal was not to break down. If I broke down, the system would get inside me and take over and it would be like *1984* and all that. And that's how I looked at the world.

"You know, I've re-read *1984* since I've been here at Paradise Cove. I've learned a lot from it. I see the other side now. When I was doing drugs, I saw myself as among the persecuted few. It wasn't as large scale as the persecution in the book, but I saw myself as victim of the system's persecution. That's pretty much what my dad taught – me versus the system. Now that I'm sober, I look at how I was thinking, and I see that, hey, this side *is* better. I *feel* better. Now I can look at things from both sides, kinda. A situation comes up and I can look back and say, 'I would have seen it like that, but now I see it like this.' And every once in a while when something goes on, I still will get back into the old way of thinking, but here I can find someone and go talk to them about it."

Paul's view of himself was what blocked him from loving himself.

I felt that I was an intelligent, creative, but *odd* young man. That felt right to me – taking my intelligence and projecting it weirdly. I got a lot of feedback. 'Being weird is your image,' they said. 'You ought to try being normal for a while. Do you see how much your image is just shock value?'

I was asked what kind of music I listen to back home. I said, 'Marilyn Manson, Jimi Hendrix.'

'Why do you listen to it?'

'Because I like it.'

'No, no, no,' they said. '*Why* do you listen to it?'

Then it came to me: It creates chaos in my life and I live to create chaos, to be weird, for shock value.

Someone told me, 'It must suck to be in the spotlight twenty-four hours a day, having to be weird so that everyone will accept you. What are you, besides this 'odd' thing that you project? I understand how you're intelligent and creative. But what inside you is waiting to take the place of this part of your image that says you should be odd?'

After a while I realized that I am an intelligent, creative, *honest and lovable* young man. And that really rung true to me. It felt so good! Now, it's something that I still combat. Like in my family, I'll still do really weird things sometimes. I'll get feedback about how I'm going off on this weird thing and people will wonder whether I'm trying to get into acceptance. But I'm dealing with it.

As Paul progressed his greatest lessons lay in facing his challenges head on.

"Dear Mom,

".... A couple of nights ago I had a dream. I was told to dig through this stack of books and find my fears. I dug around and couldn't find the book I imagined, which was a giant dusty tome with millions of pages which would take forever to read. I get two things out of this dream. My fears don't physically exist. And they consist of infinite doubt and worry.

".... Argh! Today has been stressful. I find myself in your position when I was at home. I'm family leader. I want people to do what I say. When people don't, a couple of things happen: (A) I go off and yell at them. (B) I keep asking over and over to have it done, or (C) I go and sit and be pissed and leave them alone. Remember how you used to say how you'd "dangle a carrot on a stick" with me? You'd say, "I'll take your computer away if you don't ...." I find myself doing this also. It's tough. I want to be assertive, to put my foot down, but not be controlling. A lot of stuff has been piling up, and it's just getting to me. I'll work past it, and have my leadership in order.

"It's still bothering me this morning. I am literally feeling fears weighing me down, and it makes me just want to run and hide. I'm afraid to put my foot down, because I'm afraid I'll hurt people. OK. Logic mode. My fears are running me. Feeling like I'm not worth leading is running me. And fear doesn't exist. I'm afraid of non-existent things. I think there's a saying that goes something like this: "I must not fear for fear is the mind-killer. It is the little death." I trail off there. But that's that. Who cares if they think I'm being controlling? Or if I am? 'Cause I will work past that. If I sit and fear and don't do anything, I have no chance of succeeding. So I must do something."

❖

Melissa's dream

"One thing I want to change about myself is my knee-jerk reactions. Many of us parents have this issue with our kids. I had a dream the other night, a nightmare really. Paul was home, doing something that was bugging me. I overreacted. Then I stopped dead in my tracks, looked him in the eye, and said, 'This is *not* what I've been taught to do. Let's start over. I will back down off my horse, calm down, and take into consideration all the *other* things in my life that are irritating me.'

"I have a pattern of overreacting – particularly with Paul. In the dream my acknowledgment of what was happening inside of me was so important. I don't want to go back to the way I used to relate to Paul. I want it to be different."

Jessica

About a year after Cary had been taken from Juvenile Hall to Paradise Cove, I spoke with his mother Jessica who looked at me with large, wide-open eyes and spoke with intensity of feeling and openness. I asked her to tell me how she and her family had been changed by their experience.

With deep feeling, she shared how her family became close to God. Cary had rediscovered his faith while on the island – a discovery being duplicated by his parents at home.[1] As I listened to Jessica speak, I found myself very touched by this woman and her strength.

"Cary entered the Program with a fairly positive attitude. However, he told the staff that, while he was glad he was there, he didn't need to be there and didn't think he had any issues and had learned his lesson. It didn't take long for him to realize that he *did* have issues – drug addiction, low self-esteem, being out of control of his life, and feeling that he had gone too far for anyone to forgive him. So why start over?

"Right now he's on Level Three and he's getting strong. I'm so gratified. All three of us have become Christians because of what has happened to us. That has become a big part of our lives and a big part of our communication. William and I have done the Discovery and Focus seminars and it has been wonderful. You can't even make a pretense of supporting your child and your family without doing the seminars.

---

[1] None of the programs within the World Wide Association of Speciality Programs is religiously-based. Students are free to have or establish any religious or spiritual orientation they choose. They are free to choice *no* such orientation, as well. Each choice is respected. Parents of diverse religious and spiritual backgrounds use the program.

"The biggest issue I've had to deal with is my feelings towards my own father. I thought that I had accepted my father's emotional vacancy and had moved on, but I hadn't. I didn't cry at his funeral. Not too far under the surface I was angry at him for deserting our family. Mom was very bitter about my dad. She always gets surprised when people repeat their behaviors. He'd show up at someone's birthday drunk and she'd say, 'I can't believe he's drunk!' And I'd say, 'When have you seen him that he *isn't* drunk?!' So, we always had friction because my brothers and sisters defended my dad and I thought I had reached this incredible plane of acceptance. But a lot of me was still hurting.

"In Discovery seminar I also realized that I spend a whole lot of time convincing people that I'm right. There's not a whole lot of value in being right. I'm working more now to get what I need emotionally out of life. Being right and being strong was how I survived in my family. I was *right!* There was *no question I was right.* There was no sense pounding my head against the wall about my father like my sister did or getting indignant like my mother did. *I was right!* But I still wasn't getting the love that I needed, you know? I've spent a *lot* of my life trying to be right. I still do. Someone challenged me recently on my rightness about something and, boy, did it push my button! I *immediately* went to the reference manuals: 'I'm going to show *you* I'm right!' But being right doesn't get me what I've needed in life. I'm learning just to enjoy life more and to live more outside of my comfort zone. It's just what I need.

"I've cried a lot about all the things that have happened in my life. I had a visual picture of Cary back in Juvenile Hall. They keep the kids behind metal doors with tiny little windows. You walk down this long hall to visit your son. And you see all these faces in this window. It's one of the most horrifying things. As I'm visualizing this, my heart wants to go out to every one of them, but I'm looking ahead at none of them. They can't wear shoes in their cells, so all of their shoes are lined up outside the cell. When I see my son's shoes outside that metal door, lined up with all those other shoes, I feel the most primal pain, indignation, and rage.

"Those shoes represented all the disappointment and pain I experienced during all this time with Cary. I realized that I had to go back and visualize that scene, because I realized that I'd been keeping all my rage – right there in those shoes! I was able to express my emotions before I got involved with the seminars, but I was *surprised* at how much unfinished business – rage – I had with regard to my son. I began to imagine his shoes. I screamed and screamed! And after I quit screaming, my throat hurt so bad! The rage was that Cary had done all this, that we had been in this situation, that we had so completely lost control of our lives. Because when your son is in jail you have no privileges – you see him when *they say* you'll see him. You bring him something only if you can. He was only fourteen or fifteen years old. Everything I had put into being his mother was stripped away. I knew that parenting would be a challenge, but his being in jail was *never* something I had envisioned. His being in jail was also a statement about me – that I had failed. When you're standing next to your kid and they're getting a diploma, that reflects on you. But here my kid was *in jail!* What could I have done so wrong? These were the some of the emotions I was dealing with.

"I've learned a lot about being an enabler, but I don't beat myself up any more for that. I think it's what I had to do at the time. Given Cary's state of mind, I don't think that anything would have been different. Because not only did Cary have to learn his lessons, but there was a spiritual lesson for all of us to learn. It wasn't until I saw how real and powerful God is, and how real and powerful Satan is, (Cary had practiced Satan worship) that I could come to the place of giving up my own understanding of the universe and take up another one. This is my belief and I don't say that it's right for everyone else. What I'm certain of is that it's true for me and that when my son called evil into our house, it came. I knew that I was completely helpless. It was amazing how quickly joy and goodness came when I asked God for help.

"Cary's dad has an alcohol problem. He's stopped drinking now. The whole family is drug free now. I'm really proud of that. William is going to AA and a church support group. He's always been a very functional drinker – always gone to work and done well. But every night he would drink himself to sleep. And he liked to hide alcohol. So, like what I'd see is four or five beers, but then he'd hide little martinis and stuff around, so he was putting away a lot each night. I brought this issue up in the seminars but didn't get very far with it.

"So, life went on. Then I planned to visit Cary in Western Samoa and just before I left William got arrested for drinking and driving. It deeply shook him. He managed to get the sentence reduced, but it got his attention and got him to do something. He realized that he was a hypocrite, calling himself a man of God, yet still having this secret. So now there is no more booze in our house.

"This was a big issue between William and Cary because Cary was one of the few people who called his dad on his alcoholism. Because all this time William was telling Cary not to use. William was terrified to tell Cary about the DUI so he told him in a letter. But Cary wasn't shocked. He was concerned and supportive.

"Cary was very good at playing William and me off against each other. He would get us on opposite sides of an issue and slip through the middle. We didn't agree at all. On virtually any issue. So Cary ended up doing whatever he wanted. William and I talked but never resolved. We simply passed from one crisis to another.

"William has always worked a lot and I think Cary felt left out. They've always been close, but there was a lot of resentment about the amount of hours spent at work. He tuned out in two ways, work and alcohol, and this distanced himself from both Cary and me. William is afraid of becoming his father. His own father was a very serious alcoholic, but he was a violent man, not a nice person. William has always had a real love/hate relationship with his father, whereas I had no conflict at all – I always hated his father. His father was always unsuccessful, spent a lot of time on welfare, couldn't hold down a job longer than a year. So he kept life together by being strong, silent. But inside he couldn't handle things and wasn't really strong. Whereas the alcohol made his father violent, it caused William to withdraw.

"All my life I'd tried to accomplish everything and understand life completely on the mental level. I had no spiritual life. I've realized, however, that I have a very real and very beautiful place in the spiritual world. I've realized that, when I relate to my husband and son from that spiritual place, it's a beautiful thing. We don't need to get hung up on semantics. We don't need material things to relate to each other. To see my son develop his spiritual side is a very beautiful thing to me."

❖

The cave pool

After his son had attained Level Four, Walter was able to visit his son at Paradise Cove. He told this story.

"My son had grown since the last time I saw him eleven long months ago. He had become a handsome young man. A warm smile often surfaced upon his normally controlled appearance as we swam, father and son, into the cave.

"That he was enjoying swimming with me was a reflection of the many-faceted miracle that was becoming his life. Before Richard went to Samoa he was afraid of the water, a fear he accepted at the hands of his older brother, who took much more easily to the ways of surfing I had tried to teach both my boys. But Richard had rejected the way of the surfer. I remembered a hateful letter he wrote to me upon arriving at Paradise Cove. He mocked me for sending him to 'my kind of place' – a beach far away. He complained bitterly how all the other boys would make fun of him when they saw how scared he was of the water. To him at that time it must have seemed like the ultimate punishment.

"Now as we swam to the dark end of the cave, I looked in vain for the storied underwater passage to another cave pool. After a while, a local resident came to our aide, as they often do in that part of the world. Soon he had shown us the cave's whereabouts by swimming in and back out again. I was excited.

"I could feel my own fear for Richard as I told him I would dive down to find the passage. Once down I found it quickly and could not resist the temptation to push on. Soon I had resurfaced in the new cave pool on the other side. I quickly realized that this was a poor choice as I now had an anxious son waiting for me to surface back near him. So I scurried out of the new cave and ran back to the entrance of the cave he was in, shouting for him to come over by foot.

"Richard was full of questions about the passage and new pool. I detected anxiety in his voice but I also saw a possibility to respond differently to him and be more supportive than I would have been in the past. I simply and sincerely acknowledged him for how far he had come in overcoming his fear of swimming. At that moment I saw a change in Richard's perception of me. Suddenly, I was not the father of old who always pointed out his shortcomings; instead I was affirming him for this new and exciting achievement. He seemed pleased with my affirmation and I felt it bring us closer together. He must have felt a little safer with me because he revealed that, in all this time at Paradise Cove, he had never been required to face the power of crushing waves. He said he would have to face this and other fears when he got home.

"My mind was racing now. I wondered how our experience together with the cave pool might parallel Richard's inner struggles. He was growing strong and confident in Paradise Cove but the real tests were the waves awaiting him at home. I was thankful that Richard was neither just beginning his journey here nor arriving home too soon. We were at this special place given to us both.

"I assured him that he did not have to swim the dark passage for my approval or to obtain my love. From my heart I told him that he already had that and always would. But I added that, if he wanted to go for it now, for himself, he could, and it would be his choice. He didn't think about it very long. He looked at me and asked me to swim with him, to go first and wait for him. I didn't hesitate. I slipped into the water and made for the cave on the other side. Then I waited. When a moment later he burst to the surface, it was our victory! For Richard it was another step on his journey of life; for me it was the rich experience of being a father available to my son.

"This event may not go down in any history book. But I will always hold it close, right here in my heart. This event was reflective of our entire week with each other, a week full of joining our hearts together in new ways, of supporting each other in riding the waves of life rather than being crushed by them."

Often our children want to *see* us go first, to take our place beside them, to hold up our end, to do *our part* of an experience *we're* in together. Opportunities come suddenly in unexpected ways. We can be alert to the possibility of doing things a new way. As we listen to our heart, it tells us what to do.

Raymond's message to himself

"I've been on roller coaster ride in this program, just like my son. I've come to realize that we both have to internalize important changes in our lives. Up to this point I haven't changed – not really. I *thought* I had. But yesterday I received a letter from Greg that really opened my eyes. This kid has opened his heart to me. He says that he needs to move on in his life. He's grown weary of the life he's been leading. I think he's being honest. I see him facing himself and his family. Everything he wrote brought tears to my eyes.

"Then I think I *opened* my eyes. Soon Greg will be home again. I haven't changed that much. What have I been doing all this time? Well, I've continued to try to change others. But I've ignored myself. Oh, I talk a good talk, but I don't think I've really taken to heart what I've learned. Now it's a year later. The other day I got out something I wrote about myself as I began this process. Yup. I hadn't changed like I thought. So I decided, 'OK, that was my choice. Today I'm going to make a *new* choice. I'm going to get busy on *me*.' Even through all the ups and downs, Greg's been working. Now it's my turn."

173

Excerpt from Melissa's letter to a friend

"I can see that you are struggling and fighting off feeling rotten. I was recently feeling bad and felt this terrible pressure to 'get with it' or 'shape up.' I began to have a recurring dream. It helped me get through the rough passage. I hope that it will help you.

"In the dream I was in a doctor's office. I had just been given a bone scan and the doctor was showing me the pictures. He pulled out a chart, which was like a clock except instead of containing numbers indicating time, there were different categories of images. Each image had a person in a different position. The doctor spun the hands of the dial and it landed on a person bent over, tired and worn out. He said, 'This is just where you are now. You will at some point in your life be at each different stage on the chart. No need to fight it. Everything passes.' It was simple but it sure helped me. Best wishes."

Mary Beth and Jonathan's phone conversation

"Mom, I've created a shitty environment here. I want to transfer to another facility."

"No, Jonathan. You take that shit and deal with it."

A little while later ....

"Mom, I've decided. I'm changing my shit to *fertilizer!*"

❖

The view from behind the chain link fence

One day I watched as a bridge builder in his mid-forties raised his large, thick, and rather rigid body from among a small crowd to reveal himself for the first time.

"You know, this whole experience hasn't really seemed to affect me. We've talked a lot about images. I say my image is strong. I *like* who I am. I've always liked who I am. I like being a strong man. No one can get to me! No one has *ever* been able to get through to me! *No one!* ... Except suddenly it just hit me: I can't *feel* ... And I'm beginning to see that maybe I'm missing out on something in my life. I don't feel any emotions when I'm around people ... even the members of my family."

174

Looking down as he spoke, the giant teddy bear inside of him protected and hidden by his hard exterior, he paused a moment before continuing. His voice lowered and his tense body softened almost imperceptibly.

"I don't kiss anyone. That's ... not who I am ... except that ... last night I hugged my wife for the first time. ... Ever."

An isolated man's revelation of a lifetime of self-imposed solitary confinement was slow in its expression. He continued his soliloquy slowly, tentatively, this act of revealing himself so completely new.

"I've had walls around myself ... and ... they're fifteen feet high. Now ... I've got a chain link fence where the walls once stood. I can *see* through it. ... I can *see* what I've been missing. I can *see* what others want of me. ... I can *see* my family ... over there on the other side. And to be completely honest, I guess I need to say I'm not sure if I'll ever do more than look. But at least now I know what I'll never have unless I do something to change."

This "strong" man knows exactly what the score is. I think what a privilege it is to be present when the armor cracks – even if only a little. What will he do with this experience? How will this drama unfold? Will he remain imprisoned behind his imagined fence? Or will he come out to play in the playground of the living just beyond his reach?

The lamb

A professional woman told a touching story about a little girl who once had a lamb, her constant companion after satisfying the daily obligations of school and homework. One day her father inexplicably took away her lamb. She never saw it again. Along with the lamb went a young girl's heart.

The young girl grew to become a woman. And she became a cognitive psychologist, devoting her life completely to the mind, shaping a mental model of herself and the world she lived in. She fashioned a world without much room for heart – a neat, antiseptic world of reason and research, models and data. She had an inexhaustible capacity to absorb knowledge and spent her days and nights in the cloistered rooms of her mind.

There was only one small crack in the walls containing her world. It was suspended on a wall in her home – the photograph of a little shepherd girl and her small gray lamb.

"Somewhere way back I've lost contact with that beautiful little girl ... completely," this mother of a teen in the Program said quietly one afternoon. "Except that just the other day – I don't even know why, I didn't really plan it – I went out and bought some lambs of my own. And I realized that I've had that picture hanging on my wall all these years. Now I realize why I bought those sheep."

Suddenly, passionately, and in a waterfall of tears this woman of science found her heart again and gave it back to the little girl still alive within her, waiting for permission to live again.

❖

Just back from Viet Nam

One morning a man in his early fifties rose from his solitude to speak softly. The toll of the Vietnam War revealed itself completely in gray hair, posture, and lines of sorrow written across a war-torn face.

"Ever since Vietnam, I've been holding onto my anger and all that I've been through. I've been holding onto it now for thirty years. It has affected my family, my career, everything. Well, last night I said my last "f— y—'s" to the government and the US Army. And I forgave them for everything, I mean for *everything* – for the deceit, for the betrayal, for all my buddies who died in a meaningless war. And I left it behind me forever. I'm not going to be thinking about Vietnam anymore. I'm through with it. I'm leaving it all behind. It's time to get on with my life!"

Are we in charge of our past? Or is our past in charge of us? When our past is in charge of us, we lose our present moments in this world. We cut ourselves off from the living day – a day that might have been spent holding a child or embracing a mate. If we live in the past, its business seems never finished with us. It sponges up the available fluid of our lives, leaving behind a dry and lifeless field, whereupon we stand as we rail against injustices, old hurts, and wounds that last until we are gone.

And when living in the past affects our relationships, we render those who stand at our side into ghosts of remembered wrongs and injustices. We blame a child who seeks our guidance for all that he has done to injure us. We deny our present possibility to the one who looks now into our eyes, searching and wondering. And if we so choose, we live out our remaining days in complete anger with the past, blaming it for today, mindless that with each passing day the sun dawns upon a new field of choice. For the past has *no* control but what we give it. And our living in the past *is* but living in an imagined world that does not exist. Unless we take control over our past, we will never respond freely and in present time to our families. And that choice will cost us dearly.

Anticipation

When a child is away, most parents and family members begin to wonder what it will be like when the family is back together again. Who will be different? Will we have the strength to remain together?

A man expecting his daughter home soon passionately shared the following one day:

> "I used to think that Maggie is in the Program getting ready to come home, that she's working every day to prepare herself for that moment when she gets off the plane and we start our new lives again with each other. But she's not! She's there learning to live *this day* fully and completely! And tomorrow she will learn to live *that* day, hopefully aligned with her inner purpose, her eseence, not according to some set of external factors.

> "And me? I need to do the same thing: To look at this day and what I must do today to achieve my highest potential. It's not about tomorrow or yesterday: It's about *now* and how I'm using the time available to me."

The clinging vine

Melissa was very skeptical of the seminar process. She approached it very cautiously. However, the Discovery seminar helped her realize how much she had played victim in her life. As she reviewed past decisions, it became clear that she had shortchanged herself in important ways.

Early as a mother, she had determined that she would not let Paul shortchange his life as she had. He became her focus. And once Paul arrived in Paradise Cove, he remained her focus. Melissa was a constant expression of worry, doubt, and concern. She focused on the conditions of the facility and her fears about brainwashing. One day a friend told her that she saw Melissa attempting to control Paul's experience. Melissa reacted.

> I was really mad. I went out for a walk. I noticed as I was walking in a wooded area that a tangle of vines was entwined around the branches of a tree. As I looked closely at it, I saw the tree and the vine as a metaphor. Is this enabling, clutching, controlling love – which is only going to choke the tree and eventually kill it – is this what I've been doing? I came back and determined to work on this aspect of myself.

> It took me a long time to change. Discovery seminar shifted my outlook and helped me get out from beneath a dark cloud. The dark cloud was me suppressing me. The dark cloud was keeping myself in the dark, not knowing how to get out, not knowing that I could look at something differently.

Part of the cloud was my playing a victim. I did it for years. I dutifully took care of my Alzheimer's mother but I had this incredible anger and bitterness inside of me because of it. I had the same emotions towards my marriage. And now Paul. Now that I was aware of these things I did not know how to step out of them. I began a Twelve Step program, and when I took the first step it was like stepping off the edge of a cliff, like sending my son to Samoa, and like the only step I really could take! After Discovery I realized that I didn't have to be the victimized, dutiful daughter any more. I could *live* my life. I could arrange things. I had the opportunity. My mother had money and so I could arrange things, so that I no longer needed to feel victim. I could actually *have a life!* And so I began to have one. And it helped immensely!

I also saw that I have a kind of innate power. But the issue with this power is that most of the time it is used in a manipulative way to gain for oneself. I learned how I took this negative kind of power into my life. I too had used it to gain and to manipulate others. I decided to stop it. Not to misuse power really humbled me. I think Paul also shares this power. Like me, he is learning what to do with his power. It's a common thread that we all had in my family. We're all extreme individuals who misused our power, using it to manipulate each other. I saw how important this was.

As Melissa intensified her transformation, her fear of group processes receded. She realized that no one was telling her who to be. But she waited an entire year to attend the next seminar Focus. I knew her well during this period. She was changing. Sometimes she called me and we had long talks. In her own time this intelligent, cautious woman came out from beneath the cloud of her own creation to enjoy the warmth of sunlight, equally hers.

The most important thing I got out of the Focus seminar is that there are actually things I cannot do alone. I realized that I actually do need and want the help and love of other people. That was a really *huge* thing for me. It was not easy for me to learn. I made it really tough on myself. Even though I'd gone to ToughLove, worked the Twelve Steps, seen a therapist, and put my son in the Program – all those things were like I had no choice, like the alien who just enters your chest and has a life of its own! And of course, unconsciously I must have had some awareness of my need for others but in Focus I became really *aware* of it and raised it to a level of consciousness.

There came a point in the seminar when I just gave up. I felt so defeated. I felt like I couldn't push through to the other side. But I felt the group pulling for me – the *entire group!* Now *that* was an awesome experience – to have twenty-eight people care *so much* for me to succeed and get to the other side of my own river. I felt that I was part of them and that they were part of me. And that experience of being part of a group with such intensity – it is something I have wanted very much in my life, in my family growing up, and in my own family with my children. I've had only glimpses of it in my life. My lifelong fear of groups, which came from my sense of never fitting in, from my never completing school, and from never working out right for people – I always had this big hurdle, this big fear of groups.

So this seminar was the opposite experience. It was like I came back around and realized how important people are to me. Since my husband left, I felt like I was fighting all by myself. I got really heavy into an I'm-strong-and-can-do-everything mode. That was like a necessary step to take. But I was also becoming the kind of robot that I didn't want my son to be. So the Focus seminar breathed human life and soul back into me. It made me very vulnerable.

It's been a long haul for me – to learn how to be strong, to use power only in a positive manner, to be vulnerable and open, all at the same time. Those are the elements that I have to piece together in my life and somehow balance.

The biggest thing I feel lately is that I'm in awe of my son. He's been at Paradise Cove now for over thirteen months. He's taken the hardest possible road not only in his life but in the Program, since he's been dropped back to Level One twice. But I have to say this for him: He has never given up. Not even once. He's never said, "I give up." I've had to have various reassurances along the way that things are OK – for example, the brainwashing thing. And I've asked myself many times, "Is this working for Paul?" But the biggest encouragement for me has really come from my son because he's never given up. So he's given *me* courage not to give up! It's kind of like a feeding frenzy – the two of us feeding off each other. So I just keep supporting him. That's my role: Not to get in the way, but just be here, write to him, talk to him on the phone, and say, "I know you can do it … I know you can do it."

Island reflection

As I talk with a boy in the shade of a palm tree at Paradise Cove, I occasionally look away at the white foam of the turbid surf. Its ceaseless waves cause me to think of patterns and repetition. How long it has taken to shape the character of this beautiful beach, how many poundings of surf to break up island rock into sun-bleached sand?

So are lives shaped. It is said that by the time we are five years old we have heard the word "no," or words associated with our limitations, an average of forty-five thousand times, and the word "yes," or words associated with our possibility, an average of fifteen thousand times. The relentless pounding of our environment greatly affects our lives.

What effort it takes, therefore, to change is not only an effort on the part of these boys, but a complementary effort on the part of the folks back home. I think too about my own life. Like changing the landscape of the beach, changing my life and my way of thinking, requires focus, time, repetition, and consistency. It requires a total commitment, a constancy like the sea.

REUNION

As the winter of 1996 approached, it appeared that Jacob was moving so quickly through the Program that he might be recommended home soon. To be recommended home in time to be home with us for Christmas had been Jacob's goal since his arrival on the island. But late November arrived and he was not on the recommended list.

> "My goal was to be home by Christmas because my birthday is January first and I wanted to be home for Christmas and my birthday because Christmas with my family the year before had been awful. So I wanted to mend that, right there, and I thought I was ready – not thought, I *knew* I was ready to go home. I knew I was ready for the next step. I'd done the deal in Samoa. So I knew I was ready and when everybody else told me I wasn't, I said, 'Well, you're *wrong.*' Everything that I had inside of me said, 'OK, I know I'm ready.' I was taught to go with what spoke to me inside, so I went with it. I wanted to graduate the Program really bad. So at a certain point, I had a phone call with mom and she basically said, 'You're not getting recommended out of the Program in time to be home for Christmas.'"

He tearfully acknowledged that he would miss spending Christmas and his eighteenth birthday together with us. He blamed the staff for not recognizing that he was ready. He said that he had always thought that surely mom and dad would bring him home by Christmas! But completing the work of rebuilding his life was more important, he said. He was sobered by the reality that he would be given nothing he had not earned. Soon he realized that it was not the staff who were holding him back, but himself. He faced the inevitable, and decided to enjoy the Christmas celebration being planned at Paradise Cove. Sandy and I believed that there was a reason he would not be home.

One night I dreamed that I greeted Jacob at the airport. I saw every detail of his face – his complexion, the fine lines of his hair, the details of his smile. He was a young man now – healthy, happy, and playful.

The distance of several months left it difficult to visualize his face. And of course I hadn't seen his face for several months before he left, hiding as he was behind his extraordinary hair! Yet in this dream I could see him so clearly. My dream assured me that I was now able to see my son more clearly as a person than in the past. It also revealed that I was now able to see clearly those aspects of him that were taking firm root within us both – i.e., a more playful, happy, and optimistic spirit.

A couple of days later a completely unexpected event occurred. Jacob's counselor, Sonja, abruptly told us that she would like us to explain to Jacob that he had three options available to him: (1) He could come home in time for Christmas and resume living with us, or do whatever the three of us worked out together. (2) He could remain on the island for a couple more months of additional work and return home when we were all ready. (3) He could participate in a new transition program during which he would live for a while with a family in Utah with planned week-long home visits.

Sandy and I registered our surprise. "Why is this happening? We thought Jacob would not be recommended home until later."

Sonja reported that Jacob's handling of rejection had shown that he was ready to advance to the next stage. Given he would soon turn eighteen, Sonja suggested that we let him choose what he would do.

After talking the matter over together, Sandy and I decided that Jacob's decision would tell us a lot about where he was at. So we called him and explained to an initially disbelieving young man his options and asked him to choose.

> "I had just accepted it and said, 'OK' to myself. On our next phone call home I came to the phone ready to tell you guys how I was stoked about staying and not coming home, because I felt there was some reason why I was staying be- hind, and I wanted to tell you that I was happy to be here for Christmas. There was going to be a great party and I was going to enjoy it. And then you guys said, 'You're coming home.' And I said, 'I *knew* I was ready!' But I could not believe it when you told me on the phone. I was *really* happy about it!"

Once he understood that he had a real choice of three options and that it was *his* decision, he said unhesitatingly, "Oh, no question. I'll go into the transition program. I can learn a lot from it." We were very excited about our son's choice because it indicated how much he had matured. At eight- een he was free to do whatever he wished. But none of us was ready for a full resumption of family life and he was not ready to come home. Time in the transition program (in a newly-opening facility called Spring Creek Lodge in Montana) with a couple of visits home was the best decision. It would help him internalize all the changes he had been making. Most im- portantly, Jacob had made the decision himself!

On December 23rd a Christmas celebration was held at Paradise Cove. Ja- cob and a few other boys were leaving that afternoon. One of them was a good friend of his, Joshua, whose parents lived near us in the Bay Area. Sandy and I had become very close to them. Jacob played his harmonica to say goodbye to the friends he would leave behind. Before the celebration was over, he and the others leaving were driven to the airport.

Christmas Eve arrived. Sandy and I rose early in the morning to get a jump on the day. I finished picture albums we would give to the boys for Christmas while Sandy bought groceries. Around mid-day Jacob called from the Honolulu Airport. He said he was out of money and wondered if we could wire him some. "No," I said. "It's December 24th and there is no likely way I could get you any money. Besides, I don't think you need any." I was curious to see how my impulsive kid would react. And he seemed completely OK with it. He acknowledged that he had spent the little money he had on trivialities and said that being without money is the consequence for not hanging onto it! I wished him Godspeed as we hung up.

That afternoon Sandy and I greeted MacLean at the airport, home for the holidays. We would be a family together this Christmas. He was looking forward to seeing his brother, wondering if anything would be different.

Sandy and I cleaned a house messy from holiday preparation. Ever the helper, MacLean assisted.

At last it came time to leave for Jacob's arrival at San Francisco International Airport on an evening flight. We arrived early and I paced about nervously while Sandy sat staring quietly in a chair. MacLean videotaped us and laughed at the different ways we handled the situation. After a few minutes a voice announced firmly over the speaker: "Flight 12 from Honolulu has arrived at the passenger gate."

I saw Joshua's parents Shirley and James walking slowly way down the concourse and jumped up and down waving at them to hurry up – this flight was arriving early! All attention focused towards the ramp from which Jacob and Joshua would emerge. After waiting for what seemed a *long* "deplane-ing," I spotted Jacob and yelled to the others. Within moments two strong boys, tanned and very healthy looking, were running up to us! Jacob reached his mother first and gave her a big, big, big hug. They were both sobbing. Then came my turn. I hugged my boy very tightly and he returned the hug with more physical strength than I had ever felt from him before. He wasn't a boy any longer. Together we shuddered from crying and holding each other again. Jacob and MacLean hugged; Jacob thanked him for coming. Then came time for introductions between families. It was nice to meet Joshua and for Jacob to meet Joshua's parents. We would see them again in a few days in the Parent/Child I seminar and Joshua and Jacob would spend the next couple of months together in transition at Spring Creek Lodge, a new facility in Montana. All of that was to come in a flurry of activity ahead.

Now came the time to return to our homes and begin the process of learning to live as families again. The drive home was filled with Jacob's excited observations about how very little had changed on the freeway and in our hometown. The rest of the evening was filled with stories of life in Paradise Cove, told in his usual animated way, with lively descriptions of people, events, and Program lore. We made a special effort to draw MacLean into the conversations. He was important to us.

Same yet different

What a contrast Jacob was to only ten months before! He was a blend of the strange yet familiar. He had retrieved all the wonderful qualities we knew in him as a young kid – joy, spontaneity, humor, politeness, ebullience, and natural charisma. He was a powerful magnet that attracted a desire to be around him. Yet he was sincere and passionate. I liked this young man very much.

Jacob seemed to have more purpose and maturity. He was able to sit still and be quiet. He seemed genuinely interested in the rest of us. He had passionate beliefs and strength. He told wonderful stories about the Samoan people. In fact, he could not stop talking about the Samoans and what an impact they had on him. He spoke volubly about their relative simplicity and family orientation, about conversations with Samoan "fathers."

Jacob was a far more experienced young man than the kid who had left months before. As I listened I realized how much responsibility he had been given as a leader of others his age. It had matured him. He was much more sure of himself. I remembered decades ago seeing my older brother leave for the Army and two years later return home a man. Jacob had been similarly strengthened.

But much about my son challenged standard cultural definitions of "strong man." For example, strong men in our culture usually don't reveal themselves. In contrast, my son was *very open* with his affection and emotions. Mom and Dad received hugs and kisses whenever they wanted them – and they wanted them a lot! But I could tell how much Jacob wanted our affection for himself. I experienced the energy coming from his *inside* and it was real. He seemed *secure* enough to reveal himself.

We talked long into the night. At one point he spoke about his "higher power." Each night he went to bed thinking about this power and praying. He seemed clearly connected with some spiritual energy. Although I did not know much about what this meant to him yet, I desired to understand more about this new dimension within him.

He seemed like an entirely new person in my life. "I don't think I've ever really known this person," I thought to myself. "I'm eager to know him."

Jacob was still the same hyperactive, wild, outrageous individual he had always been, moving about physically, laughing a lot, talking in a kind of wild dialog. He simply had a lot of energy. He had always been verbally quicker than I and I found myself still struggling to keep pace with the rapid flow of his conversation. But hey! We were *talking together!*

Bedtime arrived. Jacob went into his old room, MacLean into his. I felt at peace having our two sons going to their rooms with no rancor and hard feelings in the house. As I lay in bed I thought back over the evening. All indications were that Jacob had returned respectful of our home and of us. Healing tears of joy had been shed that night. A better Christmas present I have never known than to have our two sons at home and at peace. Sleep came quickly.

❖

Gifts without price

The next day we opened a few small presents together. We had told the boys that the main present this Christmas would be being together. A lot of money had gone for tuition for MacLean's last terms in college and Jacob's journey to a tropical island. Sandy and I gave each boy four photo albums packed with pictures telling their life stories. The pictures brought back old, good memories. We each lit a candle and said what we were thankful for. Everyone expressed gratitude for family.

One of the greatest blessings was to see our two sons hug and play. They were young men now, but the young men were still boys. They played with a Nerf Air Pressure SuperMaxx 3000 plastic gun that MacLean had given Jacob. Soon Nerf bullets were flying everywhere – no one was safe! There was a lot of noise and laughter in the house. I became my usual obnoxious self and it wasn't too long before the boys wrestled me down and tickled me until I screamed for mercy. A passing observer could never have guessed our struggles of the past.

But later that day MacLean took me aside. "You know, I don't want you to be set up for a fall. I'm concerned about you and Mom. Jacob has not changed at all," he declared. He saw in his younger brother that old, reckless nature – that natural wildness. Yes, it was still there! I listened carefully to MacLean and considered what he said before answering.

"Well Mac, I hope Jake will always be Jake. I wouldn't really want him any different. And he won't be perfect – that's for sure. I hope he'll live his life

185

according to the dictates of his heart, that's all. He has so much possibility –
like you, only different. If he can be true to himself and live the life I believe that he wants to live deep inside, then he'll have a good life. His life
will not be like your life necessarily, Mac, but I hope it'll be a good life on
his terms. The kid I see here with us now has that capacity and I hope you'll
be open to that possibility in him. He needs that from you. This isn't going
to be an easy time for him or any of us. It could be that he'll choose to slip
back into his old ways. Meanwhile, let's choose to see the Jacob who truly is
and give him a chance to be our beloved Jacob again."

I thought of the story of the Prodigal Son. Here was my older son before
me. Perhaps he could not remember his own darkness only a few short
years ago. From his perspective he had done everything right. And who
could argue? He had largely pulled himself out of a deep childhood depression. Not only had he completed college, he had finished a four-year degree
program in only twenty-three months! At the same time he had managed to
be editor of the college newspaper. Now he was earning good money in an
established career. He shunned all substances. When he visited home, he
took on projects to help out around the house. MacLean was the model
young man they might teach you to produce in Parenting 101! Perhaps in
the process of growing up, he had lost memory of that sad, suicidal, and
hateful youngster he had been in younger years. At some point he had chosen a different path, a wonderful path. Perhaps he did not now understand
that there is a darker side that casts its shadow over all our lives, that no one
is a source only of light. And now perhaps he could not understand our
celebration of delight in our new-found son. I sought to say, in the best
modern language I could find, the equivalent of these concluding words of
the father in the Prodigal Son story …

Son, thou art ever with me, and all that I have is thine.

*It was meet that we should make merry, and be glad: for this thy brother was dead, and
is alive again; and was lost, and is found.*

Luke 15:31-32

Suddenly I had great compassion for my sons. In their lifetimes, they will
suffer from judging and being judged in return. We create the world we
choose to see. When MacLean begins to believe in his brother again, I
thought to myself, he will find a new brother there waiting to be believed
in. Jacob might choose to slip back into his old ways. But with open eyes
we can choose to see without blinders the real Jacob who truly is and always
can be – the young man living again in these familiar rooms, happy, loving,
at peace for once in his life – and hold him to that possibility.

Many gifts were given and received on this traditional day of celebrating new birth. But the greatest gifts were those without price. My heart was full.

As for Jacob everything invoked memories of how life used to be. Old surroundings brought back old hurts. He walked by my open wallet on my bedside table, a reminder of money for the taking. Later on, a walk past an empty field reminded him that he and a friend accidentally had set it on fire while doing drugs. Hard, unpleasant reminders of a not too distant and very painful past. Hard on everyone. As he revealed his emotions towards those old times, I realized that he had been hurting far more than I ever knew. It felt good to be able to let the past fade away by telling it and letting it go.

Continuing journey

Togetherness was too short lived. The following day MacLean headed back to his home in Boise while Sandy, Jacob, and I flew to Las Vegas, then drove to southern Utah for the Parent/Child I seminar.

During the next few days we got to know each other more and more. Jacob was *intense*, that's for sure! He was a young man who had lived in a structured, very intense program, giving and receiving feedback all day, every day – for months. By comparison Sandy and I had lived laid back, relaxed lives free from the pressures and tensions of children. Sure, we had been working hard on our end attending seminars and ToughLove meetings, going to counseling, etc. But the intensity of our lives paled by comparison to the intensity of his. Being around him was being around a loved one overexposed to a large dose of radiation! I *wanted* to be with him; but I wasn't always sure I could take the dosage! I was happy for opportunities *not* to be together! We all needed a healthy break now and then.

However, having long conversations with Jacob on important family and personal topics gave me great peace of mind and hope for our future. We discussed thorny, long-standing family issues. We each received feedback about ourselves in the seminar that we didn't like to hear – like, "Dad, my experience of you is that you're still too tightly wound up." And some that was very *nice* to hear – like, "Dad, I like how it feels when I'm around you. I feel I can tell you anything and you'll understand." The family held up together well; honesty and directness *helped.* We talked with each other openly and with empathy. Each of us could understand and be understood, tell and be heard. Rather than hiding from each other in pain, each of us was reachable – *very* reachable. We began to develop confidence in *us* as listeners and participants. My son and wife are two intelligent, savvy people. Conversations were *interesting.* I looked forward to them. We gave each other high

187

marks for communication as we built our new family structure upon foundation stones of honesty and openness.

After the seminar we headed north to Salt Lake City where we would stay with Susan, Greg, and Ryan – friends we had met in the Program. Jacob and Sandy shopped for clothes with Ryan, now working at a clothing store. Jacob selected clothes that reflected the positive image he wanted to present to the world. He had a realistic understanding that images exist and wanted to create an image for himself that would work best for him. He joked about his old hippie image. The image he now wanted to present to the world was consistent with the congenial young man he is. He portrayed a responsible and attractive young man you might want to hire – or date! He quickly learned that girls liked his natural way of dressing more than his old I've-got-to-make-a-statement look.

Visiting our friends turned out to be a fun but challenging experience. After all that we had been through, it was wonderful to laugh, play, dance, and sing together. We had long conversations over dinner. Ryan had been out of the Program for six months, had earned enough money to buy a used car, and excitedly drove us around in his Mustang. We went to a substance-free New Year's party in Salt Lake featuring salsa dancing. It was so much fun to watch Ryan and Jacob dancing with cute girls their age.

We were having so much fun that we weren't thinking about the ironies. The next day, New Year's Day, Jacob turned eighteen. It would *not* be a day to celebrate his independence. Instead, we would drive him north to Montana to finish his Program. Yet here he was tasting the free life. All the delicious dancing, playing, and cute girls proved to be *far* too tempting a smorgasbord to put before a young man with unfinished business.

That day we celebrated his birthday and shopped for clothes. During a breaking in shopping he announced that he had been thinking it over and had changed his mind about going through internalization. He reviewed what we already knew – that, after agreeing to participate in the transition, the Program had totally changed what it meant by "transition." We had all been told originally that transition would consist of Jacob's living with another family, going to school, doing chores around the house, playing with their children, having family meetings, etc. This would be accompanied by a couple of visits home. He would remain with the transition family until the Program recommended him home. Jacob had agreed to that plan for a transition experience, since the concept of living with a family appealed to him very much. In his mind transition amounted to getting on with his life – a notion which had become very important to him. But the Program's *new* definition of transition consisted of working as a "junior staff member" in a facility just opening up in Montana! While Jacob had originally made his peace with that change, suddenly he wanted out.

Sandy and I responded in unity. "We understand your disappointment. But our agreement was that you would go through at least two months of transition. And you yourself had agreed to that, even after the definition changed." Jacob would not let go. At various times during the day, he brought up a matter we thought settled and kept pushing it. After a while, Sandy called him on his manipulation. It was that old, uncomfortably familiar feeling of being pushed towards an end we did not want, yet being unable to convince him that "no" meant NO. It was complicated by the fact that when a child turns eighteen everything changes – particularly the energy given to the tempting sweetness of independence! Sandy and I became immediately fearful that all we had worked towards could be undone. We were not ready as parents for Jacob's return. We had more work to do on ourselves and our relationship. We wanted a transition period for ourselves. We wanted the safety of home visitation where we could experiment with being together then return to a sanctuary, assess what we'd learned, and maybe lick some wounds. We wanted to take it all more slowly. But Jacob thought he was ready to come home. Right now!

Fortunately, Susan, Greg, and Ryan were on hand to assist us with their wise counsel and experience. I learned in a new way the value of support! Our friends were invaluable in assisting us to get to the next stage. Susan and Ryan told Jacob that they experienced him as manipulating us. Ryan was the most helpful, since he had the benefit of a few months' out in the world. He told Jacob that he wished he himself had gone through some kind of transitional experience because there was too much to assimilate all at once "out here." He helped Jacob look at his own purpose and what he was trying to accomplish at this point in his life. When he said that his purpose was to rebuild his own family, Jacob knew at once that he needed to continue with the original plan.

As parents Sandy and I learned an old lesson in a new way: We are engaged in a journey not a destination. Our son would emerge from the Program not as some completed product we could label, proclaim "finished," show off, and produce as some cookie-cutter model for families in similar circumstances. He would return with issues and challenges. He would have to be strong enough to face them and we would have to be equally strong to face them with him. Together we had faced a test and survived. Sandy and I could have attempted to hide the issue from our friends; instead, we sought their assistance. We were deeply proud of our son and the maturity he showed in realizing that it was in everyone's best interest for him to complete what he had begun.

As we drove north out of Utah and headed for a destination Jacob was not thrilled about, we stopped at a gas station. Without a second thought we left him with a tank to fill, the keys to a rented car, our credit cards, and our luggage as we visited the mini mart. When I returned to the car, I realized what we had done! A year ago we could not have left Jacob alone if we were taking him somewhere he did not want to go! He would have walked off – with a little spare change! Trust means *everything* in a relationship. It would grow from an accumulated evidence of small things.

We stopped in Idaho Falls, Idaho, to visit with my mother and family. Grandma made a beautiful cake for Jacob, "her birthday boy." The next day we continued our trek to Montana. We kept hearing reports about the terrible roads ahead and an ominous snowstorm approaching, but we kept moving forward in our rented sports utility vehicle. Some benevolent force seemed to anticipate our journey and sent warm rains to melt the snow and clear the roads, enabling us to drive up to the remote lodge buildings buried in four to six feet of snow and housing the new facility. I finally spun out as I tried to park at the lodge! We toured a facility still very much under construction, then drove back to town for dinner at Granny's Diner with Jacob and the director Cameron. Then Sandy and I left for home while they drove back to the lodge. As we said goodbye, Jacob seemed excited to be at the new facility and to be part of opening up something new. The resistance was gone – a tribute to his new-found ability to be flexible and open to possibility. We all looked forward to our first home visit soon.

Our first few days together had been fun, exciting, hopeful, nervous, tentative, confidence-building, and challenging. Jacob no longer hid behind a mask. We could see the handsome, friendly face of the real, wonderful person who has always been our beloved son. Still the same kid, he seemed to love being himself now, without the need to live some cartoon-ish pretense of what a human being might be like. Jacob was living on the fuel of his own life purpose and an awakening maturity.

First visit, first challenge

Early in January Jacob flew home for his first home visit, including participation as staff in a parent Discovery seminar held in Los Angeles. Jacob affected many lives with his power. At first, many openly resented him because he expressed his thoughts and feelings with the directness he had been taught in the Program. Many were obviously uncomfortable with this directness, especially if it hit too close to home. I overheard one fellow muttering, "Who is this arrogant kid?!" It takes a lot of *chutzpa* for an eighteen-year-old to stand toe-to-toe on an adult-to-adult, patient, and rational footing with a fifty-year-old man not liking what he's hearing. But Jacob did not waver. Only recently he had stood toe-to-toe with Mr. fifty-year-old's *son* who most likely had Mr. fifty-year-old wound up tight like a pair of knickers left *way* too long in the dry cycle! Suddenly, the tables were turned: Little Johnny received feedback daily; it was time for Johnny's dad to hear a few things. Many parents seemed to come to the seminar thinking, "Yes, I have a kid in the Program – but hey, what have I got to do with that?! I'm here to support my kid. This isn't *about me!* No thanks – everything's just fine with my life." Well, Jacob didn't buy it. (Neither probably did Mr. fifty-year-old's son!) The family is a *system.* When the system breaks, *all* the parts to the system are affected. All contributed something to the break.

At one poignant moment in the seminar most of the participants demonstrated such fierce resistance to real honesty in our lives that Jacob broke down sobbing. All of a sudden a room full of a hundred people hushed. Moms and dads leaned forward to listen. What was going on?

"I can tell you right now that I don't *want* to come home if this is what I'm coming home to!" Jacob sobbed. "I'd rather stay in the Program where at least I know there are *some* people willing to be real and tell the truth! I've *had* it! I don't want to be around this anymore!" His breakdown was completely unexpected. He was not staging some kind of entertainment. He really *cared* about an honest, no-bull approach to living. Here was a teen wide open and *real* enough to express his real feelings in a room full of hostile adults. I watched his words penetrate into the vulnerable, soft space of everyone in the room. This could have been *their* son or *their* daughter crying out for a little honesty in a world of pretense and self-deceit.

I had not seen him cry like this – this freely – since he was a small child. And these weren't just a couple of tears: He sobbed for several minutes with the innocence and vulnerability of a small child. Duane, our seminar leader, cradled Jacob in his arms until it was over. I believe that in that moment we were privileged to see what kids *really* want when they put aside the games they've learned to play. *They want the truth from us!* Not the duplicity, pretense, faking, and game-playing we give them all too often in so many different ways, pretending everything is "OK." "Yes, I've got a son whacked out on drugs so bad I had to put him in Samoa – but hey, man, my life is OK. There's nothing I need to change." Suddenly, the seminar transformed from an interesting, albeit irritating, experience to serious engagement. Perhaps for the first time in many lives, people began to talk about themselves with *honesty* instead of BS and to say how they *really* felt about their lives. Individual processes of healing old wounds were kindled. It was a beautiful sight.

After the seminar many told me that they saw in Jacob a power lacking not only in their children but in themselves. How refreshing it was to see a kid so willing to be vulnerable! They singled him out as the one who had assisted them the most.

On the flight home I reflected on how grateful I was to have had this experience with my family. Staffing reinforced our commitment as a family to be involved in a healing process. I also reflected that we were constantly meeting people whom I could learn from and respect. Their experience and knowledge would rub off on us. Ours would rub off on them. We would infect each other with the will to heal. It was good to be part of an infectiously healthy process. I wanted others in my life. I didn't want to go it alone anymore, for that was just a long road to nowhere. I appreciated a strong son, a committed wife, and friends who saw possibility in me and would challenge me if they saw me selling myself short.

We arrived home exhausted. During the remainder of the visit, we recouped and had fun together. We played board games, went to movies, went for walks, and visited friends. We made up for a lot of lost time.

But when Jacob boarded an Alaskan Airlines flight to return to the transition program in Montana, I was full of fear again. My wake-up call had arrived on the way to the airport. If I had been before, I was no longer in illusion that my kid would return some perfect, completely powerful, kid of my dreams.

We had agreed to periodic drug tests as part of the home contract in order to establish Jacob as a drug-free individual in our eyes. Rebuilding trust was a critical family goal. On the way to the airport we dropped by our HMO to administer the first test. As we approached the registration desk, Jacob began to be agitated and say how much he hated being drug tested. "I'm not going to be doing this for long!" he muttered.

I stiffened instantly. "Oh yeah, you *will!*" I said. "For at least six months."

"*Six months?!*" he shot back. He was giving me a *hard time* about this! I thought we had agreed about all of this. In fact, I *knew* we had!

We waited in this uneasy state in the foyer until it was time to go into the bathroom with the specimen cup. We had all stipulated visual verification of the pee test because he used to drop yellow food coloring into warm tap water to give the appearance of submitting urine for test. The HMO testing procedure tested for everything *except the presence of urine!* Months of positive drug test results had been based upon *yellow water!*

Meanwhile, Jacob was reminding me of how "degrading" this was. I was uncomfortable with his attitude.

"So you think this is *not* degrading for me?!" I asked in reaction.

After he finished peeing in the cup, he showed me its contents and in a punk voice of old said, "Here! You want to drink this?!" At that point my emotional registers went wild. "What a smart-assed, disrespectful *punk*!" I kept my words and emotions in check until we got to the car.

Then I let fly. Jacob listened quietly to an explosion lasting several minutes. After my storm blew over, he said, "I can't understand where all this emotion is coming from!" It turns out I had more emotion left! "*What?!* You make the comment to me about drinking your urine, you give me a hard time the *entire* test, and you wonder where *my* emotions are coming from?! You've got to be *kidding!* This is just like you were before – a smart-assed kid trying to make me feel bad for doing something you agreed to do!"

We went back and forth for several moments. There was some real heat in the air. At last, the storm dissipated and we began to talk rationally. Sandy assisted us.

For his part, Jacob was having lots of feelings about the drug test. He felt inside like he *was* trustworthy. *He* knew what his commitment was to himself. Why should he have to satisfy someone else of what he knows inside of himself? He felt degraded having to prove something that he already knew and having to take a drug test under inspection. His punk comment was venting his emotions – just what he'd been taught to do: Vent your emotions so you don't feel like you have to *act* on them. His buddies in the program would understand him immediately, he said.

I told Jacob that I didn't discern any feelings *at all* in his words. All I heard was intimidation and "running his number" on me. He would have to figure out how to express his feelings in a way that I could identify them *as* feelings – because this way wasn't going to work at all for me. Jacob listened calmly and seemed to understand where I was coming from. As we spoke we realized that doing the urine test in the old setting under supervision evoked really unpleasant memories and emotions for both of us. I realized too that Jacob would often have negative emotions about things. He needed a safe place to vent them without my reacting out of my own negative emotion. Would I be a safe person for Jacob to open up to? I certainly wanted to be. However, I needed respect from my son, not an attitude. We agreed that we had a communication problem to work on. We ended up giving each other a long hug and telling each other that we were sorry this had turned out so poorly. But we knew we had a lot to ponder.

I realized how fearful I was of my son and a relapse. In our next scheduled phone call home we all reviewed the incident. Both of us had gone immediately to battle with a back-and-forth exchange of salvos; neither had stepped back to observe the conflict on a more objective footing. It was good to learn together, even though getting there was messy and hurtful.

Second visit, second challenge

The next time we got together, we learned that too much togetherness is not a good thing. We were so excited about being together again that we didn't allow ourselves space to breathe. We needed to learn to *relax into* each other again. Our first priority was to reestablish family cooperation. To-getherness would come naturally as we relaxed and let it evolve.

Old issues came up all the time. Our family would not suddenly transform into the Waltons! We were a real-life family. The difference was that we now seemed to have a better tool set to deal with issues as they arose. Sometimes we didn't use the tools right away. But eventually, we dragged them out and applied them.

One night the phone rang. I was in my home office on the computer, Sandy in the kitchen fixing dinner. Jacob answered the phone. It was the girl across the street – definitely not a friend who would necessarily support Jacob in a drug-free life style. Jacob asked me if he could go see her for ten minutes before dinner. Worn out from spending the whole day with my intense son, I mumbled my consent, totally absorbed in whatever I was doing on the computer. In two or three minutes, Sandy came in to ask me where Jacob was – she needed help with setting the table. I had an immedi-ate, uneasy feeling of being caught at something I didn't exactly want to understand! I feigned, with blank innocence, "Oh, across the street ... he'll be back in ten minutes." Sandy told me she was upset with Jacob because this was a violation of the home contract he had been working on. Exas-perated with talking about but never actually *seeing* a typed home contract always in some perpetual state of revision, I angrily replied, "*What* home contract?!" and retreated to the safety of my computer. When the wanderer returned exactly on time I heard them exchanging words in the kitchen. I laid low, preferring to remain in an unconscious sea of tranquility.

Later, everyone chose to avoid the situation – an old family pattern. Every-one had feelings about the incident, but no one really *said* anything. After I allowed myself to think about the incident and review my involvement, I became depressed. Avoidance was a big deal. I started to ruminate about it. Soon I was talking to myself in an old, depressive soliloquy. "Oh no! We're not good parents! We're not partners! Jacob will just find a way to manipu-late us! He's slipping back! This is all coming unraveled!"

Happily, I recognized the old familiar song of panic and depression. I called Greg who listened with empathy and objectivity. What helps his family in their issues, he said, is simply to ask his son, "Do you acknowledge that you have a broken agreement, yes or no?" Greg helped me recognize that, again, I was reacting out of fear from the past. I shared this conversation with Sandy and we were both able to get back on an emotionally even keel.

As a threesome we reconstructed the scenario: (1) Jacob violated an agreement. (2) Preferring only calm waters, I "went unconscious," giving Jacob permission to do whatever he wanted. Therefore, I was an accomplice in his violation of the agreement. (And by the way, insisting that a home contract didn't exist just because it wasn't typed was my perfect way to feign ignorance!) (3) Sandy saw the situation clearly but lacked the personal confidence and integrity to take us on effectively. She expressed herself to Jacob but did not take a risk with me. Hence, (4) Sandy and I were divided by negative emotions felt toward each other. And, the bottom line: (5) Jacob, who had likewise been unconscious, got off "scott free." This seemed like an uncomfortably familiar scenario.

The result of our review? Jacob and I acknowledged our broken agreement, Sandy took accountability for her powerlessness, and Jacob paid the fine he had stipulated for violating his contract. We all learned something.

As I reviewed my behavior during the second home visit, I saw that at times I was serene and tranquil, but at times I was up-tight, defensive, and paranoid. I began to judge myself very harshly. I let myself believe that Jacob was probably glad to escape from me and get back into the Program. However, I now had a support system and I was more savvy to the games I play with myself. There were several people I could call when I got down. I could create my own small miracles. One night Sandy and I called Susan to talk over all the emotions which had come up. Ryan was there too. Soon all four of us were in conversation.

Susan told me that these kinds of things came up between her and Ryan too. "This is something we're going to have to learn to handle," she said. "However weak or strong when they return, our kids will test us. Parents have to learn to be strong and to hang in there with their kids." Over time things will get better if we both stand firm in our commitment to make this work. Falling into my emotion will *not* help, I realized. Susan stressed the positive and reminded me that we had worked this out by talking it through. Why feel depressed about it? Actually, why not feel *great* about it? Each of us has something to learn and we would have plenty of opportunities to learn ahead of us. We were in a *process*. She recalled my own words in an article I had written. I had expressed everything she was now telling me. As she recounted my words to me, I wondered aloud, "Who is this wise

195

man who wrote these words? Surely, it's not *me*!" We shared a hearty laugh about *that* one! To make matters funnier, Susan herself had slipped up on holding Ryan to an agreement that very day – the same day when she had been thinking about my words!

I realized that there will be trying moments when we fall back into our old ways. The strength of our family would be determined *not* by a studious, planned, iron-willed avoidance of trials. It would be measured by how we handled these trials and their aftermath. Will we succumb to fear and negative emotion? We will learn to communicate? Will we reach out for assistance from others? Will we hurry through each trial, hasten to give it a perfunctory burial, quickly erase its memory, and live in the pretense that everything is OK? Or will we stop to examine each moment and draw from it the lesson it contains? Will we forgive ourselves, pick ourselves up, and move on? Our response to *these* questions will determine our strength, I realized. I also discovered that I (like most of us) already have the wisdom within if I will only consult it.

Ryan spoke next. He shared with us how fearful he had been to return home. He told us how split he was – how comfortable he was in the latter stages of the Program, how much he wanted to get on with his life, yet how fearful he was to take up life with his family again. He stressed the importance that we hold Jacob to his agreements even if he is struggling against them – "because there is where Jacob's greatest comfort will lie."

Then Ryan "pulled me aside" and we talked privately. He said that each kid has a primary struggle with one of the parents – a long-standing encounter that continues after homecoming. His was with his mother. There were times he hated her. They would blow up in anger. Now they hung in there with each other.

"Now she's my best friend," Ryan said. "We're so close. I love her more than anyone. Tim, I know you guys pretty well now. I know what part each of you plays in your family. The primary conflict in your family is between you and Jacob. You are both powerful leaders and your big egos are going to clash. You've got to hang in there with Jacob and be there for him." He urged me to make a pact with Jacob to hang in there with each other forever, no matter what. He said that he knew we would succeed because of the kind of people we are. Comforting, hopeful words.

The next morning I realized how severely I had been judging myself. I still felt like a "bad father." I didn't *have* to feel that way!

After all was said and done we pronounced the home visit a success precisely *because* these issues came up and we were learning to deal with them. We weren't hiding out, pretending everything was tranquil and perfect. We were becoming stronger as we faced ourselves. These incidents were like being in a boat in the middle of deep water. Occasionally, someone would rock the boat really hard. We wondered if we would stay afloat. But we were gathering confidence. As we worked through problems, we refused to give them meaning. Instead we worked them as problems to be solved, nothing more. We refused to be drawn back into a vortex of old fears and anger. We began to calm down. After all, one loose thread doesn't mean the whole cloth is coming unraveled. Better to live in present tense and take care of the one loose thread!

Parent/Child seminars

While the earlier seminars we attended focused on our own lives, the Parent/Child seminars emphasized rebuilding the family as a unit, with an emphasis on home preparation and specific skill development.

We all worked hard to come up with statements of family purpose and values. We worked further on Jacob's home contract, his binding agreement between himself and us. We assisted with comments, suggestions, and declaring what we could and couldn't support – which led to contract changes. For the most part we worked easily and productively.

We quickly agreed on a statement of our family purpose: *We are a fun, loving family with constant growth, integrity, and awareness.* It felt good and complete to have a written statement of what we were about. If we lived that purpose, we would create positive results as a family.

It was only a little more work to come up with family values – i.e., the values we would keep and honor together during our remainder of time together. The spirit of cooperation and enthusiasm for undertaking this project were great. We seemed to enjoy thinking about what we value. The values applying equally to all three of us are:

1. Unconditional love.
2. Integrity, honesty, and self-disclosure.
3. Respect for people and property.
4. Striving for greatness.
5. Substance-free (drugs, alcohol, and tobacco).
6. Cooperation first, togetherness second.
7. We do not abuse or act judgmentally towards each other.
8. Family activities are vital to the family.
9. Feedback is valuable to the health of individual family members.

Many families struggled as issues came up in the first Parent/Child seminar. One Level Four boy, whose parents were bringing him home early, never looked at anyone directly when he spoke, which was only when spoken to. He joined in the general horseplay that enthusiastically accompanies any crowd of excited teens, but never shared anything about how he was feeling. After observing him a couple of days, the seminar leader, with a lot of compassion and heart, openly challenged the parents to leave their son in the Program a while longer.

"I can tell you right now he is not ready. He is weak; he has not internalized yet all he has to internalize to be successful at home," he said.

The parents seemed divided – the mom very emotional, the dad inexpressive and controlled. Only an occasional irritation with his wife broke the unrevealing blankness of his face. She spoke a lot about her fears of her son coming home. She liked what the Program had done for her son and herself. But dad had said, "Enough is enough." A compromise had been reached before they ever arrived: The boy would go home.

In another Parent/Child seminar, Margaret and Art were delighted to meet their Level Three son, Nathan, whom they had decided to bring him home after several months at Paradise Cove. His letters indicated so much improvement! But when they saw their son next to upper-level boys being recommended home, they saw their choice more clearly. The other boys were open, confident, and more independent. By contrast, Nathan seemed still to lack confidence (one of the reasons they enrolled him the program in the first place). They had difficulty getting agreement on home contract issues they felt strongly about. And Nathan did not seem ready to express how he was feeling to his parents like the other boys. They wondered, "Just how much is cooped up inside him? If we can't access how he feels here, how will we *ever* access it back home?" Art and Margaret decided that Nathan wasn't ready. They also wondered whether they were strong enough as parents yet, given their earlier decision. They decided that day to re-enroll Nathan. The next day an escort service arrived at the seminar and, before several on-lookers, transported a reluctant Nathan back to Paradise Cove. This decision proved to be a great one for the family. Nathan lasted another full year in the Program. A much stronger young man was reunited with much stronger parents.

It was through lessons like these that I learned not to underestimate the challenge of reuniting a family once broken. Even with a family focus, personal issues came up with me all the time – issues that would have a direct bearing on my family relationships. At one point during a Parent/Child seminar, we had an opportunity to learn and practice a technique invented by John Bradshaw for working with emotions when they arise between people. The technique allows you to express what you see or hear in a given situation, how you interpret that information, how you feel as a result, what you want, and what you learn from the experience. We were instructed to practice this technique with our family. I used the opportunity to work through an issue with Sandy I felt emotional about. I expressed it something like this:

"Sandy, whenever I want to give you feedback about something, you seem to roll your eyes or turn away from me as I talk. I interpret that as an unwillingness to receive feedback from me. As a result, I feel hurt and blocked from a relationship with you. What I want is for you to ...."

I stopped myself mid-sentence! No sooner had I blurted out the phrase, "what I want is for you to ..." than I realized where I was taking this. The process was supposed to be focused on *me* and what *I* want or learned. But I was turning it into an opportunity to tell Sandy how *she* has to change. "How *dare* I try to tell her how to be!" The beast of my old desire to change others and not myself had risen again from under the bridge where it lived. I was using an exercise designed to express and understand my own feelings as a means to attack the woman I love. I realized on a wholly new level how challenging it is to keep the focus inward where true change is possible. How tempting it is to externalize! How easy to avoid looking at myself in order to point the finger of judgment at another! I gathered myself together, looked at Sandy again, and let my heart do the talking:

"Let me back up. Sandy, what I *really* want for my life is to have your trust and to have it because I *deserve* it. What I want for my life is to be completely intimate with you, to share everything with you, and for us to share everything with each other. What I *really* want for myself is to be completely harmless so that I will never hurt you and so that you'll feel safe when we talk together."

There ... that felt a *lot* better! I really *felt* the words as I spoke them. I was recognizing what I want for myself, rather than making Sandy once again the reason why things aren't quite right for me. It seemed to feel a whole lot better to Sandy, too!

I don't think I'm much different than most of us. When we are at our best we are sharing our *inside* with each other. When we are at our worst, we are telling others how to live their lives or saying it's not OK to think a certain thought. "If I continue to 'run my number' on Sandy, I'll run it everywhere else, that's for sure!" I thought. I began to understand at newer and deeper levels how anything that upsets me has its source *within me*. When someone "pushes my button," he does *not* cause anything in me to occur! He only provides an occasion for my response. How I respond reveals nothing about the other person – but everything about me.

199

We each choose a reference point, a vantage point from which we view everything that happens to us. The reference point can be either *outside* or *inside* us. When I feel angry or blameful, do I look *outside* for the cause, for whom to blame? Or do I look *inside* to see why I am so upset? Do I look at the button pusher or the button being pushed? I began to practice this idea as a simple, moment-by-moment choice. I had complete control over my choices. When I lived by it, this way of thinking was *empowering*.

I worked hard and focused on healing. I worked with such tools as the Bradshaw technique and developed my own simple ways of looking at things – like the button and button pusher. *It helped to think on my own and create a process that worked for me.* The effort began to add up for my life.

Throughout this journey, I learned from lessons like these. I was glad for all the time we had apart – a son, a mother, and a father learning about ourselves so that we would be stronger for each other. As we allowed ourselves to be ruled by the emerging quality of our lives, not by time, increasingly over time we began to feel ready to be together again full time.

In my room

In a dream I stand at the threshold of an old house. I am struck that it seems both foreign and familiar. A friendly sign reading "Welcome Home" hangs over the front door that has been left slightly ajar. I put out my hand to push open the door and, through the narrow opening, feel the warm air within.

As I pass into the interior space, I feel both a stranger and at home. A fire surrounded by a large hearth reminds me of a distant, unplaced memory. Was I here a long time before? Or just a few moments ago?

I tour the house, passing several rooms with open doors. I am looking for something. But at the end of a hallway is the room I am drawn to enter. It pulls me, although I realize that I could easily resist and go somewhere else. But I want to visit this room. As I enter it, I realize that it is my bedroom. I look around. Yes, this is my bed. And these are my clothes hanging in the closet. This is indeed my room.

As I look about, I notice that a small card has been placed on a small table beside my bed. This being my room, I believe that the note was left for me. I open it and read: "Room restored to its original condition."

New Beginnings

We returned home with a mission: Healing the family was our priority during at least the first four months of Jacob's return. As part of his contract we had mutually agreed that he would spend that time primarily reintegrating into the family. Girls and friendships would wait. I was concerned whether my lover son would stick to this agreement. After all, nothing prevented his choosing to thumb his nose at the whole family healing business.

I was pleasantly surprised! Jacob signified his true intention to reunite with us and to adhere to much of his contract.

We had some real quality time together. We went frequently to movies and dinner. I spent time listening to him play his guitar. Often I came home from work, went into his bedroom, and sat down for a chat. This was more like it! This is what I had always imagined being a father could be!

We had to learn not to smother each other by trying to be together all the time. Finding a good balance between being together and having our private time felt healthy. We took time to work on issues as they arose. Jacob was available and didn't have strong outside preoccupations. After a while, things sort of evened out in terms of time spent together, time spent apart, and emotional energy expended.

When I saw that Jacob intended to stick to his agreement not to date, it helped me as a parent to replace the trust that had been lost. I trusted not only that he would keep his word but that his relationship to me and his mom was the most important thing to him.

Of course, we had unpleasant moments when something would come up and we would end up giving each other feedback. But these always ended being positive, constructive moments. We worked through those moments and achieved a sense of resolution and solidarity. Openness and honesty lived, and along with it a growing trust!

I began to experience Jacob as a completely honest kid – someone who would tell the truth even if it cost him. And because he was abiding by his contract and we were actively monitoring his contract, he created very few situations where lying was a temptation. At first, we monitored him more often. As he proved himself trustworthy, we relaxed.

This time together was a little bit like three people learning to dance with each other. No partner could dance faster than the other partners could follow. Each had to take into consideration the other and dance as fast or slow as the other needed at the moment. To make this dance successful everyone had to finish. But when one of us faltered, the others helped out. To stay focused in the dance, no one had time to worry about our failure to dance in the past or a possible failure to dance tomorrow. Dancing required movement in present tense.

One of Jacob's top priorities on arriving home had been to get a job. His second priority was his education. He also wanted to join NA, do a Twelve-Step program, and get a sponsor. He soon got a job at a grocery store. It was good to see him get busy with his life right away and I enjoyed spending a few moments together each morning before we went off to work.

It was difficult for Sandy and me to realize, though, that Jacob was not really serious about completing his education. We both earned graduate level degrees. Education is important to us! We had to accept, however, that at this point in his life education was not important to our son. At first we fussed and gave ultimatums that had little effect other than to create distance. Sure, he would *go* to a class but he would have little heart in it. Finally, we decided to turn the problem entirely over to him. "It's your life. You'll decide what's best. When and if you're ready for an education, you'll get one."

"However," we continued, "our decision not to charge you rent when you got home was based on an assumption that you would complete your education. Now that you've decided not to finish school, you can pay us rent." He readily agreed.

After attending NA for a while, Jacob decided to drop that as well. "What's this all about?" we wondered. Jacob explained that he didn't want to be part of a process that reminded him of his addiction. He wanted to get on with his life. We were concerned that he would have no ongoing process for staying in touch with his inner power.

Per agreement, Sandy and I monitored the home contract. For example, we checked up on him to see that he was indeed at work. He was always there, working hard. We administered drug tests. We lived up to our part.

However, monitoring the contract was one of the hardest parts of family reintegration for me. When it comes to my kids, I let things slide easily. Because of what was at stake, I had to light a fire under my behind several times! Making demands of myself helped Jacob. He knew that my relationship with him meant so much that I would consciously make unnatural choices to assist him. I even carried his contract with me to work in case he called with a question! One day I referred to it when he called. I was proud of myself. I was serious about keeping my commitments to him.

On his side Jake helped the most by being faithful to his contract. It became easy to monitor him. He eagerly welcomed the drug tests now. We used a very stringent hair follicle test. It was a joy to experience him living at home, living in peace, living with energy, and living drug free! He was that magical child who once had disappeared and now was among us again!

As parents, I think that we learned to become approachable and easier to live with. There were times I was out of sorts. I could see that no one wanted to be around me. As I learned to deal more effectively with my negative emotions, I noticed that Jacob and Sandy wanted to be around me more. I was no longer the person that my family wanted to escape from.

We worked as a team. We shared a commitment and lived our family purpose. Often I felt a kind of excitement being with Sandy and Jacob. "This is the way my family life is supposed to be!" I said to myself more than once. When we went to our final Parent/Child seminar four months after Jacob returned home, we performed a "ten thousand mile check." We knew now that we had a very strong relationship with each other.

As we evolved, I wanted Jacob to know that I really had no program of my own for his life, no particular way that I thought his life should turn out. I did not feel that he must fulfill any dream that I had for him. My happiness was no longer even linked to his "success" or "failure" on returning from the Program. I had learned by this time that my happiness was my exclusive responsibility and choice. So I became very open to his differences and determined to support those choices if they looked to be "working choices." I had no "plans" for Jacob – only plans for myself in relationship to him. I planned to be lovingly detached, emotionally balanced, receptive to feedback, and without need. I was working on all of these aspects of myself as part of my own growth process. "If I am working on myself, he'll have the best chance to succeed given any influence I might have one way or another," I counselled myself.

❖

What might have been

On June 12, 1997, Christopher Landre killed himself by a gunshot wound to the head. I interviewed his parents Cathy and Lance four months after the tragic loss of their son. As they told their story a deep sadness spread its long shadow over their faces – even in smiles that occasionally replaced the natural gravity of their expression.

Christopher was an adopted child – a very bright and precocious youngster who learned easily and quickly. Parents and relatives alike doted upon the boy. Lance spoke in fond remembrance of his early years with Christopher, of skiing while carrying his son in his backpack. Christopher was exceptionally bright and was placed in the Gates program (a one-day-a-week program for California school children who test at the gifted level). He also excelled in soccer, baseball, skiing, archery, and street hockey.

But as bright as Christopher was, he also "lacked common sense," his parents told me. "He was bored quickly in school and easily distracted in class. He often didn't want to do the work and took the easy way out in things." They also reported him as very good at manipulating. Over the years, he became more and more of a challenge to raise. In high school he fell in with the wrong kids and began to use. Eventually, the Landres enrolled their son in Paradise Cove.

But his stay there was only six months' long. Due to extreme financial hardship his parents could not acquire the necessary funding required to keep their son in the Program. Christopher had not had enough time to internalize all he needed to learn at a deep level.

Upon rejoining his family, he took home school for a while and then returned to his old high school again. His parents described Christopher as feeling very lonely after he came home from the Program. Over time, sixteen-year-old Christopher began to hang out with old friends, at first with the notion that he would assist them in not using, but then he began to use again himself.

During the last month of Christopher's life, he slid downhill rapidly. One Friday night after a party he did not return home and stayed away three weeks. He was arrested for theft and legally confined to his home – kind of a house detention. Lance and Cathy recognized the direction the boy was headed in and were attempting to arrange for emergency finances to return him to the Program. They decided to wait until his court appearance.

But one afternoon before the hearing, he huffed gasoline. Huffing, which was Christopher's drug of choice, is achieved by pouring gasoline into a plastic bag, then putting the bag over your mouth and nose, and inhaling the fumes. Huffing induces a quick and cheap high but can be accompanied by physical and emotional shutdown, paranoia, and a collapse of thinking and reasoning. After huffing, Christopher climbed into the attic and reassembled an old .22.

Alerted by Christopher's sister that she smelled gasoline on her brother, Cathy rushed home from work. Christopher had locked himself in the bathroom. Shortly after his mother demanded that he open the door, Christopher shot himself. He remained unconscious for a short while before dying.

Lance told me, "Two days following his death, Christopher gave the gift of life to five people. Five Lear jets landed at the local airport and left with seven major organs from his body. Perfect tissue matches enabled Christopher to save two lives. A friend told us in a eulogy that when a pebble is dropped into a pond, there is a rippling effect. Those families are as grateful to Christopher as we are to have known and loved him."

In commemoration of their son, the Landres created the Christopher Landre Memorial Fund to provide assistance to needy families to keep their kids in the Program through approved zero-interest loans.

To me, the story of Christopher's brief life is a story of lost potential. We can only wonder what might have been in a life so full of possibility. The promise of a new beginning for the Landres ended in tragedy. And yet Christopher's possibility lives on whenever contributions in his memory assist another child to realize that he too was born bright as a radiant star and that his life is worth living.

Letting go

After Jacob had been home for four months, we all agreed that it was time to review the contract. We decided to replace the five-page contract with a few lines of text to be written on a single sheet of paper. We thought about this new agreement not as a "contract" but as a kind of living agreement between three adults living in the same home together. It was a powerful shift for us – a shift from having everything specified to having most things understood. The honesty and openness, values, family purpose – all were assumed requirements now. We felt like we were living those things with each other. Now we should be able to move from living according to the strict letter of the law to living its spirit.

After about six months home, Jacob (now eighteen-and-a-half) began dating a girl from his acting workshop. This was another experience in letting-go. We knew that he was ready for this, but we also knew that time spent together would diminish. We were uncertain what kind of girl Jacob had chosen. The kind of girl he chose would reveal a lot about him.

One weekend, MacLean brought his girlfriend Nancy home from Idaho for a visit. We arranged dinner and Jacob invited his friend Rebecca to join the party. He wanted us to meet the girl he'd been telling us about. We were very pleased to meet a beautiful, poised, fun, and thoughtful young woman!

Their relationship evolved quickly. It was not long before they spent most of their available hours together. They talked about going to Los Angeles to pursue acting careers. I loved it when Jacob would share with me the deep, intimate feelings he had towards her. She was the first real love of his life. I admired the high respect he had for her and his unwillingness to push her — not only past her own boundaries but what he believed she was herself ready to handle. Rebecca had been deeply wounded from an abusive relationship with a previous boyfriend. Jacob was clearly devoted to assisting her in recovering from those old wounds. I was a little nervous about what might happen if this relationship ended. It seemed to become everything to him. "Let go, let go. It's not your life. Have faith in him," I counseled myself. Besides, through watching Jacob in his relationship with this vulnerable young woman, I gained respect for his strength and ability to live purposefully rather than from passion and craving.

We had a couple of meals out with Jacob and Rebecca. I suppose young couples never feel completely comfortable with parents, but they seemed to. We joked about double-dating! Rebecca was adorable and sweet. When it was time to go separate ways, she always left with a warm hug for Sandy and me.

But there was a kind of trouble and sorrow in Rebecca's eyes. She lacked confidence and belief in herself. She seemed afraid to take risks. Jacob encouraged her to attend a Discovery seminar. It really didn't require much selling. Rebecca wanted some of the power she felt from Jacob in her own life. The Rebecca who walked into Discovery was unsure of herself and impatient with herself for being unsure. The Rebecca who walked out of Discovery knew that she had great, untapped potential. That was the Rebecca who walked into the Focus seminar that followed. Emerging was a Rebecca who glowed with self-knowledge about her awesome possibility and a determination to move forward in her life.

When it's time to move on

During the first twelve months Jacob was home with us he worked hard, went to acting classes, hung out with Rebecca, played harmonica and guitar, and wrote songs. Jacob and Rebecca continued to talk about L.A. and acting careers, but they did not seem in a hurry to do anything.

One morning before going to work, over a year since he had returned, Jacob told me that Rebecca was having trouble in the relationship. He was very vague about what was going on. Explanations about what she was going through were really sketchy. His description portrayed a girl who was frightened and unable to make a commitment. He seemed willing to talk about it but understandably confused and struggling to make sense of it.

I struggled with my own emotions that day. I had feelings for my hurting son. And I was concerned that this would be Jacob's greatest test. How will he deal with the stress? If he could survive a broken heart, most likely he could survive anything! It was a good sign that he chose to confide in us.

But later that evening over a beautiful candlelight dinner that Sandy prepared for us, Jacob said, "Oh, there's one thing you need to know, because I don't want to hide it from you. I'm smoking cigarettes again."

My heart sank; my fear immediately rose. Both Sandy and I spoke to him from our hearts – or was it our fear? – about our feelings towards cigarettes. Both Sandy and I each lost a parent to emphysema. We reminded him of our family value. "Substance-free" included no cigarettes. Jacob just looked back at us. He was going to smoke anyway. We told him that he must not smoke in our house or on our premises.

Later that evening I was talking to someone on the portable phone and wondered where Jacob was. I opened the front door and there he was, standing by the cars parked out front, smoking and (I could tell) not feeling very good. It felt just like old times – my kid in pain and alone. My offer of assistance was declined.

Jacob had begun to hang out with an old friend whom we knew to be at least an occasional user. Jacob said they were jamming together – he on the guitar, his friend on the drums. I had known and liked his friend ever since he was a little kid. But I knew what he and Jacob used to do together. I stopped myself, reasoning, "Well, I don't really know anything about Jacob's friend today. I'm judging him without cause." One day I expressed to Jacob my concern about this renewed relationship and told him that I had caught myself judging someone I didn't even know anymore. Jacob only responded with a gesture conveying that, hey, I might have a brain after all! I didn't like his attitude. I spent some time by myself focusing my energy on remaining balanced during this period of challenge.

One Monday evening I was in my home office writing. Sandy was meeting in the kitchen with women from her Codependency Twelve-Step group. Jacob came home early from jamming. Rather than leave what I was doing to make contact with him, I decided to just let him be. He went directly to bed without saying a word. I heard him coughing in his room next door.

Suddenly within two or three weeks, Jacob's attitude had shifted considerably. Sandy and I began to experience more anger and distance from him. Jacob would come home and go directly to his room without much of a greeting, if any at all – unusual for him. He wasn't even his usual talkative self after his morning shower. He was more irritable. I thought twice before approaching him.

I was concerned and talked to a good friend. I remember saying several times, "I can't allow myself to go to the fear place." If Jacob was having problems, how could I assist him if I was in fear? If he wasn't, then what was my fear all about?

With the pain of a broken heart, being shaken was all too understandable. But if he was beginning to use again to cope with his pain, that was unacceptable! No problem, however, great or small, could be resolved with a substance! That was our stand, our commitment to him and to our home.

Later that week Sandy spoke to me before leaving for her morning exercise. "All the warning bells are beginning to ring in my head," she said. "We've got to have him drug tested." I agreed.

That night Sandy and I went out to a movie. When we returned home I heard Sandy and Jacob in the kitchen having an argument. Sandy then stormed down the hall saying, "He's smoking in the family room. He had been smoking out on the patio, he said; some of the fumes must have drifted into the family room. But damn! The fumes smelled like marijuana!

"Have you been smoking pot?!" I demanded.

Jacob looked really startled and hurt. "No!" He made sure I heard him loud and clear. He was glaring at me.

I asked for one of his cigarettes. He handed over a pack of cigarillos. I removed one from the pack, got a box of matches, went to the garage, and lit it up. I had to know! I took a drag. It had been twenty years since I'd smoked anything. At first I inhaled gingerly. This smoke was remarkably smooth and bland, almost tasteless. It was almost like smoking nothing at all. When I didn't cough, I inhaled again. And again. A little deeper each time. Nothing. No sensation, no dizziness, no rush. Finally, I inhaled as deeply as I could. Again, nothing. I know what marijuana tastes, smells, and feels like. This wasn't it.

I returned Jacob's pack of smokes. He looked at me with a very piercing look and said, "I want a drug test and I want it right now! I'll pee in a cup. I'll do anything you want. I'm so *frigging mad* that you would accuse me of using, after all this time and all we've been through together! I consider this a *major* problem between us!"

I asked for a family discussion. We spent the next hour-and-a-half talking. It was the usual kind of conversation between us – Jacob and I the more talkative, Sandy the more quiet with an occasional attempt to get a word in. Jacob was often sarcastic. I had to work at remaining calm at first but managed to controlled myself with slow, deep breathing. But soon I relaxed. Jacob stopped being sarcastic and we began to have a good talk.

One issue for me was that Jacob was letting his hair grow long again. His hair is exceptionally curly and had become fairly ragged. Although far shorter than in his hippie days, his hair still reminded me of the days when I couldn't see his eyes. I told Jacob how I felt about his hair. He said he didn't really care too much *what* I felt about his hair, but, just so I knew, his talent manager had asked him to grow it out for studio pictures. Hmm…I didn't know this. If he had simply informed me, it would have been much better, I pointed out. I also told him that I didn't like his attitude.

"I'm eighteen. I don't *want* to tell you everything anymore. My hair is *my* business!"

Jacob seemed mostly hurt by the fact that we'd lost trust in him so quickly. He said, "What I see is that, after all I've done to establish trust with you, this is what I get. I can't *win* this game!"

"You've got to understand," I told him, "that you've never walked in our shoes. You've never had to live with an addicted child! Don't be surprised if I have questions or fall back into distrust. Don't expect me to be perfect because I will always fail you if you do!"

We went back and forth for a while. Sandy thought to renew our stand.

"Look Jake, it's simple," she said. "We will not tolerate use of substances in our house. You cannot live here if you're going to smoke cigarettes."

Jacob said that he would think this over and asked us how long we gave him to think it over. We said that the next day would be fine. He said that he saw us as controlling and wanting to run his life. "Besides," he said, "I've been reaching the conclusion that it's time for me to get out of here, to move to L.A. to work on my acting career."

I told him that we had been saying the same thing to each other. "Not that we want you to move away from us! We just realize that the time is arriving for you to strike out on your own. We've got mixed feelings about it. We're going to miss the hell out of you when you're gone, but we'll also enjoy the quiet time we'll have together. We've probably accomplished most of what we need to accomplish together. Now we're starting to annoy each other. The time has probably come when all of us should move into the next phase of our lives."

"But in terms of cigarette use, we're not being controlling at all. We're simply holding you to an agreement that we all made together in freedom."

211

"At your age," I continued, "it probably *is* difficult to have to live in our home and obey rules. I remember how difficult it was for me at your age. You should strike out on your own. But we hope you'll never choose to smoke, even in times of stress, because it doesn't enhance your life."

After a while, the conversation became very pleasant. We talked about the future. It had been a long time since we'd talked. We needed to clear things up and set a direction.

The next day, I bought a drug test kit, cut the usual lock from Jacob's hair, and mailed it in for the test. Jacob seemed glad to do it. He reiterated, "Get this, Dad! I personally don't care about the drug test because it will prove nothing to me. However, it will prove to you that I'm drug free. I expect an apology from you when the drug test comes back negative!"

The next day Sandy and Jacob got into yet another skirmish. Sandy had a lot to do that day. She wanted to organize her classroom. She needed to pack some things into her van to take to school and asked Jacob to help. He agreed but there was a misunderstanding. He did not understand that she wanted help *now*. Feeling no immediate pressure, he resumed playing his guitar.

I was on the phone when I heard Sandy scream. Worried that she was hurt, I rushed out to see if she was OK but found her screaming at Jacob to get off his guitar and help her. Suddenly, the air was thick with traded insults and hateful remarks. After awhile, Jacob relented and performed the minimal tasks required. The mood between them was dark and unresolved. Sandy drove off to her classroom in a state.

Later I sat down to talk with Jacob in his bedroom. He reiterated how much he longed to strike out on his own! He was feeling the power of the drive to independence inside him. He did not want to be told what to do, and when – especially by his mother!

"I've matured enough now to where I don't *want* this anymore. I don't want all this family stuff now. I want to fulfill my own life and my own dreams!"

He said he would probably move to L.A. in three months; meantime, he would live here and respect our agreements, including no smoking. We agreed that it really was time for him to move on into his own life. I said that I only hoped that he and Sandy would choose to work things out between them. I pointed out to him the things he did to push his mother's buttons. He indicated an unwillingness to let his life "be run by her emotions." He said that the next time she blew up at him, he'd blow up back at her. He was still operating out of his anger. I pointed out that he had been taught to express his anger and not hold it in but that he had not necessarily learned how important it is to resolve relationships fully. I caught myself succumbing to the temptation to meddle in their relationship and mentally slammed on my brakes.

Once again he raised the issue of my suspecting him of using. He said that this took away so much from our relationship. "You and I will get our close relationship back in a short time," he said, "but do you really know what that does to me?"

He went out to visit a friend and was gone all afternoon. Sandy remained away all afternoon as well. When both had returned, each left the other alone. Together, but apart. "Just like before," I thought. They were fully capable of working it out. They either would or wouldn't. I talked a lot to myself while they were upset with each other. I made a commitment to myself to remain conscious of myself and my condition. I insisted that I remain emotionally balanced. I told myself to be attached to the highest possibility in this moment, not to take sides, not to rescue, not to become angry, not to become depressed, not to compromise our values – but to soar as high as I could soar in this situation.

Nevertheless, the next day-and-a-half were difficult! I was still not free. I would not let go of their conflict! I kept up the inner dialog, the higher part of me counseling a lower part ready to explode. "You love these two so much. But love isn't running their lives for them. It's trusting them to do it for themselves. Especially after all you've been through with them, you must not interfere in their relationship. Learning to love includes freeing yourself from the arrogant belief that *you* know best for them but *they don't!*"

The next day I came home to find that they had sorted things out between themselves. They didn't need me at all. In any conflict they had ever had with each other, they never needed me to "help them."

It had been over a year since Jacob had returned home. Despite occasional storms, each of us felt that living together had been a success.

But Jacob was changing. His relationship with Rebecca was soon back on track. But I couldn't help feeling that I did not like the direction his life was going. Sure, there was the "eighteen-year-old thing." Yes, he had passed the drug test. But I did not see him working towards goals. I did not see him living any particular purpose. Further, I did not see him engaged in an ongoing process that might sustain him through the tough times and help him soar through the good.

Life tests

One late Sunday afternoon, a few weeks, later I returned home exhausted from a fun weekend of zany-ness with a half dozen of my crazy male buddies — two eighteen-year-olds and four middle-agers. On Friday my friend Kyle had borrowed a camper. The rest of us piled in with our stuffed animals (yes, men have stuffed animals), crackers, and sodas. We drove from the Bay Area all the way north to Seattle for a cup of coffee at an espresso joint owned by parents of a kid in the Program and then drove back again! Yes, all in one weekend — we *were* that crazy! Occasionally on the road we had deep talks, but mostly we just had a lot of fun! At a truck stop in Oregon we gobbled down steak and baked potato topped with what must have been an ice cream scoop of butter. But no one could have had a heart attack from the food because there was too much laughter! Our trip was a testosterone pilgrimage on wheels replete with dirty jokes, oinking, and copious farting. All I can say, ladies, is that it was the *perfect* male weekend!

I was having a lot more fun these days. I *liked* being crazy! It had been a long time since I'd allowed myself the freedom to be *me* — the little kid as well as the grown-up.

Sandy also had been away that weekend, staffing a parent seminar. I returned to an empty house and saw some dirty dishes on the kitchen table. As I reached out to collect them for the dishwasher, I noticed a coffee cup saucer containing loose change, a movie ticket stub, and a burned-out fragment of a marijuana cigarette paper.

Sometimes reality prepares you and sometimes it doesn't, I guess. In this case, reality had been preparing me for some time, but I had been too busy ignoring it. What I had been overlooking was that the powerful kid who returned from the Program was now discernibly less powerful than before.

Before long he came through the door and we greeted each other. Then I said what was on my mind.

"What's this?" I asked as calmly as I could, holding out the saucer and its contents.

The concern on his face was obvious. It was an "Oh shit! I didn't want him to see that!" look. "It's really nothing for you to worry about," he replied with a nervous laugh. "It's really nothing, Dad!"

"What do you mean, it's nothing? Look Jake, we've been around the block together. I can see what it is and it certainly isn't nothing!" I replied.

"Well, I don't want you to get involved in this."

"But Jake, I live here. I *am* involved in this! Did you smoke this?"

"No, I didn't." He looked me straight in the eye.

"Well, who did? And why is this here in my house?"

"I'm not going to get into who did it," he answered.

The conversation was going nowhere. Sandy and I talked that night. Clearly, Jacob was using again. The increasing lack of eye contact, the growing lack of communication, the unexplained absences, the renewal of acquaintance with old friends, and now this. We could ignore an accumulation of signs no longer.

We asked for a meeting together, which didn't seem to take us very far. Jacob seemed uncommunicative. Sandy and I regrouped and began talking about how best to respond. We wanted to respond firmly but with love.

A few days later I opened a card from a friend. It read simply: "Dear Sandy and Tim, our thoughts and prayers are with you both and Jake. If we can be of any help, please call. In love …." It was written with care and love, but it also had the feeling of a sympathy card. No one in my family had died! I determined not to take it that way, to call our friend, learn what this was about, and thank her for her concern.

Something was wrong and I knew that I wasn't going to like it. But I felt strangely serene and calm. This was simply an obstacle. Did I ever think there would *not* be obstacles?

I called her the next afternoon. She seemed surprised that I didn't know that Jacob had been arrested. She had read it in the local newspaper. Jacob had been picked up by the local police one evening at 10:24 P.M. for driving under the influence, transported to a "First Chance" program, and released. But it wasn't surprising that we didn't know. Jacob had not shared much with us lately; why should he begin now? I thanked our friend for reaching out to us. When I hung up the phone, I felt strangely calm. Whatever Jacob would go through wasn't going to alter what I was building for myself inside. My new way of thinking, my new way of dealing with emotion, my new tools, my growing faith in an inner power – these would see me through.

We asked to meet with Jacob again and told him that we knew about his being arrested. He talked about the whole scene calmly. He seemed relieved to have it out in the open now. He was in the process of contacting a lawyer. He knew this would cost him a bundle and a lot of time. He seemed to be facing it square on.

For our part, we reaffirmed our family value of no substances. To paraphrase our approach, we said: "We love you and we always will, Jake. We see that you choose to use drugs. We do not support drugs – a value we all agreed is important. We want to support you in being the great person you were born to be, the person you truly *are*. We *believe* in you, honey! And we love you. We see your struggles and want to assist you to be great again if you will allow us to. How can we do that best? We all know that, if you continue to use, you'll need to live elsewhere. If that is your choice, then how can we assist you in that transition with love?" We asked him to consider counseling at our expense. We required a weekly drug test, starting immediately. We requested that he check in with us for just ten minutes a day to share with us how he was feeling emotionally. We affirmed that we would be available to assist him however we could. We requested that he stop seeing friends who would not support his sobriety. And we told him that we could feel his sense of guilt toward us and himself. He had recently mentioned the possibility of working for a time in the Program. We told him that we thought that was an excellent idea. "How can we assist you in doing that?" we asked.

Jacob agreed to little at the time. So we asked him how we could assist him in making preparations to move and requested that we set a date. He asked for three weeks' time. We agreed.

Meanwhile, his relationship with Rebecca seemed to suffer again. They weren't hanging out together as much and, when they did, their meetings seemed to have quiet, quick, and unplanned endings. Rebecca confided in Sandy and me. She reported that she knew he was struggling, that she would attempt to get close to him, but that he would push her away – not physically but emotionally. Our experience of Rebecca was that she was now more powerful than Jacob, more open and revealing, more honest, making greater strides in her life. She was doing things with her life. She had been in an experimental film. She had recruited several kids for the acting workshop. She was planning to move to L.A. and now seemed to have the confidence to go without Jacob.

One day she tearfully confessed to us in our kitchen something we had suspected: It was she who had brought the marijuana into their relationship and had, in fact, left the burned out paper in the saucer on our table.

"You know," she said, "It's something I just do occasionally and it's no big deal. But I was surprised at him, how it was such a big deal to him."

"You mean, you didn't realize how powerful it was in his life and how fast it would take over?" I said.

"No!"

"You mean, that you didn't really realize that he is an *addict?*"

She hung her head. "Yes. I really didn't understand."

Now she *did* understand. Now there was a kind of emotional distance between them. She had committed to him earlier and now committed to us that she would stop all use of substances herself. Jacob didn't seem to take it seriously, however. One day, we all shared our concern directly with Jacob. He remained uncommunicative in a verbally elusive way – saying lots of words which, added up, meant, "stay away from me ... I'm gonna do what I'm gonna do." A few days passed by.

Soon Rebecca broke up with Jacob. In essence she was saying to him, "Hey, when you get your life together I want to be in it. But not until then. And if you decide not to get your life together, I'm moving on."

We watched as Jacob responded to this, trying to be strong. Rather than come down hard on Jacob, we chose to let him be for a while. "Let's see if he sorts this out himself," Sandy and I said as we took walks together. "Let's keep practicing the art of letting go and see what he makes of it. He'll need to leave as scheduled but let's give him the space to right himself."

A few weeks earlier I had called Jacob's buddy Joshua who had graduated from the Program with him. I told him that I was concerned that Jacob was using again. "My advice to you, Tim, is to be optimistic. If he's using, he isn't feeling too good about himself right now. But that doesn't mean things won't turn out OK for him." That wise counsel *sustained* me.

Sometimes Sandy and I possessed a kind of serenity, and sometimes not. One day when he walked in the front door, I saw his eyes and began to cry. I could tell he had been stoned sometime earlier in the day. I let all my feelings go. Tears I wasn't ashamed to cry gushed down my face.

"I love you so much, Jake," I blurted. "I can't stand seeing you do this to yourself!"

I asked him why he wouldn't talk to me anymore, why he couldn't turn to me in this time of need. "I'm here for you, Jake! But you won't talk to me. I feel like a failure as a father again! I see you suffering and I don't know what to do and I keep wanting to *do* something!"

Jacob listened quietly. Then he reached out his arms and held me close. "Dad, you've *never* failed me as a father! I *love* you. I admire you. And I know that you love me. I've always felt loved by you. You're the *greatest* dad in the whole world! I want you to know that it's going to be all right with me, dad. You'll see. It's going to be all right. I promise it will." He was tender, and I was vulnerable. That moment brought us closer together, I think,

217

than ever before. After a time, we were laughing, actually. We were a father and son caring for each other and sharing a difficult time together.

Overall however, Sandy and I approached Jacob's relapse with a new attitude and unity. We took long walks together and held hands. We talked about our emotions. We affirmed ourselves for giving Jacob two years of a drug-free life, a time when for he first time he experienced the fullness and power of his life. We affirmed that our task was not to burden Jacob with judgment, fear, or anger but to lift him with our love. We believed that Jacob's higher power was at work within him. We believed that there was a *purpose* in his relapse, that there were lessons yet unlearned, and that he would learn them in time. We made it clear to him that, while we could not support his drug use and while it was time for him to leave, we nevertheless loved him beyond measure. We refused to panic, to become angry, to simply kick him out of the house instantly. Instead, we gave him time to sort things out and trusted that he would. We often said, "Jacob, we *believe* in you."

A few days passed. One evening I was taking off my shoes after work. Jacob walked into my bedroom and stood in front of me. He looked at me seriously.

"Dad, I'm pledging this to you right here and now. As of this moment, I'm not going to use any more! It does nothing but tear me down! It's costing me *everything* – my relationship with Rebecca and with you guys. If you want to drug test me, fine, but I'm moving on in my life."

The following day he called Cameron, the director of the Montana Spring Creek Lodge facility where Jacob had lived during transition and asked for a job. He told Cameron what was going on in his life. He needed a break and he needed some money. He knew he could work with the kids and be helpful. After a drug-free period of several weeks, of getting his life in order again, of stabilizing himself, he left for Montana.

One night he called for a lengthy talk. We heard the strength returned to his voice. It seemed easier to talk together as he moved out into his life … his world of plans, fears, disappointments, and dreams. He enjoyed working with the boys. He played his guitar and was anxious to share his new music with us soon. He had good days and bad ones, days when he felt part of things and days when he felt lonely and disconnected. He was restless, wanting to get on with the life he planned in Southern California.

"Mom, Dad, if you had handled this situation (the relapse) any differently, you would simply have pushed me over the edge," he said. "I appreciate the way you handled it a lot." Sandy and I acknowledged Jacob for having the strength to redirect his life when he saw that it was not headed in a direction he wanted. How much he had matured in two years' time! All three of us found ways to communicate our unmistakable love and respect for each other.

In a few months Jacob would have enough saved to follow his dream of going to LA. He would drive home to visit a few days before heading south. It would feel different to think of him as a visitor. As MacLean before him, Jacob would enter a passageway to a new life, uniquely his. We couldn't wait to see him again. The time would pass quickly before he left to find his first apartment, a place he would call "home," hopefully a safe haven for the challenges ahead.

For he will be tested. Life tests us all with a wisdom we can never fully comprehend. We are given the challenges we need and no more of them than we can handle. Our children challenge us and in turn are tested by life. It does not appear to be our parental right to spare our children the ordeals of their lives, nor does it seem to work when we try. I guess we never stop worrying about our children. My mother, somewhat an expert in these matters, says that she *still* worries about me!

One day in a future they do not quite understand, our children will hold their newborn infants in their arms and call them "son" or "daughter." They will give them names and wait anxiously for their first smile. As untested parents they too will watch anxiously as their children confront the frightening challenges of the age in which they live. The hour will change. But the process of living, awakening, and becoming ourselves will be the same.

It is a strange process. For what we discover inside us was always there, always true, yet we knew it not. It is an extraordinary and ineffably beautiful journey of birthing. I give thanks to my family for being part of my own birthing and for being my companions on the road. I give thanks for the joy they bring into my life, for the sadness too, for the love and understanding, and for the forgiveness. I thank them for it all.

JOURNEY INTO POSSIBILITY

From the experiences of the past few years I am beginning to understand some of the multifaceted dimensions to healing, at least as they apply in my own life. We give our lives meaning by making sense of our experiences. But it takes more than learning or writing to change a life! Unless I assimilate the lessons inherent in my experiences, I doom myself to a life of recurring pain. One of my favorite sayings used in the seminars is:

That which is not acted upon is not learned.

How profoundly true! Any insight I might have would be little value without its real impact on my life. If I realize that I have lived my life in judgment over others but do nothing about it, then I will judge again in the next experience. And the next. And I will repeat the cycle until I finally *get it*. And "getting it" puts me in no special position. I do not think that anytime soon I will loudly proclaim, "Well, thank God I'm beyond that now!" In my experience, it doesn't work that way. Every day is a challenge and an opportunity to live *this* day anew. Life humbles on a daily basis and humility is the great antecedent to learning and growing.

Another antecedent is our attitude towards experiences. For years my friend Jerry and I have backpacked in the beautiful Sierra mountains of California, in awe of their imposing granite peaks and pristine lakes. Carrying our packs and heading up the steep mountain trails is truly hard work! This summer MacLean joined us for a trek to Peeler Lake.

As I put my body into the 2,600 foot vertical climb, my legs registered their quick complaint – with, oh, I'd say about 2,500 feet to go! For a long time I thought of nothing but my legs and breathing. I was in immediate agony! After suffering for awhile, I instructed myself just to enjoy the moment – this special moment of being with friend and son in this rugged terrain of resplendent, snow-capped peaks, glacial moraine, and snow-fed streams. "What a wonderful life this is! What a privilege to be here!" I thought. As I focused on aspects of the trek more profoundly *real* to me than even the complaints of my body, pain receded into the background and *love of the experience* took over. Hot and dusty trail, dry mouth, and scorching sun became accepted parts of the journey, even part of its beauty. After a time we would come upon a shady place, catch our breath, perhaps pump stream water through our filter, and renew ourselves for the next push. Water, shade, and enjoyment of the moment healed aches from the climb.

While treks like these are demanding, they *strengthen* me. They take me out of the ordinary and stretch me to capacity. From transforming my viewpoint, from turning struggle into opportunity, comes the reward of fully appreciating this awesome terrain, experiencing oneness with the setting, and enjoying my companions.

So it is with our lives. The attitude I take towards my experiences defines their very nature. When I choose to focus on the pain of an experience, I encounter pain more than the experience itself. When I choose to focus on the positive aspects of the experience, it is a different experience altogether.

As I review the experiences recounted in this book, I don't really regret anything. But I would respond differently were I to encounter the same experiences again. For example, I would not make my son's drug addiction the center of my emotional life. I would not focus on the pain of my relationship with MacLean and Sandy. I would not allow myself to feel separate and lonely. I would see more clearly that *I* create my world. *I* determine my experience *with* the world. Sure, I don't control a son's addiction or a wife's depression. But I *am* in charge of my emotions and attitude.

Were I to live this experience again, I would focus instead on what the experience contained for all of us – and particularly me. I would ask basic questions: Why do I have an addicted child? What am I supposed to learn? How can I respond to my son with the highest love? Once I realized that there was something each of us had to learn from this experience, I began to see the possibility that maybe – just maybe – Jacob had done us all a *favor!* That insight opened a door to other possibilities. Perhaps none of us was a victim. Perhaps no one was *wrong.* Perhaps we were being challenged simply to wake up and change our lives. Perhaps these events were part of a grand opportunity for our lives.

Awakening

Many people believe that life consists of a sequence of random events. I no longer share that belief. If it is true, then we are all victims living in a purposeless, capricious, and random world. There is *far* more to life. And we are capable of achieving far more than victims can ever achieve.

Experiences do not just happen to us: Something within us, something wiser than our narrow, small, and egocentric selves, *creates* the experiences we need to grow and expand – to become whole and complete – to become who we are, which is our inborn potential. This is the reason we meet the people we meet and have the kids we have. Sandy and I did not just meet by happenstance. Somehow I *attracted* her into my life. Our sons did not "just turn out to have problems." Sandy and I lived unconsciously as parents and created these two boys to teach us to be more conscious. Likewise, MacLean and Jacob did not "simply happen to be born to" Sandy and me. They created parents like us to teach them to rise above themselves and see life from another point of view. Each of us is a gift to the other, a teacher who will teach us what we need in order to become complete individuals. As we become more complete, we heal ourselves from our sense of being less, *far less*, than actually we are.

It is as if we are transmitters broadcasting an inaudible signal into the atmosphere. In my life I was given three very special people to teach me about love and acceptance. Notice that I did not attract a wife and two sons who made life *easy* for me. The message of my broadcast was: "I need you to come into my life. I *need* to understand something that only my experiences with you can teach me. I need your assistance to awaken to who I really am." For the most part, we are unconscious of our own broadcasts. Others often sense the signals we put out long before we do.

In a sense, when we are challenged by people and events, we have already set the stage for the challenge! And with each challenge, I have two choices: to *respond* or *react*.

When I react I simply act or think out of habit and conditioning. I learned nothing. I get angry. I judge. I pretend a problem doesn't exist. I attack. I feel separate – a victim of the world.

But when I *respond*, I align myself with an energy that completes me, or makes me whole. I begin to *awaken* to all kinds of possibility that might otherwise be blocked from view. I have a strengthened awareness of people around me. I have clearer vision and insight. I see the learning opportunity in every moment. And I act differently. That process of alignment is my *higher power in action*. Freely choosing to align myself with an ever-accessible power within, a power that helps me manifest my highest potential, seems to be the overall intent for my life.

I believe that this is how the system works for all of us. The price for ignoring it is costly. Each day I am out of alignment with my greater power, I create pain in my world. You and I are energy systems. Our "playing small," judging, controlling, striking out in anger, turning our backs on those in need, tuning out and turning on – it all has power. We think that we are small and don't count. But ... *everyone counts!* Our lives matter. Our energy has widespread effect. When we put out healing energy, it accumulates toward the healing of our families and planet. When we put out harmful energy, it too accumulates and everyone suffers. Each one of us has enormous power — the power to be a block or a channel for a powerful energy promoting life, consciousness, and healing. And with each small awakening, I affect much more than simply my own life.

While my life may have a different purpose and contribution than yours, I believe that the aggregate purpose of our lives is to overcome our smaller selves by becoming the special individuals we were born to be — loving, caring, whole and complete, alert and aware, intelligent, creative, and responsible. Every life can be like a flowering lotus, continually opening.

No magic is involved. No bolts of lightening are required. The only thing required of me is my choice to activate the awakening process of seeing, aligning, and responding *in my life*. That one choice *is the only miracle I need*, the one act of personal creativity required. From activation of the higher power in my life, everything flows. The system does the rest.

❖

Door to within

My life has been a long, slow movement from slumber into a process of awakening to a true inner life. I have simply been *blessed* with crises providing the catalyst and motivation to begin the awakening process! Each day now, I have an opportunity to live a little more consciously than the day before — to love more deeply, to surrender my fear more completely, to let go more fully. At a certain point I came to understand this. And I understood that everything I had been through was simply what it took to wake me up. I realized that the same is true for Sandy, Jacob, MacLean, and for all of us. We get what we need to open a door to within.

Arousing a slumbering human being like me to a continuous process of awakening is not easily done. It is harder than raising a child! The most difficult child I have raised has been *me!* In trying to change myself, I have often felt like a small David pitted against Goliath! Change requires a sharp intensity of motivation. Becoming conscious is an intangible and elusive concept for experienced grown-ups, not just confused adolescents trying to find their way in a bewildering world. At fifty-two years old, it was an annoying indignity to admit how unconscious I was. The prospect that the journey of self-discovery just might be the most wonderful journey of all, a journey into my own possibility, was a hard sell. So I found resourceful ways to avoid it.

It took a crisis in my life – watching my son deteriorate before my eyes and realizing that I contributed mightily to unhappiness within my family – to generate the willingness to examine myself with complete honesty, and to decide to change. The word *crisis* comes from the Greek *krisis*, meaning decision. In the inner realm, deciding is an absolute – I don't "sorta" decide. I either do or don't. Truly deciding means choosing – closing some doors and opening others. All the way! Hinges off the hook! Deciding requires that I cut away what isn't useful, and nurture what is. Deciding means going for it with everything I've got!

Amazingly, even profound family breakdown and crisis often are not enough to trigger change. When I suggest to people that they take just a few minutes out of their busy day to meditate, to get in touch with that which is deep within them, I often see the sense of being overwhelmed in their eyes: "Where would I begin? How will I find the time? What will it really *do* for me, anyway?" their eyes ask. I sometimes see the fear of losing control: "Is this some kind of cult-ish idea? Will I be able to handle what I turn up? What if I start to think about bad stuff from my childhood?" I have a lot of compassion for these fears, for I have had all of them myself. The fear of change, they say, exceeds the fear of death itself!

I have overcome my resistance to a true inner life by understanding it a little better. It helps me to think of life as existing in different dimensions at once. One realm, *the outer*, consists of the bustling world of events and facts. My outer world is what I do and how I present myself to the world. This domain is for the most part visible, discernible, tangible, and intellectually embraceable. The outer level answers many questions such as ... "How did that happen? When did it happen? Where? Who did it?" The outer world is full of opinions, conclusions, solutions, reports, and facts. It is full of other people. And here's the problem: *It is infinitely easier to focus on everything outside of me rather than what is within me.*

I can live my life entirely based upon an outer reference point, or a continuously looking outside of myself. When things go wrong, I can look outside myself for causation – for someone or something to blame. "Jake's ruining my life! And before him it was Mac! And Sandy – she's *never* been on my side! And what about Jake's friends and, oh yes, that damned school system!" There are countless ways to live from an outer reference point. I may obsess with how another person angers me. "How could she have *done* that to me?!" I may spend all my time performing good deeds in hopes that I'll be thought highly of. I may spend all my energy waiting for everyone else to change or act first.

It is *easy* to focus our energies on the outer. We're trained to do it! For example, it is easier for a mother to obsess about her daughter's low grades than to reflect on how attached she is to her daughter's success and to disengage from that attachment. And it's easier for the child to focus on her oppressive mother than to look at why she achieves so little. Mom's attachment and daughter's resentment lie within themselves. Neither can change the other. Best to give up that useless battle and focus on what we truly *can* control: our inner selves. This is focusing on *cause* rather than effect. I can respond to the outer world by looking within and seeing what I want to create for my life in response. I can be the cause of my life rather than simply a steel ball in a slot machine bouncing wildly off everything I encounter.

I have spent much of my short lifetime obsessed with how I look, whether I get promoted, who is angry with me, how inadequate I seem, whether people will approve of me, whether they'll think I'm smart, and on and on. The payback for this misplaced focus was a relatively powerless and unfulfilled life, an unhappy marriage, and a kid in Samoa!

Only by refocusing have I begun to understand how important my one life is and to understand what I *really* want to do with my life. In contrast to the limited space and perception of the outer world, the inner realm is a vast, interior space of endless and unlimited *becoming*. The world within us is more vast even than the outer world itself because inside we were not built to be finite. When we access our true inner nature, we discover how limitless we are! Within us resides our highest Self where the spirit of individual identity and possibility quietly breathes beside a *higher power*. The world within us is our most fertile and creative center. It the center of true objectivity and, not coincidentally, a place where personal power, detachment, mindfulness, natural knowing, and deepest love are born. It is the locus of a third eye, another way of seeing, which monitors how we relate to the world. Living from its guidance, I make course adjustments in my life aligned with my most essential being. When I have an internal reference, I *first* direct my focus on the quality of my inner state of being and *then* act. Inner *drives* outer. I create rather than react. I become purposeful and focused.

In the inner realm I ask for and receive answers to profound questions. Harry J. Rathbun defined the inner quest this way:

> "If I am to realize the greatest possible meaning for my life, I must know what I have to work with. The matter of first importance, therefore, is to know what is the nature and what is the destiny of mankind in general, and of myself in particular. What am I? Who am I? Where am I in the life process, and where am I going? What is my built-in potential? What can I *be* at my highest and best? What choices are open to me?

Aristotle's comment is helpful: 'The true nature of anything is the highest it can become.' By that standard, the true nature of man is what he can be at his highest and best...." (Harry J. Rathbun, *Creative Initiative: Guide to Fulfillment*, [Palo Alto, CA, Creative Initiative Foundation, 1976], p. 10.)

This drive to understand my true nature has to be *activated*. It requires a commitment on my part. When it is active in my life I find very practical results in the here-and-now. My attitude changes. I am loving. I am purposeful. I resolve conflict. People respond to me and want to be around me. My job is to keep the door to within open at all times.

Once the door is open, there are many ways to explore the interior landscape of the Self. Several processes in this book have been useful to the people involved: attending and then staffing personal growth seminars; support groups; therapy; daily spiritual study; prayer; meditation; writing; doing a Twelve Step Program; etc. The important element is *committing to and sticking with an ongoing process* that directs us inwardly.

You may wonder if so much focus on *me* isn't just egocentricity carried to the extreme. Not in the sense that I mean it. I'm not advocating self-absorption, catering to my every whim, or believing that I'm at the center of everything. The internally-referenced life is rather pursuit of the higher power flowing through me and defining my individual purpose so that I might manifest that purpose through loving, serving, teaching, and giving. An internally-referenced life is not selfish! It is a gift of selflessness to our families and the world around us. Only from within do I begin to understand what love and forgiveness really are. Only then can I extend them to others, can my action in the world be truly meaningful and powerful. Vast social problems await this simple realization in each one of us. Our families – indeed the world – can only be saved by individual decisions to open doors to within.

Identity

Learning about my own true nature and allowing my inner purpose to be in the driver's seat build within me a sense of my *identity*.

Sandy and I take long walks on a levee on the edge of the beautiful San Francisco Bay near our home. As we walk we pass by a delicate marshland populated by slender green reeds. There is something about the simplicity and elegance of the marsh grasses that captivates and inspires me. Strong bay winds blow and the tide rises and falls, but the marsh reeds respond with the elasticity that is a part of their essence – not with resistance. Reeds take nourishment from their environment and do nothing to harm it. They possess all the information they require to grow and flourish. A reed has an inborn *identity*. It knows what it is.

We humans, however, have to discover our identity. If I gain a sense of my identity (my true, inborn nature) I possess a certainty of who I am and a consistency of being. The person you encounter in me today on the street is the same one you greet tomorrow on the levee. If I have identity I have a clear sense of my values and what I'm all about. People and events cannot shake or break me. A wayward child cannot destroy me. Others' opinions cannot deter me if I know myself completely.

A person with a strong sense of his/her identity acts differently in the world than one who does not. For example, Sandy uses a wonderful Sufi technique that she learned many years ago which illustrates what it means to have identity. When someone says something angry to her she visualizes the anger as an arrow coming straight at her. She visualizes moving aside to let the arrow pass. She does not allow it to harm her nor does she allow herself to retaliate. She simply gets out of the way and responds rather than reacts. This is responding from a position of identity. The inner statement is, "I know who I am. I cannot be harmed unless I choose and I choose *not* to be harmed. I also choose not to be harmful in return. I choose to respond with love because I know myself and I am a loving person." To respond to another's anger with love rather than react from anger or fear is powerful and creates a *presence of being* that is remarkable in this world.

Recently, a parent shared this observation in a support group meeting: "Being a parent of these kids and dealing with our anger is like surviving a tornado. It is our obligation to remain centered in the storm." Identity is the ability to weather the storm and stay the course.

Identity is not living in resistance to reality – i.e., in a state of objection to something that has happened. Identity is not reacting; it is *being*. Identity is making decisions based on a deep sense of who I am, then declaring myself, and standing calmly and with assurance upon that foundation.

Identity is not some kind of solo act. Identity enables me to partner confidently and authentically with others around a shared set of common values, to stand strong within a social context.

Identity is not acting out of *I should* or *I ought*. Groucho Marx once said, "Those are my principles. If you don't like them, I have others." Well, sometimes I have felt like this in my life! I will be whatever you want me to be. But identity is not acting from a need for approval, retaliation, subservience, or control. It is acting from a basis of *I am*. Identity is an affirmation of my being or essence rather than a negation. Identity is what distinguishes my individual uniqueness or greatness. And yours. It's what sets each of us truly apart in the world.

Identity is having a clear sense of my individual life purpose and living it. Living a purposeful life requires that I "go inside" to discover myself and what I'm passionate about. But it also requires something more than a deep and rich internal life: It requires living in alignment what I find inside. If I'm continuously replowing inner ground, but never make basic decisions about myself, I never find what my identity is. Identity is buying a round trip ticket – departing to an inner place of discovery *and* returning to act from what I find and to share that knowledge with the world.

Light and shadow

Our children need our optimism and hope. Yet how many of us deep down have little hope and lead lives of "quiet desperation" as I did? To give our children hope, we must be hopeful people to begin with and lead lives that inspire others with hope.

We choose to see the world as a place of light or darkness. Interestingly, when I choose to see a world of darkness, the people around me wear the troubled, pained visages of the darkness I choose to see. But when I choose to see a world of light and hope, I see the light within everyone I meet.

The light in a friend's life may be very obscured by a darkness of his own choosing. Optimism is not a blind, take-me-my-pockets-are-open kind of naiveté. I never give up the obligation to be aware. But when I see also the light of possibility in the eyes of my family and friends, I respond differently. I develop faith in them and their higher power that, after all, is the same as mine. I encourage them in directions that emphasize their hopeful qualities. I hold out for their highest possibility in a positive spirit and do not cater to their dark urges. Being a hopeful person based on faith in others is coming from a position of strength, not syrup and sentimentality! It is coming from a powerful conviction that it's all going to work out OK.

To have a strong foundation of hope for my children is one of the greatest gifts I can give them. Living in hopefulness creates a kind of inner serenity and allows me to "let go and let God." Suddenly, parenting (and life) is not as difficult as it was when I lived in fear. I don't have to control my children's lives anymore. I can focus instead on what I *really can* control – my choices, values, and way of seeing.

To have hope in my children allows me to be free from fear of them and *for* them. No one really *wants* my fear! It accomplishes nothing. My fear adds an unwanted burden to *their* lives. It's amazing that I've spent so much time indulging in my fear! You can see how learning to live with hope paid important dividends to Sandy and me when Jacob began to use again. If you reread how we handled his relapse, you can observe how differently Sandy and I were able to handle a family breakdown than before. Notice the focus on the profound love we have for our son, our affirmation of his inner greatness, our *stand* for his life, and our lack of hysteria and negative emotion. Sometimes during this test, we responded in panic and fear, in anger and disgust, and with hopelessness. We weren't perfect! But as we responded from an optimistic faith that all was as it was intended and that things would turn out OK, the results were favorable. We were able to let go, trusting that Jacob's higher power was in charge.

I have had frequent difficulty being hopeful because of beliefs and judgments about success and failure. Jacob's relapse forced me to confront these energies within myself. There were times I judged myself a failure as a father – "playing old tapes" that I'm not good enough, have not done enough, etc. There were times I judged Jacob a failure for going through all he has gone through only to use again. But my higher power quietly spoke to me and I listened. It whispered words of healing. "This is the perfect place for you and Jacob," its voice counselled me. "There is nothing you cannot handle. You were born for this moment. There are but lessons still unlearned. All is at it should be. Do not panic. Do not use silly words of *success* and *failure*. Your task is to love and respond, not judge. Generate faith. Generate hope – hope born in understanding and compassion. Breathe them deeply into yourself and exhale them with kindness into your loved ones. They need your hope."

Hope is a powerful energy we can give to others. And the surest way to give hope to someone is to live a hopeful life – one worth copying. Our children need our *leadership* as parents. We took on a lifetime responsibility and obligation, as will they in their turn. Our children need us to "walk the talk" – 'til we drop. They need to see us *doing* what we want them to do – to love; to listen to our higher power; to live honest, responsible, trustworthy, and sober lives; to mature; to deal with our anger and fear; etc. As we grow, we give them hope for their own lives. If I see you deal with your anger and transform a moment from darkness to light, it is *noticeable*. It creates the possibility within me that I can do the same.

Finally, hope is self-renewing. When I radiate hope and lead a hopeful life myself, I feel good about life. When I feel good about life, I feel hopeful about it – a kind of replenishing effect. In a sense, life comes back to me with the same energy I put *into* it! When I give hope I get it back and build an internal reservoir I will need for the future.

❖

Love

Learning to understand love and to live a life sourced in love is a lifelong task. Understanding love is like dipping into a well: As I drink I am replenished from an inexhaustible source. There is always more to learn and know.

Loving myself. I recall boarding an airplane shortly after MacLean was born. As we taxied out to the runway, our stewardess went through the usual instructional litany. When it came to the part where "in event of a decrease in air pressure oxygen masks will be released from the compartment overhead," she got my attention. If we are accompanying children, she said, we should place the mask first over ourselves and *then* place it over our child. A new father very much in love with his son, I immediately objected. "I love my son *more* than I love myself," I thought. "I would give my life for him." Then my brain kicked in. "Despite your good intentions, Tim, if you don't take care of yourself first, you won't be available to help Mac!"

It has taken me years to discover the general lesson imbedded in this simple example. If first I don't learn to love and care for myself, how can I possibly extend love and caring freely to others? How can I have the energy required to love another human being unconditionally? The great teaching, to "love thy neighbor as thyself," implies that I learn to love myself first and then extend that love out into my world.

Not loving ourselves has implications in other lives than our own. Sandy made this point very succinctly one day. "As a mother I wasn't modeling a person who loves herself. So how could I expect *Jake* or *Mac* to love themselves?"

One day after Jacob had returned home, he saw that Sandy was still feeling depressed. He said to her, "Mom, I wish you would get over your depression and just love yourself." Sandy thought about this a long while and realized that, as she persisted in her depressive refusal to love herself, she communicated to him that somehow her depression was at least partly his fault. Again, we are power centers that broadcast messages and energy. Sandy realized that her depression was a negative energy she put out into her world.

Sandy added that, "Loving ourselves results in understanding that when things don't turn out so well, we're not bad people unworthy of love!" Living from a sense of shame only results in guilt, self-recrimination, and self-condemnation. Constantly beating up on myself is a masochistic and perverse form of self-indulgence. Not loving myself is actually an act of self-

231

ishness because I am not free to give love fully when I do not *really* love myself. Not loving myself created a reservoir of guilt so large that I was immobilized when it came time to raise children. I did not feel worthy of being an adequate father. In contrast, loving myself means that I'm *wholly worthy* of the love I give myself and of the love of my family – even when I have done things to suggest otherwise.

Loving myself means learning to embrace my negativity. When I observe myself in a negatively-charged emotional state, I neither condemn myself as someone bad for having those feelings nor allow myself to linger in negativity. If I have to, I can vent my emotions in a way that isn't harmful to someone else. Then I tell myself to "get over it!" I talk to myself and establish a kind of ongoing interior dialogue. I ask myself challenging questions such as, "What is the creative response required of me?" The answer is always at hand. When I completely succumb to negative emotion, I wake up sooner or later, forgive myself, start the inner dialogue, and charge myself to get right back in alignment with a course of direction based on love. This is the method I have learned to practice. The more I practice it, the easier it gets.

Unconditional love. When I am not free of factors that block love, the frequent result is love with strings attached. Sandy and I raised our boys with a lot of conditional love – "If you get good grades in school, then I'll love you! If you don't, I won't!" Of course, we never actually *said* that. We were well-intentioned parents who *never* intended to broadcast that message. Nevertheless, our boys *experienced us* as loving them with strings attached and that they were unworthy of our love simply as they were. In the economy of love, the script that counts is how we experience the attitude of another. I have learned not to take love too lightly. Love is much more than bidding Sandy good night with a routine "I love you." Love is something I communicate from my being. Or not. Conditional love is not real love because it is never *felt as love*. It is felt as the manipulation it truly is. When I love my children conditionally, I teach them to be manipulative. True love is unconditional and for all time. True love has no connection with what another person does – whether I approve or disapprove. Even if I do not agree with something my son does I can communicate that, while I cannot support his actions, I nevertheless love him as a person – for all time and without strings. And if I love unconditionally, it will be felt and understood more from my attitude more than my words.

The economy of love. The more I give love, the more I get it back in my life. Love has a kind of "economy." I must spend love in order to gain it. One of the seminar leaders, Bill, said in a recent seminar that Sandy staffed: "There are two ways to have love in your life: to give it and to ask for it."

How simple and how true! We are completely in charge of the love we get in our lives. I have no excuse for feeling unloved. Because I understand this principle, one of the things I am proud to have achieved in my life is that I *never* feel unloved anymore – no longer separate and alone. When I want love from MacLean, for example, I tell him how much I love him. What I feel back, although in his own words and in his own way, is unmistakably love. Or sometimes I ask for love. Just the other day I was feeling out-of-sorts. I felt that I needed love from Sandy and wasn't getting it. I have spent so many years resenting that even my simplest needs weren't being met. No more! I simply said, "You know what I need right now, Sandy? I need your love. I need your affection. I need you to tell me and show me how much you love me. I need you to hold me." She responded immediately. For most of my life I've expected others to read my mind! I've learned that I'm in charge of my life – no one else!

Recently I was privileged to experience a moment of true healing. I met the adopted son of a physician and his wife, a boy who had been abandoned first by his South American mother, then again by her relatives after he had bonded with them as a child. Emelio stood before a small group of parents and Program graduates, one of them his sister. The pain of a lifelong belief that he was not, nor would ever be, loved was etched already upon his youthful face. Despite the misfortune of his early life, Emelio had received a wonderful gift: his adoptive family. His new father and mother had cared for him and given to him all his life with great love. But they are not expressive people. The father, a good man, was nevertheless analytical and emotionally remote.

Standing before him was young Emelio. With a *need*. Emelio needed something from his father to heal a lifelong pain that he felt profoundly – a pain that would not go away, a pain that said, "I am not loved. I am not lovable." I watched as Emelio struggled with what to do, with how to get what he wanted from his father. At last, it was suggested that he might simply tell his father what he so desperately wanted from him. And when his father realized that his son wanted something from him, he *ran* across the room to stand before his son. With tears falling onto his cheeks, Emelio spoke finally the unvoiced words.

"Dad, I want you to tell me you love me."

His father looked at this miracle in front of him and said, with great feeling, "Why son, I love you with all my heart."

The two embraced and cried, holding each other tightly. Their love filled an entire room. Love asked for, given, and received – what powerful teaching for us all!

233

Love is responding to reality. Love defines my relationship to reality. As my own story illustrates, I've spent a lot of energy in my life objecting to what-is or what-just-happened. But objecting to reality is a form of insanity. We cannot change what happened, yet many of us believe that our anger, whining, frustration, retaliation, resentment, and so on, will make a difference, will set things right, will make us feel better. Love has nothing to do with this kind of magical thinking! Love is *responding to reality*, not reacting in objection to it. Love is being grateful for all that is – even those things that have caused us great pain, for embedded within those things is invariably that which can teach us the most about ourselves.

As a wonderful spiritual teacher, Emilia Rathbun, put it once, "Love is being in a constant state of responsiveness. To object to reality is to curtail my own capacity for responsiveness." Learning to love is learning to respond to others without negative emotion and with positive feeling. There is a profound objectivity to love. Love is quite beyond my narrow and petty self-interest. Love embraces the interests of all. Love is an alignment with my inner purpose (which is *always* positive and objective) and a response emanating from that source. To be responsive does not demand that I *like* everyone I encounter in my life. The demand is far greater than that! The real workout is that I *love* everyone I encounter.

We are culturally trained to believe that love is a form of attachment to another person or a love object. It's not. As I learn more and more about love, I have come to see it both as a form of detachment to people, events, and things, *and* a bond with the higher power operating within and through us. This dual nature of love is expressed beautifully by the Twelve Step principle, to "let go and let God." "Letting go" is detaching from all the illusions which I have made real and important – i.e., the events, people, and things that I have let have complete power to run and control my life. "Letting God" is attaching myself to the higher power accessible within me and within all of us. When I "let God," I am in alignment with reality and the highest possibility for everyone in my life.

Love's classroom. You and I have been invited into a classroom. Our families, our friends, our neighbors, and the people we work with – all are enrolled in this class too. It is the most important class we'll ever attend. It combines lecture and lab. Living in a family is one of the labs we will be required to take. This class has no walls – the classroom is the world we live in. And this is not an ordinary class. Everyone is both pupil and teacher. No one will fail. However, everyone will remain in the course until the material has been mastered. Learning will be completely self-paced: the material will be presented to each of us at precisely the moment we are ready to receive it. If we refuse the lessons, that's OK. We can, and will, repeat the course until we learn its content. This course is likely to last a lifetime. So we might as well get to work! The subject of the course is: *learning to love*. It is the most rewarding and demanding course I can ever take.

As a student who has only recently committed to studying love, what I have learned thus far is that I can never cease learning more about it. Life is inexhaustible and exciting! And learning to love my family more each day teaches me what it means to love everyone who crosses my path.

AFTERWARD

Last week Jacob returned from Montana. We visited a little bit, caught up on stories, and dined at Max's Opera Café with Rebecca. Two days ago he drove to Los Angeles.

This afternoon he called me to give me an update. He's found his first apartment! It's small – maybe a little bit larger than our living room, he reports, but hey, it will be his first place on his own! It has a small kitchenette at one end. It's located in a good neighborhood where he feels safe, he assured me. And it's just minutes away from where his acting workshops are held. He has to put down a deposit tomorrow.

I love hearing the excitement back in his voice again. I love to hear him talk about getting a job and a place of his own, about his acting and music, about working on his goals and facing his challenges.

Sandy and I just returned from dinner at a new Italian restaurant she found. We enjoy our moments together and take them often. I had fun telling her about Jacob's phone call. We'll always be a couple of doting parents who love talking about the endless details of our kids' lives. During the school year Sandy is very absorbed in her work with kids with special needs. At the end of the day she is tired and turns in early. But tonight the news of her son's activities erased the fatigue on her face.

MacLean loves his life in Idaho. He loves the outdoors and is minutes away from bike trails. He has rented his first house – a little two-bedroom bungalow in Boise. I imagine him puttering ceaselessly about the house – something he loves to do. And when he isn't puttering, he cycles, works in community theater, holds down a regular job, and consults. He is already saving for a house of his own.

Sandy and I are beginning to plan how we'll all get together soon.

I enjoy my career in information systems. I also lead workshops offered by the World Wide Association of Specialty Programs for other parents who have taken the same journey we are on. It feels good to give what I can to others. I feel very touched when I hear people talk about their lives. I am one of them and humbled by all there is to learn. Nothing separates me now. I'm on a trail we all walk together. I like to assist people in making the most of this experience. I wish the same healing in their lives that we have had in ours. Still I take one day at a time. I no longer live my life through my children. They will have their struggles and triumphs. Our boys are older now. I can move into the next phase of my life, the next turn around the bend.

I had a dream the other day. And in my dream I was a young man lying in a meadow and having a dream of his own. Or perhaps I should say that he was having a nightmare, for his dream was a succession of the darkest images of fear and separation. In his nightmare ...

he walked the streets of a city lined with the homeless and drugged lying at his feet ... and each day the children of the city slept beside them in greater numbers ...

a city where they turned up the violence and punishment ... but it failed to fix anything ... and the children sensed their fear and were afraid themselves ...

a city whose sons and daughters lined the walls of the schools, eager to be first in their class to learn how to become victims or executioners ...

a city whose increasingly irrelevant institutions built monuments, proclaimed initiatives, and made new laws ... but the children had less hope than before ...

a city where daughters sold their innocence for a fix and sons fingered their fathers' wallets for credit cards ...

a city where most everyone got stoned – on drugs, power, sex, or work ... and the children watched them ... and learned ...

a tortured city where children abused their parents, then roamed beneath street lights leaderless and satisfied their longing for family in gangs ...

a lost city where families and marriages were swapped as easily as jobs ... and the sons and daughters looked in all the empty places for a little bit of constant love ....

And just as the dream had reached its worst point, he heard a faint, irregular, and metallic sound. It came from outside his nightmare. There was an unspecific familiarity about it. And at first he did not recognize it, so groggy and burned out was he from the horrible dream. It was a kind of music, a warm and inviting sound, like something he'd heard before, maybe somewhere tucked away back in his childhood in a time he almost couldn't remember. It called him out of his dark dreams into the land of the waking.

And when he awoke he discovered that he was lying on a high mountain meadow. He heard the strange sound again, not too far away. It sounded like a wind chime swinging freely from a tree. Its mysterious and exotic music reached him from somewhere further up the trail. Its chime responded to the sighs of the wind and played an enchanting, Aeolian peal of notes. Its music was like a calling, inviting him to awaken from his unhappy dream and follow it to some new place, a place it seemed to understand and give voice to.

So he set off in pursuit, with the music of the wind chime always ahead of him, always a little bit farther up the trail, mysterious, elusive, and haunting. And after a time he realized why it is said that the gods wear masks. Because we are never intended to see them fully – just as he would never quite see the chime, though its music would always call to him. He realized for the first time that his life task was pursuit not attainment. The pursuit itself would transform him. It was where he would find happiness. And he realized he would never be the same. So he followed faithfully for a long time until one day he realized that he was no longer a young man.

And on that same day he happened upon another trail merging into his. And a few days later another. And then another. And at each junction he met other travellers. They were walking a network of interconnected, interdependent trails. His fellow travellers seemed willing to accompany him on his journey and happy to meet him. As they walked they told their life stories and talked about all that mattered to them. And soon they all realized that each had dreamt nightmares of their own making.

The travellers had long discussions about the music they followed. And after a while they came to an understanding. The chime, they said, calls to all who dream – to brother, sister, mother, father, neighbor, friend, and enemy alike. It has called us long before we were born, they said, and will call us long after we have died, when other travellers will take up the trails and hear the wind chime that will ring forever. Its sound will beckon all to rise up, each according to the miraculous plan of his birth and the perfectly formed chaos of his life. Its ringing will bid them, as it has bid us, to awaken to their yet unborn possibility as conscious and loving human beings. It will celebrate all that they can be. *If they will.*

If … they willed it so, they said, all could hear its music simultaneously everywhere on their now-small planet – from the high rise canyons and wasted slums of the inner cities, to the slumbering suburbs, to the midwest farmlands and plains, to the granite mountain tops of the Sierras. There is no place where the song of the chime could not be heard, they believed, no dream too dark that it could not ultimately be penetrated by this music singing the haunting song of their possibility. The bell could always be heard right there in the living chambers of their hearts where, once wounded, they could be whole and healed again.

The companions decided that, even though few in number, if they healed the wounds that beset their souls, they could change not only their lives but the world they live in. And so they rose up with a conviction and a sense of destiny to create the ultimate and only freedom there is — the freedom that comes from realizing how wonderful this life is when we are aligned with a power greater than ourselves. They had nothing to lose, they reasoned, and everything to gain.

As mothers and fathers, as the *leaders* of their families, they gathered together their children who, when their hearts were equally touched, told them that they too longed to walk beside their parents on these rugged mountain pathways. They too had heard the sound of the wind chime calling, felt the longing in their hearts, and wondered what was out there awaiting them. Someone said that if all the world has the same vision, if they all hear the Aeolian bell, ultimately the earth's people will respond and there will be no more dreams of darkness. And when they truly hear the bell in their hearts, they said, they will know what to do.

And so these few rose up freely and awoke — one by one by one. Men and women looked into each other's faces with unrestrained love, a love they no longer felt embarrassed to feel or show. And they took their beloved children by the hand. And they formed a happy band of loving-kindness dancers — unchained, joyous, and free — and left behind the collective dream of darkness they had made. It was unable to hold them when they but gave the word. As had always been the plan.

And choosing their heart life — a life of passion and love, of caring and commitment, of individual power and perpetual forgiveness, a life where they proudly beat their drums to the pulse of each other — they made their way into the healing sunlight of their becoming, and ascended unto that holy place where the music plays still a little further ahead and where a father meets his son, and the son becomes a man, and the mountains touch the sky.

❖